PENGUIN BOOKS

MONEY MATTERS FOR WOMEN

Helen Baker was born in deepest Somerset, educated at Ilminster Girls Grammar School and earned her first wage as a Saturday girl at Woolworth's. She holds a degree in economics from the University of York, a bilingual secretarial certificate from the City of London College, and a Certificate of Education from Wolverhampton Technical Teachers' College. She qualified as one of Her Majesty's Inspectors of Taxes. Employers include champagne shippers, shipbrokers, solicitors and the National Board for Prices and Incomes. Following an enjoyable spell as a technical college and polytechnic lecturer, she joined the Civil Service as an Inspector of Taxes. After four frustrating years she joined a firm of chartered accountants as Taxation Manager. For seven years she advised clients large and small on all aspects of finance. With her husband she left for New Zealand on the day the Chernobyl fallout reached Britain. There she taught tax at the Technical Correspondence Institute (New Zealand's equivalent to the Open University). She now lives in France with her husband and Siamese cat. She wrote this, her first book, in her second attempt at retirement.

GW00703324

HELEN BAKER

MONEY MATTERS
FOR WOMEN

PENGUIN BOOKS

PENGUIN BOOKS

Published by the Penguin Group
Penguin Books Ltd, 27 Wrights Lane, London W8 5TZ, England
Penguin Books USA Inc., 375 Hudson Street, New York, New York 10014, USA
Penguin Books Australia Ltd, Ringwood, Victoria, Australia
Penguin Books Canada Ltd, 10 Alcorn Avenue, Toronto, Ontario, Canada M4V 3B2
Penguin Books (NZ) Ltd, 182–190 Wairau Road, Auckland 10, New Zealand

Penguin Books Ltd, Registered Offices: Harmondsworth, Middlesex, England

First published 1993
1 3 5 7 9 10 8 6 4 2

The moral right of the author has been asserted

Set in 10.5/13 pt Monophoto Janson
Typeset by Datix International Limited, Bungay, Suffolk
Printed in England by Clays Ltd, St Ives plc

No woman can be a beauty without a fortune.

Dr Samuel Johnson, 1709–89

CONTENTS

Introduction   ix

1 Financial fallacies   1

2 What money is and how to get it   5

3 Income from employment   9

4 More income from your employment   23

5 Income from self-employment   32

6 Understanding your accounts   49

7 Capital   62

8 Keeping your money   80

9 How (not) to squander   90

10 Saving   103

11 Borrowing   113

12 Investing   138

13 Your choice of investments   149

14 Marriage and after   170

15 Retirement and the generation to follow   180

16 Overseas   192

17 Inflation   199

18 Fraud   206

19 The other side of fraud   211

20 What you learned at school: some basic arithmetic revision   218

21 Glossary   235

22 Conclusion   265

Index   273

CONTENTS

INTRODUCTION

Money is a blessing that transforms our dreams into reality. It provides everything from the food we eat to the luxuries we drool over. Those pretty pieces of paper make the difference between misery and affluence. They make the world our oyster. They give us joy and fun and power. Money allows us to hide our mistakes, our shames, our stupidities, and start again.

Money is a curse that keeps people awake at night, tossing frantic with worry. It stirs up more quarrels between loving couples than any other reason. Money provokes the sort of jealousy that can smash a family apart or drive people to the cruellest of crimes.

Money – which is it for you, and for all the other women reading this?

The young woman looked up at me with the eyes of a whipped dog. 'I lost my lovely home,' she sighed. 'All because I signed a piece of paper. I'd never have signed if I'd known there was the tiniest chance. But my husband told me to.' I shook my head sympathetically. This was one client I could not help.

Eileen's husband had set up a **limited company.**[*] He had installed her as a **director** and told her to sign a **personal guarantee** for the bank. The company's business failed, so the bank used the personal guarantee to get its money back. Eileen

---

[*] Words printed in **bold type** are explained in the glossary in Chapter 21.

lost her home. (Don't worry if you don't understand any of this. You will after five more chapters.)

'Now we rent a poky flat. If only I'd known.' She stuffed her handkerchief back into her bag and shuffled out of my office.

It is women like Eileen who provoked me to write this book. We women handle money all our lives, yet nobody tells us how. Schools give no guidance. Most books on finance overpower you with jargon or else recommend you to save twopence by turning your husband's shirt-cuffs.

We women rarely talk about money among ourselves. Maybe we moan about rising prices or rave over a wonderful bargain we have discovered, but we never discuss money itself, still less wealth. When did you last speculate with your friends on how to get money, on how to make the most of your present resources or turn your pittance into opulence?

Men, by contrast, spend profitable hours on these subjects, during working hours and in the pub afterwards. Women are interested all right – who hasn't watched the transforming hand of money? – but few know where to start.

In twenty years of working professionally with money, I met hardly any women with practical knowledge about money. Time after time, I would phone a bank, a solicitor's office, a government department. A girl would answer. Perhaps she would hand over to a female clerk. But always, always when she realized what I wanted to discuss, a male had to take charge. I grew to dread the change-over.

We women have taken huge strides this century towards independence. But not in the field of money. **Finance** remains overwhelmingly controlled by men and run in their own interests, as you will see later. Don't be deceived by the presence of flocks of girls shelling out banknotes over counters.

Show me the most liberated woman you know. I can guarantee that when she needs help or advice on how to invest, borrow, run her business – anything short of walking into a shop and forking out cash – she turns to a man to provide it. I will also guarantee that, by and large, she does not understand the advice she gets. Outwardly, she may think herself liberated. Financially, she is as helpless as a baby.

Yet how can this be? We women have managed the family finances and balanced the budget for centuries. Traditionally confined within the home, it is easy to think small, and not to plan beyond the end of the week. It is easy to be penny wise and pound foolish. Even worse: we are conned by the old wives' tales, the ten financial fallacies I list in Chapter 1.

In the chapters to follow, we will consider wealth: how to get it; how to stop it frittering away through your fingers; how to save it; what are real and what are false economies; how to invest it to make it grow; how to borrow it. Then we will look at problems most women can expect to encounter: divorce or widowhood; retirement; handing over to your children or grandchildren. Next, because it is a wide world we live in, a little about money overseas, inflation and fraud. To follow, there is a chapter on the easy maths you need and a glossary of all the terms I have used. We round off with a review of progress to date.

I have designed this book for women aged from 16 to 80, rich and poor. The rich face problems too, but they are different ones. I aim for it to be useful to you throughout your life. Despite the ever-changing jargon, most of the basic facts don't change. One thing I promise: not a word on the sober drudgery of budgeting, or on how to enjoy your wealth. You must have a million ideas of your own on these topics. If not, other people will soon suggest them for you.

1

FINANCIAL FALLACIES

So what are these beliefs that steer women away from the mention of wealth, let alone the reality? They are taboos acting so subtly that sometimes more women believe them than men.

1 *'Talking about money is not feminine.'* This was always implied behind the 'Don't bother your pretty little head about that, dear' of the Victorian father and husband. They should try it on a Frenchwoman or a Thai. Both nations boast some of the most glamorous and feminine women in the world. They also expect them to learn the art of driving a hard bargain with a winning smile.

2 *'Talking about money is not polite.'* This depends on the time and the place. What would be shocking at the graveside becomes perfectly proper among the same people in the solicitor's office half an hour later. All we British act coy about money. None of us would dream of asking a stranger at a first meeting how much he or she earned. An American would not hesitate. British men beat about the bush in public but in private they soon launch into precise figures. It is your choice. Would you rather be considered a perfectly polite little lamb ready for fleecing – or astute and well informed but a little outspoken?

3 *'Careers connected with money lack that magic ingredient, glamour.'* Good looks count for nothing – that is true. As soon as a woman talks knowledgeably about money, men grow so interested, they forget she is a woman. A few words on finance can halt a Romeo in mid-seduction. Some women take this as a reason not to choose such a career. In fact, it offers a golden opportunity. What qualified women complain of – the youngest and prettiest more than any – is not being taken seriously. Money gives you that chance.

4 *'Women cannot understand figures.'* Twaddle. Say rather that women, and many men, don't like the look of figures. I have spent hours poring over columns of numbers but I still look away whenever I see one on the printed page. This does not stop me looking back and puzzling out what it means. Why should this happen? In Britain, where most of the primary teachers are women, it is girls who are bad at figures and good at languages. In East Africa most primary teachers are male. There, the boys are good at languages and bad at figures. Draw your own conclusions.

5 *'You need to be a maths genius.'* Chartered accountants need to add, subtract, multiply and divide. They must understand fractions, decimals and percentages. This is all I ever saw them do in nine years working alongside them. You learned all that before you were 14. Besides, everyone uses calculators to take away the drudgery. In case you have forgotten since or never really understood arithmetic, you will find it explained in Chapter 20.

6 *'I can't understand the language.'* You will find a glossary in Chapter 21 to explain the technical words I use. You should then be able to follow the explanation a commercial dictionary gives for any other words you come across. Incidentally, have you read the blurb that accompanies skin-care products or lists the contents of some food packets? How much of that did you understand? Did it stop you using the product?

7 *'I've been handling money all my life. It's common sense.'* Life is not so simple. What we call common sense is not common. Perhaps, like the French, we should style it 'good sense'. You find as many old wives' tales about money as you do for curing hiccups or freckles, increasing your bust or reducing your hips. I have sprinkled them throughout the book and explained just why they are wrong.

8 *'Men know better than women.'* This fallacy is only held by women. No man ever refused to let me handle his affairs, even when it involved juicy divorce details or facts about him that his wife did not know. But a woman refused – purely on grounds of gender.

9 *'If you need help or advice, someone will always give it to you.'* The girl who pronounced this to me was 15. That must have been her excuse. She said she had learned it from her mother. Clearly, Mother never reads a newspaper. The papers trumpet to the world what befalls innocent people; either they do not realize they need advice, or what they receive proves useless. What you don't know *can* hurt you.

10 *'Men and women treat money just the same, so any advice on money will suit women too.'* Not so. Women receive money at different times to men, for different reasons. Their career patterns, hence wages, differ because of bringing up a family. They may receive a lump sum on divorce or inherit on widowhood. Few women get 'golden handshakes' (a lump sum to soften the blow of dismissal), large redundancy payments or 'golden handcuffs' (lavish perks to discourage them from changing jobs). Women cherish different aims for their money from men. Besides, they have quite a different approach, say, to investment.

You will handle money for the rest of your life, whether you read this book or not. How well do you manage it? Are you using what you have available to give you the sort of life you want? Luxury items, fine, but also the sort of basic security that comes from knowing everything is insured and your old age is as well provided for as possible?

We females enjoy one great advantage. We can appear ignorant. My husband always asks me to drive a car to the garage if one develops a fault. I find out in detail just what is wrong, what that involves and what is needed to put things right. I write all this down at the garage, taking great trouble with the technical words. Why? Men are expected to know about cars *whether they do or not.*

The mechanic who will eagerly explain to me in detail if asked nicely would just grunt, 'Big end,' at a man and expect him to understand. And – because they dare not lose face – most men would pretend they did understand. Then they would pay any bill at the end of it.

Money is just the same. Men assume that other men know all about it. Disguised male ignorance causes monumental blunders.

Besides, the more you – or any woman – know, the more intelligent the questions you can ask, and the more you can pierce the smokescreen of jargon that costs you money and restricts your financial freedom. That is what this book is all about.

2

WHAT MONEY IS AND HOW TO GET IT

When we talk about money, most of us think of banknotes and coins. We think of crisp clean tenners new from the cash dispenser, or ragged greasy fivers from a back pocket; a golden sovereign sparkling in your hand, or a tarnished, bent penny lying in the gutter.

Although money means cash, you own many other things which are 'as good as' cash. You can write a cheque. It is only a piece of paper, but you know you can hand it over just as though it were actual banknotes. Or you can go to the building society and produce your dog-eared old passbook, but the girl happily hands over the money you want. Perhaps you have a **credit card** or even a season ticket. They are all as good as cash, in the right place.

The first thing to grasp about money is quite straightforward. It is the difference between **capital** and **income**. One wise old judge said, 'Capital is like a tree, and income is the apples on it.' You plant the tree once, but you pick apples from it every year.

Suppose your building society balance stands at £1,100. If you drew it out, all the notes would look the same, but they might represent different things. If you had only paid it all in the day before, so it had not earned any **interest**, all £1,100 would represent your capital. If you had paid in £1,000 a year ago, and the **interest rate** had been 10 per cent, then £1,000 would represent capital and £100 the income your capital had earned you in that time.

Why does it matter when it all looks the same? For a start, only income suffers **income tax**. More than one person has written down the total amount in their bank account, their **balance**, on the income tax form and then paid tax on the lot.

Just as important, unless you know how much of your money is income and how much is capital, you have no way of judging how good your investment is. Similarly, if you run a business, this is how you calculate whether your business is profitable or not.

So capital is what you started with, and income is what you earn from it. Sometimes people talk about your **principal**. Then they mean the cash you started off with.

Sometimes they refer to your **assets**. Then they mean the money plus the things that are 'as good as money' that you started with – like the **shares** in the diamond mine Aunt Freda left you, the winning lottery or raffle ticket you are about to cash in, the brilliant invention you have just patented which will earn you a fortune. In everyday talk, assets and capital mean pretty much the same thing.

Not all assets are the same. Some are more **liquid** than others. This just means that you can convert them into cash more easily.

Suppose you need cash in a hurry. If you have money in a bank account, you can rush to the bank (except at the weekends) and get it there and then. If you own some British Telecom shares, you can tell your **broker** to sell them. There will be no problem, but you will have to wait a few days before you receive your money, and the broker will have deducted his **commission** from it. Unlike withdrawing money from the bank, you can never be certain just how much you will get.

If you own a country cottage, you can call in estate agents to put it up for sale. You may have to wait months for a buyer, biting your fingernails and lowering your price. Then finally when you do find a buyer, what you receive will be reduced by the hefty fees of estate agents and solicitors. The sum may be far less than you hoped for when you first decided to sell.

So, money in the bank is a more liquid asset than a share certificate, which is still far more liquid than a house. You should always bear the **liquidity** of an asset in mind when deciding where to invest. We shall look at this again.

Finally, assets can be quite invisible but still worth having. For instance:

A bold young man went to pester the famous millionaire J.J. in his hotel. He demanded a loan to start a business.

'Never,' laughed the rich man. 'But I like your nerve, so I'll do the next best thing. Come on.' J.J. put his arm around the young man, walked him down to the hotel lobby and shook his hand at the entrance. Outside the door, several strangers rushed up to the young man as he stood alone scratching his head.

'You're a friend of J.J.,' they beamed. 'Any friend of J.J.'s is a friend of ours. Want to borrow some money?'

J.J. had certainly given the young man an asset – confidence. When people talk about 'confidence' in money (financial) terms, they don't mean faith in yourself. The young man had that before he tackled the millionaire. They mean that other people (**the market**) have confidence in you. They believe you have a great future.

HOW TO GET YOUR MONEY

The most likely ways to get money – capital or income – are to earn it, borrow it or inherit it. Beyond that, you may be showered by gifts or outright windfalls, which we shall consider later. Meanwhile some people settle for stealing their lucre or, more subtly, engage in fraud. Most of us, unfortunately, have to earn it, so the next two chapters will cover income from a job – employment income – and Chapter 5, income from **self-employment**.

If working for it sounds too tedious, turn directly to Chapter 7 to discover how to get capital. On the other hand, maybe you have propped this book against a spare mound of the neatly docketed tenners that cover the table. In that case, you should turn to Chapter 8 to learn how to keep it.

3

INCOME FROM EMPLOYMENT

So far, everything you have read applies equally to men. Now things change a little. Figure 1 is a graph covering the life of a typical woman. We'll call her Eve. A graph is only a picture, so there is nothing to worry about, and the only figures in this one are her age. The picture shows when, over her lifetime, Eve is most likely to have spare money.

Go to the bottom left-hand corner of Figure 1 (overleaf), marked 0. The bottom line (called an axis) starts at birth and measures years. The vertical line also starts at 0, but this time it means £0. The higher the wavy line climbs up the page, the more money Eve has to spend at the age shown below.

So the graph tells us that Eve enjoyed virtually no money until she started to work at 16. There was no silver spoon; no fabulous earnings as a child star; no **income** from Granny's **trust**.

Eve did not earn much even then, because she was unskilled. Matters improved when she turned 18 and started to earn a full adult wage. From then on, Eve's available money started to increase quite nicely until at 25 she married Jeff. What reduced

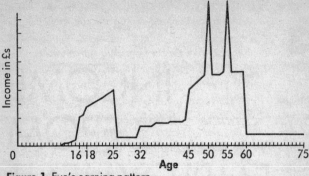

Figure 1 Eve's earning pattern

her income was not the fact that she married, nor the fact that the new couple started to buy a house. It was her pregnancy, because it stopped her working.

So until 32, Eve had little money again. Then her younger son started school and she could manage a part-time job. But part-time workers normally earn little, with no chance of promotion. So Eve's income hardly increased until she reached 45. Then, with both children working, she too went back to work full-time.

Now the family income really started to improve, because the **mortgage** was nearly paid off. Compared to earlier years of struggle, the payments seemed tiny. When she was 50, Eve's father died and left her some cash in a **legacy**. She took the whole family to the United States and, while it lasted, had a marvellous binge.

At 55 Eve had a shock. Jeff left her and started divorce proceedings. The solicitors pointed out that they both worked full-time now and had no dependent children. They suggested that a lump-sum settlement (cash) would be better than regular payments of **alimony**. Jeff and Eve agreed. The family home was sold, and part of the proceeds provided the lump sum for Eve. She enjoyed a lovely cruise to get over the shock, then went on a spending spree to furnish the new flat she rented.

At 60 Eve has retired. Now she can claim some state pension because of her own **National Insurance** contributions when she worked and those of Jeff before the divorce. She never thought she might need to provide a private pension for herself because she relied on Jeff. Besides, she never had the money, except when she was very young, could not even imagine growing old and was more interested in a good time. Now at 60, she has little to live on and the prospect of another twenty comfortless years ahead of her.

Sad? Of course, but not uncommon. All the fault of the divorce? Only partly. If Eve and Jeff had stayed together, they would still possess the home they worked so hard for. In a year or two, as they are much the same age, Jeff would retire too, and they could share his job pension. His state pension for the two of them would probably amount to less than they now receive separately – a lot less if Eve claims supplementary benefit.

Blame it all on Jeff? He kept Eve all the time the family was growing up and gave her a fair divorce settlement when he left. Honest and hard-working, he did as much as anyone could expect. He does not reproach himself.

Perhaps he should have taken the promotion the firm offered him in his twenties, but it would have meant moving, and they were happy where they lived.

Perhaps he should have accepted his brother's offer when he was 30 that the two of them should start up in business together. Their father wanted to lend them the money. But neither could manage the paperwork. Eve said she was too busy with the new baby and wanted Jeff at home.

Perhaps he should have thought of the future when he won that few thousand on the football pools in his thirties. But he'd always fancied a sports car, and Eve enjoyed being seen out in it too.

No, the problem is that whenever Eve or Jeff had money or the chance of earning money, they did not take advantage of it. When you have read this book, you should be able to plan better.

Eve's life history may be nothing at all like yours. But her graph illustrates the problems that face all working women. So we will look at it again in more detail.

Take the period from 16 to 25. This is the first time when Eve is affluent. Obviously, the longer you can make this period last, the better. This period usually sets the scene for your future lifestyle. This may well be the most important time in your life to earn.

It finishes, not because you get married or because you start a mortgage, but because you start a family and so cannot earn. If you have children in your teens, the period is over almost before it began.

Eve started untrained work at 16. If, instead, you continue your education and don't start work until 21 or 22, after your university course, or even later after professional training, you have squeezed your peak earning time still tighter. One female barrister I know never earned a penny until she was 25 and then peanuts until 30.

Besides, we all suffer the loss of money when our career hiccups because we lose our job, retrain, get married or have to follow our husband's career. My cousin Margaret's little boy had already started his third school at only $5\frac{1}{2}$. His father worked for a bank. Every promotion involved a new branch and a house move. At this pace, Margaret could not possibly have worked herself, even without a child.

All right, many women decide, I will have my family. But I will employ someone to look after the children out of my earnings. So they do. Jessie, for instance, handed over her entire salary to her nanny because she was so desperate to work. Was it worthwhile? She thought so. From a financial point of view, I wonder. If Jessie had been a well-qualified high-flyer and it was a short-term arrangement, maybe. But she was a secretary with no prospects. Her biggest asset was her determination. She worked herself to a frazzle when the nanny was ill, on holiday or needed transport.

Some employers do provide crèches where workers can leave their children, but certainly not all. Small firms will never be able to afford such luxuries, and the government will never finance them as long as there is male unemployment. In wartime, when every worker is needed, of course, things are different.

Most male employers have no idea how much effort their female staff put into ensuring their children are well taken care of. What is more, they don't care. It is no more their business than whether a female employee locked the door before leaving home. They look on child care as a woman's problem.

All right, you say, we know the problems. Tell us the answers. Sadly, if you decide to have children without capital or high earning capacity of your own, nothing has changed. You are going to stay financially dependent on your husband – or the state – for a very long time. Anyone who tells you differently is deceiving you.

Equally, the dream of a wage for housewives is too expensive ever to be practical. What political party dare introduce it? How many working women, let alone men, would accept the much higher taxes it would demand – simply to pay someone to do in a week what they have to cram into their 'leisure' time? This is a practical book, and you need to know the truth.

When Eve was 32, she started part-time work. This is the compromise many women settle for. Unfortunately, part-time work, and work at home for that matter, is normally shabbily paid compared to the wages of full-timers.

Part-time work can also be a blatant con. As a lecturer, I spent twenty-four hours in a classroom a week. My unfortunate

– and always female – colleagues taught for thirty hours. Yet they were officially part-time. And they received no pay until after the end of term! This continued, uncertain year after uncertain year, because a part-timer enjoys less job security. If times turn hard, businesses always sack their part-time people first. This is one reason why they employ them in the first place. They can increase or reduce the workforce quickly and cheaply.

Why do so many women fall into this trap? Because there are too many women in the same position. In other words, **supply and demand**, which I will explain later on. The college always ran a waiting-list of women keen to lecture part-time.

Things are improving. The **Civil Service** now allows full-time workers to work part-time and keep their job security and seniority. They are also experimenting with **job-sharing**. If your skills are in short supply, employers are more willing to help. For example, computer programmers can work at home, choose their own hours and earn high wages. This is another good reason to make yourself as well trained as you can before you start a family.

Look back again at Eve's story. Her income only picks up when she can go back to work full-time. She enjoys better job security and better pay and stands a chance of the pay increases which reward promotion. But Eve is 45 and in competition with people of 25. Besides, much of what she knew before is out of date.

There are lots of books on how to return to work, so I will say no more except that there are problems and there are also solutions to them.

WHICH JOBS PAY THE MOST – AND WHERE?

Wages always stay lowest where most of the workforce are women (or, to be cruelly frank, male immigrants), as with shop workers or nurses. This is true regardless of the level of training, if you compare the wages with what others earn who have undergone the same length of training.

A woman may spend three years at university studying French, and one more year actually in France earning peanuts as part of the training. But translators and teachers – mostly female – are poorly paid. The girl studying economics in the next room for three years will fare much better, not only in the salary she earns but in the range of jobs open to her.

Why should this be? For a start, women have in the past either refused to join trade unions that were run by men for men, or worked in areas where it was difficult for unions to organize. (Secretaries, for instance, are spread over thousands of employers. You can imagine the chore of trying to organize a sudden union meeting.) When they have joined in sufficient numbers to play an active part in running the union, they are often reluctant to take industrial action on pay. A strike involves unpleasantness and loss of wages. It may drag on for months with no guarantee of success. Men usually think extra money alone is worth the risk. Women may be more concerned with safety, conditions at work, the right not to wear uniform or a moral issue – like the Irish shop girls who held out for months because their shop sold South African apples, or the Liverpool manageress who was sacked after trying to protect her staff from their randy boss. Perhaps you have seen Glenda Jackson's marvellous performance in the film of the successful strike for her reinstatement.

Most pay increases are based on a percentage of last year's pay. If you miss out one year, you never catch up.

Also, you would be surprised (and men would be amazed, some downright scornful) how many women are frightened of getting a pay increase if it means they earn more than their husband.

'My husband only earns the same as I do now, and he's a chartered accountant,' declared Lucy, blushing. The fact that she herself was a fully qualified programmer, and therefore in great demand, cut no ice at all.

Also – let's be honest – many girls and women don't really *believe* they have to work, whatever they may say in public. Or at most they think they'll have to work for only a few years, especially those in dead-end jobs. Perhaps they don't really expect Prince Charming or a miraculous pools win to whirl them away from the factory and into a paradise of idle luxury. But there is always the chance of release, through pregnancy, family commitments or their husband's job move, perhaps tomorrow. As a result, many consider mundane work a passing chore, as it was for Cinderella, and they don't take it seriously.

Men, on the other hand, *know* they are stuck with work for life. They take it seriously, and this means they relax. No one but a fool wears himself out in the first few months at a job he knows he will be doing for the next forty years.

The different time scale explains why so many highly thought of men at work appear infuriatingly lazy. It also explains why many female graduates are criticized for being too 'keen'.

The next reason why jobs done mainly by women pay badly is supply and demand. I will mention this again. Broadly, the more people there are willing to supply a service, or to do a certain job, the less employers need to pay to hire them. This is the supply side.

Conversely, the more employers need workers for a job, the more they will have to offer. This is the demand side.

So, from the supply side, women cannot expect to earn much if they can only offer skills which half the population is expected to possess by instinct, like cleaning or looking after children. They face too much competition. This forces the wages down. A man who can only offer his strength, as a labourer, has the same problem.

My young neighbour Dawn tried to build herself a career as a professional baby-sitter. She worked hard, exceptionally long hours, and dashed from one client to another. Everyone marvelled at her Mini. She decked it out with 'Baby on Board' signs, two baby-seats in the back and umpteen mirrors so she could watch over her charges as she drove. Several cuddly animals swung from the roof to entertain the infants. Boxes of wet-wipes and nappies sat ready. She had created a mobile nursery.

If Dawn had only done her sums beforehand, she would have realized that her dream was impossible. She could work around the clock but never earn a living wage. People were very grateful for her care but they would not pay her more than the going rate. Why should they? Common sense said that any schoolgirl could do the job.

The moral is to find an opening with less competition where one's skills are highly valued. If advisers try to channel you into 'traditional' women's work, remember that there is no such thing. Traditionally women, certainly educated ones, *didn't* work. Take typing. The typewriter was invented in the 1890s, but female typists were not allowed into the City of London until the mid-1920s. The male clerks fought tooth and nail to keep them out.

You cannot expect high wages if you can only offer what most people don't want or value. Mary was a qualified milliner, but who buys an individually made hat nowadays? Mary thought her skill guaranteed a job for life. How many girls leave college even today, thankful that they will never have to study anything again? They could not be more wrong.

Logically, you would expect people with greater skills to earn more. This is not necessarily what happens. Bilingual secretaries often earn less than ordinary ones. Professors may take home less pay than the people who were their students not long before. Why? Supply and demand again.

Clean hands often mean lower wages. The graduate book-seller in the smart shop may take home much less than the car mechanic round the corner. Perhaps the graduate really has the better prospects he or she was promised as compensation.

On the other hand, many industries and professions run on the backs of a succession of young hopefuls. Always try to find out just how many have been promoted from your job in the past.

Then take working conditions. How many of us would accept the isolation of a lighthouse keeper or a submarine crew member? I recently met my first female driver of an articulated lorry. She told me she had trained for eighteen months, found everyone very helpful and did not mind a life on her own on the road and in transport cafés.

In our society, unlike some countries, the filthiest and most dangerous jobs are normally done by men. As long as we are content to let this continue – and it is not used as an excuse to pay men more – 'danger money', 'dirt money' and 'overtime' money will always keep the average male wage higher than the average female.

Where you work influences how much you can earn. Everyone knows that wage rates are usually far higher in London and the South-East than in Scotland and Northern Ireland. So if you work for an employer, like the government, who pays on a nationwide scale, your wages appear relatively low if you are working in central London or the South-East. They seem reasonable if you live in Birmingham and a downright fortune in Newcastle. Yes, I know they offer a London allowance, but it does not make up the difference.

Why do the wages vary from place to place? Our old friends supply and demand: the more people available and willing to tackle a job, the less they will be paid. Higher house and flat prices, rents and travelling costs reduce the supply of people in London, so employers have to pay them more to overcome this. The more employers in an area who need people, the more they will have to offer them. Most big firms keep their prestige head office in London.

This effect does not stop at Dover. Everyone knows the fantastic tax-free salaries, perks and free accommodation that secretaries and nurses earn in the USA or the Persian Gulf.

They have tempted many women to work abroad, at least for a few years.

Bear in mind also, when you choose a job or a training course, that some skills travel and others do not. A good typist can step into a job readily anywhere in the English-speaking world. An English solicitor is rarely of any use outside England and Wales, because every country has its own laws, even Scotland.

When I left Britain for New Zealand, all the detailed tax knowledge that clients cheerfully paid £30 an hour for was suddenly worthless. My teaching qualification provided a job straight away.

Of course, if you just consider pay when you decide which job to choose, you run the risk of spending a vast part of your life doing something you hate. Just remember, it is possible to use the same skills under different conditions for many different employers. You can nurse the sick under the National Health Service, in a private hospital, in uniform in the armed forces, in a factory, in a boarding school, in the Persian Gulf working for an oil company – or even plane-hopping in the Australian outback or in Hollywood on a film set.

The same applies to pounding a typewriter or sitting in front of a computer screen – but not to operating a sewing machine, or smearing synthetic cream over a conveyor belt of Swiss roll in a cake factory.

If you choose to work for an international, male-orientated employer, you too obtain all the perks that other employees have negotiated and insisted on.

There is an old saying: *don't marry money; marry where money is.* The same applies to choosing a career.

We all know which job really pays a woman the most. Even in our civilized society, the highest-paid women follow the oldest profession. Prostitution is legal; and in practice, although not in law, earnings usually come tax-free. The amounts earned can be astronomical. This explains the many highly organized criminals and 'protectors' ready to take their cut, using violence where necessary.

I have never had a prostitute ask me for tax advice – she would hardly need it – or for investment advice. Yet she would need the latter desperately with her highly paid, high-risk, uninsurable and short-term career.

WHEN WILL YOU EARN MOST?

Modelling, advertising, sales, hostessing, anything where looks count and glamour is everything means you earn most when young. Often by 25 you are a has-been. The same goes for any job where you use your strength. A man may earn high wages at 20 because he can endure lots of overtime on a building site. The same man, worn out at 64, will struggle to drag himself through an ordinary day. Of course, then he only manages the basic wage.

At the other end of the age scale you find the professions. You will earn a pittance for many years but really coin it when you are older, say 40 and above.

It is not so very long ago that people had to pay to be trained, say as a solicitor, even though they produced valuable work for years as they trained. Entire industries, from accountancy to hairdressing, still run on the cheap labour of a succession of hopeful apprentices or articled clerks.

Again, this late reward tells against women. Just when the men of the firm are sitting pretty at 40, the women are starting again at the bottom of the ladder, with their children only just off their hands.

WHAT IS AN EMPLOYEE?

An employee is anyone who works under a **contract of service**. This is simply a written agreement telling you the job, the hours, holidays, pay, etc. It may be just the letter offering you the job. Big employers, like the Civil Service, produce large manuals spelling out in detail exactly what their employees are entitled to.

Basically, the boss tells you what to do and how to do it. Employers provide all you need to do the job. If anything goes wrong, they are responsible. So if you, as a waitress, trip up and pour scalding tea into a customer's lap (as I once did), it is your boss and not you who picks up the dry-cleaning bill.

Employees receive their wages under the **PAYE** (short for **Pay As You Earn**) system. Employers must calculate how much **income tax** and National Insurance to deduct from each employee's wages. They use tables and a tax code given them by the **Inland Revenue**. Employers also have to pay National Insurance contributions themselves for each of their employees to help pay towards their pensions, etc. This may cost them as much as 10 per cent of the employee's **gross** wages.

Employees who are paid straight out of the till, like casual barmaids, and whose employers do not deduct tax, form part of the **black economy**. Sometimes the numbers of people and amount of money involved are huge – but not among women.

In a secret survey of black-economy women in London, many claimed they worked that way to avoid tax. In fact, when they quoted their wages, most earned so little that there would have been no tax or National Insurance to pay. So they were not in the black economy at all. These 'employees' had simply been conned by their 'employers'.

They were cheated out of job security, health-and-safety-at-work protection, perhaps pension contributions and any possible career prospects. Why? Higher-level people are never treated like this; with them, tax-dodging is more sophisticated.

How do you know if you have fallen into this trap? Broadly, you can forget about tax if you are earning less than £3,000 a year or £57 a week.* Details on tax and National Insurance change every year. How do you find out? Phone or visit the Inland Revenue (the Inspector of Taxes' branch, not the Collector's). Simply ask what the current figures are. The number is listed in any telephone directory. These people don't bite, and the offices are mostly staffed by women. For NI details ask the telephone operator for National Insurance Freefone, or again you can pop into the local **Department of Social Security** office.

You will find a big difference between the two departments. The Inland Revenue are used to dealing with the wealthy – people who will stand their ground or call on lawyers and accountants to argue for them. The DSS are used to dealing with the needy and the helpless.

The Inland Revenue will not answer questions like, 'If I buy a house and rent it out, how much tax will I pay?' If they did, all their time would be spent helping people to avoid tax.

So much for the job scene in general. You want to know how you can improve your own position, whatever your job. This is the subject of the next chapter.

---

*These are 1992 figures. I have tried to avoid quoting figures. I aim for this book to be useful to you in ten years' time.

4 MORE INCOME FROM YOUR EMPLOYMENT

It is easy to say how much you earn, *you may think: either the amount shown in your* **contract** *of employment (your* **gross** *wage) or the amount you take home (your* **net** *wage). Not so.*

HOW MUCH DO YOU REALLY EARN?

A colleague, usually male, may earn the same as you on paper, perhaps even less, but receive considerably more. How can this be?

He may have a salary package. In other words, he works for a wage just like you, but he is allowed a car, perks like an expense account, a pension.

Take Jane, who earns £9,000 a year and does the same job as Bill, who only earns £8,000. Both travel around on business; but Bill has a company car, while Jane just gets petrol money.

To make life easy, suppose the **PAYE** deductions are 10 per cent of the gross wage. Therefore Jane takes home £8,100

(£9,000 − £900), and Bill takes home £7,200 (£8,000 − £800).

This makes a difference of £900 between them (£8,100 − £7,200). Could Jane buy or hire a car, insure it, service it, pay for petrol and oil, perhaps even pay to have it cleaned and garage it for £900 a year? Of course not. So, though on paper Jane is higher-paid, in fact Bill earns a lot more. And he pays less tax too.

Besides, the employer may be much better off paying Bill this way. Why? Remember those employer's **National Insurance** contributions? They are based on wages; so the lower your wages, the less the employer has to pay. Also, the employer still owns the car; Bill is less likely to change jobs if he has to leave it behind.

So why does Jane not get similar treatment? Perhaps it never occurred to her to ask. Perhaps she never looked beyond her wage packet. Her boss will be surprised, and impressed, when she does ask. He never thought women were interested in perks. Men are the serious earners. Women are only after 'pin money' in his experience. Now he must think again.

Big public employers must treat all employees as laid down in the agreed manuals. Otherwise the unions, who have spent years fighting to get these agreements, would soon complain. Even so, this does not always happen automatically. You may still have to make a claim, and this means reading the manual first. You have to know your rights before you can exercise them.

Small employers, by and large, can come to any agreement they like with each employee individually. If you work for one of these, it is up to you to try to improve your position. In Jane's case, she would be better off asking to reduce her salary in return for a car.

There are all sorts of perks an employer can provide: from luncheon vouchers to business suits; from pension schemes and private medical cover to a subsidized canteen or the chance to buy company products cut-price; from an entertainment allowance or contributions towards your home telephone bills to a season ticket or an interest-free loan towards one.

Remember what we said at the outset? Money is much more than the cash in your pocket.

Here are two more very valuable perks that may appeal to you. Banks and building societies make house-purchase loans to employees at ridiculously low rates of interest. Travel agency staff can roam the world for a few quid.

Most of these perks are taxable if you earn more than a certain amount. In this case, your employer must inform the **Inland Revenue** about them on a form called P11D. Don't let that put you off, because the tax comes to far less than the benefit to you.

For instance, suppose your employer provides you with a suit that cost £200. You pay tax as though your extra **income** had been the value of a *second-hand* suit. And what is a second-hand suit worth? Can you sell it, even?

You will hear lots of company **directors** moan about the tax on company cars. Just try suggesting to them they give up their cars and pay themselves extra salary instead to buy and run similar cars. They will soon change the subject. They know, despite the tax, that they are on to a winner.

EARNING MORE: PAY, PERKS AND BENEFITS

How can you persuade your boss to provide perks, pay you more or improve your conditions?

If you work for a large organization, the union does all the bargaining for you, whether you belong to it or not. If you work for a small concern, you stand alone. Let's first consider women who work for large employers.

Your starting point is to find out what the union has already negotiated for you. You should find this in staff manuals. Alternatively, union officials should know. You also need to know how what they have achieved compares with the legal minimum you are entitled to, if there is one: for instance, the length and amount of maternity leave and how long your job is kept open for you, or help with child care.

Next, are you actually getting it in practice? Sometimes perks and entitlements are left for people to claim, according to grade, not handed out automatically. No claim, no perk. Sometimes benefits agreed at national level get 'overlooked' or plain forgotten at local level, especially if it is an item in which the boss or union official is not interested.

Finally, find out what improvements the union is currently trying to obtain. A male-dominated union may be quite uninterested in asking for benefits which would make life easier for its female members, even though employers might be willing to grant them because they would cost little or nothing. Here, a determined group of women acting together can make an impact.

How you work is more important to women than to men. Men have the happy knack of combining work and play. A man can be drinking at the bar and at the same time collecting a valuable client for his firm, or solving a problem with a colleague. He can be getting a new contact with inside information while they scrub off the mud together after the rugby match.

For women, outside activities – collecting the children, going to the hairdresser – are usually an intrusion not an extension of work. So arrangements like working flexible hours ('flexitime') or being able to share jobs prove particularly worthwhile.

With flexitime, there is a core time when you must be present. Say, 9.30 to 12 and 2 to 4.30, Monday to Friday. Other than that, provided you complete the agreed hours in the week, you can do them when you like. With some schemes you can accumulate hours to earn days off. The choice to start late or finish early to fit in with family commitments, or for a disabled person to avoid the peak-time crush, can be a big bonus, even if it does not put a penny extra in your pocket.

Women who work for large organizations can often benefit from opportunities which no small employer can give. Like the chance of a sabbatical – this is unpaid time off, usually a year, with your job kept open for you. People use it to update or broaden their skills, perhaps on a training course, in another country or working for another organization altogether. Then there are exchange schemes. A teacher may work in Canada for a year while her place is taken by the Canadian teacher she replaces.

Alternatively, there may be the chance to work in your home. There is all the difference in the world between an underpaid out-worker struggling to keep up amid domestic chores and a skilled worker operating a computer terminal in the spare bedroom linked into the employer's computer system.

This has only become possible within the last few years. The advantages are clear: saved travelling time and costs to the employee, saved office space to the employer. Disadvantages that American males, the pioneers in this field, complain of include loneliness, fear of getting out of touch and, greatest of all, fear of being overlooked for promotion. Also, you would expect extra salary for the perks you are missing out on: heating and lighting paid for while you work, perhaps a subsidized canteen, luncheon vouchers, free coffee.

The woman who works for a small concern has more scope to improve her salary and perks because she is a 'one-off'. The boss is not restricted to national agreements. The thing to remember is to look at your ideas from the boss's point of view, and with real figures.

As the saying goes: *use soft words and hard arguments.*

With many jobs, like accountancy, you record your time regularly to charge it to the right client. The number of hours you worked multiplied by the amount your work is charged at gives you the total you earned for the firm last year. It is always a good starting point if you can remind the boss just how valuable an employee you are. Of course, they know this already, but may wish to play down the fact.

For every idea you raise, point out the advantages and the money saved for the firm.

Jane might say, 'I would like a company car, like Bill, and I would be willing to accept a lower salary in exchange. This would save you National Insurance contributions and the petrol money you pay me. Of course, the cost of the car and all the running expenses and the **hire-purchase interest** are legitimate business expenses. So they reduce the tax the firm pays on its profits. Then there is the **VAT** on the cost of the car which you can claim back, as a business. I as an individual can't.'

She should produce figures to show how much buying and running the car would cost. A show-room can tell her price and hire-purchase details. She can work out how much she spends running her present car. When she hands a copy of all this to her boss, the battle is half won.

Don't rely on your memory. Scribble a few notes of all the points you want to raise and take a pen to note anything else the boss might ask you to find out.

Never raise your voice and never act aggressively – if you do, you have lost. You need your boss's help. He may have to persuade his superiors. Sit diagonally, not four-square in your chair. Use the we-are-all-in-this-together approach, not the hammer-and-tongs approach.

There are other little ways in which you can get the boss to spend money on you besides your salary and perks. Perhaps you would like more training. Remind your boss that such expenses are all tax-deductible and the firm benefits when its employees keep up to date. Be as specific as you can. Find out who runs what courses and get their brochures. Many organizations offer a pleasant day in a smart hotel with lunch thrown in. There is tax relief too for in-house courses (run in your own offices) and even for training videos you can hire. John Cleese of Monty Python fame is just one of many comedians who have produced training videos which are fun as well as informative.

Being passed over for additional training is an easy way for women to fall behind their male counterparts. Stay on the look-out to take advantage of what is available. Even if your employer is unwilling to sponsor you for long-term training or release you during working hours, he may be content to pay for evening classes or correspondence tuition. This, with increased use of audiovisual and telephone techniques, is fast proving the easiest way for busy executives to learn. If possible, aim for a course giving a recognized qualification. This way, your new skills will be easier to sell to other potential employers.

Books and other training materials are also tax-deductible, and there is no rule that the books have to stay in the office. Perhaps there is some equipment that would enable you to do a better job, or an exhibition where it might be demonstrated.

Even an electric fan or air purifier or ionizer for the summer will be tax-deductible. Does the office need brightening up? How about a contract to provide flowers for the reception area; after all, you benefit if you work there. Someone has to take the flowers home at the weekend – why not you?

Many firms run incentive schemes or reward good ideas. Perhaps you should suggest it if yours does not. By and large, any money or goods you receive as a reward are tax-free. It is up to the firm to decide how much their business has benefited before they pay out.

Similarly, the Inland Revenue accept that it can be a legitimate business expense for employers to provide taxis for late-night staff. Perhaps your boss is not aware of this.

These are just a few ideas. Perhaps your employer will reject every single one. Even if he does, he will end the meeting with a very different idea of you. You will have shown yourself to be imaginative and dynamic, someone who thinks about their job and the good of the firm.

Always be specific. It is much easier to sell an idea when it is clear in your own mind. If you cannot write it down beforehand, you certainly cannot spout it face to face.

This chapter has told you how to get maximum income from your employment. There is one more organization you may not have thought of. It pays out money which is as good as income every day of the week, and you don't even have to work for it: the welfare state. Are you receiving all you are entitled to?

The best book I know for explaining what benefits are available, to whom and for what is Tolley's *Social Security and State Benefits*.* I don't claim it is easy reading. But it is better than the DSS's own pamphlets, which always send you chasing off after umpteen other pamphlets. The people who write Tolley's guide deserve a medal – if they are not in straitjackets!

One other earnings-related source of income or **capital** which is more common than people suppose comes from an insurance claim. Have you been involved in an accident which impaired your earning capacity or prospects? Did you claim? Is it too late? Only a solicitor or the Citizen's Advice Bureau can tell you for sure.

Finally, if you think working for others is a mug's game and

---

*Tolley's address is Tolley House, 2 Addiscombe Road, Croydon, Surrey CR9 5AF. If you don't want to buy the book, ask your local library to get it; but it must be the latest edition, because the rules change every year.

anyone with an ounce of initiative wants to work for themselves, then off you dash to the next chapter.

But you are not quite correct. Some of the most successful people run their businesses through a **limited company**. They act as directors, and company directors are employees. So they still need to refer to this chapter afterwards.

5

INCOME FROM SELF-EMPLOYMENT

Sally runs her own business.

A glamorous hairdresser in her thirties, she bubbles with energy and ideas. With a mind quick to take decisions and the determination to see them through, Sally typifies the self-employed businesswoman. If you had to sum up Sally in one word, it would be 'organized'.

Traditionally very few women take the plunge into **self-employment**. Part of the reason is that girls opt for the sort of training that leads to employment. The only apprenticeship commonly open to girls is hairdressing. As a result, many women go on to run their own salons with great success.

Another drawback is that to start many businesses you need **capital** or to be able to borrow it. Yet most women find the biggest deterrent is the complete commitment the business demands. As the Americans say, starting a new business is like producing a baby. For success, the whole family must want and prepare for it.

Sally knew before she started that she would need to work very long hours with no guaranteed wage waiting at the end of the week. She accepted that she would not know whether the business was successful for a long time – not even if clients came flocking and she was run off her feet.

Besides, she would have to record every penny in and out in painstaking detail, then prepare **accounts** for her salon or pay someone else to do it. She would have to contend with **VAT** on what she bought and sold and calculate **PAYE** for her employees. At least, in a cash-only business, Sally does not have the additional worry of customers who don't pay.

On top of all this, Sally knew what could happen if her salon flopped in favour of that up-market branch of a national chain of hairdressers down the road, or the cut-price barely trained girls who call on people at home. Debts would mount faster than she could earn the **income** to pay them. If she found herself overwhelmed by more debts than she could pay, Sally might have to sell everything (including her home) to pay them off.

No one would volunteer for all that worry and hassle if there were not terrific advantages to compensate – and there are.

WHO IS SELF-EMPLOYED?

Remember that an employee has a **contract of service**? A self-employed person has **contracts for services**, one with each customer or contractor. These contracts are simply agreements – they need not even be written down – between the self-employed person, like Sally, and the person who wants their services. You have made dozens of such contracts.

Every time you visit your hairdresser and pay them to tint your hair, you enter such an agreement – just by making an appointment. You would not dream of telling them *how* to wash your hair, let alone cut, perm or colour it. They provide the salon, the basin, the hot water, the shampoo, the drier, the magazines, the cup of coffee, everything down to the appointment card.

If the owner, like Sally, or anyone she employs, makes a botch of the job or stains your clothes, it is the owner who must compensate you out of the business money. You never employ anyone in the salon, although they are doing something for which you pay them. Sally herself enters a contract of service when she calls up the self-employed plumber to unblock her sink.

Sally is genuinely self-employed. In addition, you will meet a growing army of 'sham' self-employed, with no real business behind them, the vast majority male. Why?

The distinction between employees and the self-employed, between one sort of contract and another, grows more blurred all the time. Hospital doctors are employees of the NHS, but no one stands over them in the ward and tells them how to hold their stethoscopes.

In fact, any male who could possibly claim to be self-employed fights tooth and nail to be accepted as such by the **Inland Revenue** because of the tremendous advantages. I have even seen petrol-pump attendants try it on. Their boss, the garage owner, will support them too. If you take on a self-employed person to do work for you, you don't have to deduct PAYE tax or **National Insurance** contributions. You avoid employers' National Insurance. You don't even have to bother with safe conditions at work.

Next time you pass a building site, look around at the carpenters, bricklayers, painters and plasterers hard at it. Virtually every man-jack of them will be officially self-employed. Yet they may work for one employer for twenty years. Probably the only employee in the place – the only one to pay PAYE – will be the girl in the office. Here you see the 'sham' self-employed. They are really employees but enjoy all the advantages of being self-employed.

WHY BE SELF-EMPLOYED?

If you talk to anyone who is self-employed they are certain to complain that they are hard done by and penalized by the Inland Revenue and the DSS. Reach for the salt and take a good pinch. The opposite is true. Otherwise, people would not rush to be self-employed – people like contract milkers, who just drive from farm to farm fitting rubber suction pads on cows' udders, farm secretaries, private nurses, insurance agents and pools coupon collectors.

So what are these marvellous benefits that the self-employed enjoy?

1 You pay your taxes much later. Employees have already paid their taxes before they can even open their wage packets and count the notes. When a self-employed person starts up a business it is usually nine months before the Inland Revenue even contact them. The Revenue do this deliberately. They leave you in peace to get established. For ever after, you pay your tax very late.

Take the year from 6 April 1990 (tax years always start on 6 April) to 5 April 1991. Monthly paid employees pay tax from their wages at the end of April 1990, May 1990, June 1990, and so on, up to March 1991. The weekly paid pay even sooner. But self-employed people pay half their year's tax on 1 January 1992 and the rest on 1 July 1992.

Don't worry if you don't understand *why* the dates should be so different. Take it from me, they are. Any tax office or accountant can confirm this.

2 Employees spend a lot of their earnings just travelling to work. But a self-employed person effectively runs their car (and maybe their spouse's car) out of the business. In other words, the buying and running of the car are treated as a business expense. This expense reduces the amount of tax that self-employed people pay on their **profits**. Very nice! And the rules are even more generous. If you are self-employed, much of your private motoring is treated as a business expense too – taking the family to the seaside, for instance, as long as you stop off to deliver some samples to a client on the way.

3 Many of the self-employed live out of the till. All the receipts of the business are under their control, and they are also responsible for record-keeping. So it is not difficult in a cash business, like a shop, for owners to take money directly from the till to spend on themselves and their family. Unless this money has been recorded already, it is not included in the sales of the business. So the owner never pays tax on it.

This is, of course, dishonest and illegal, because you are cheating the Inland Revenue. But it does explain why the average self-employed person declares profits which are below the old-age pension level! Otherwise you might wonder why anyone would work so hard and such long hours for nothing.

4 Depending on the type of business, owners can benefit from what they sell. A pharmacist will not go to a rival pharmacist to pay cash for her make-up, her soap, her perfumes, for cough syrup for the family, or house-cleaning products, or for Christmas presents – or to swap for the fruit and vegetables sold by the nice woman next door. She will take stock from her own shop, perhaps damaged stock, and maybe she will record the fact. Again, she may order articles from her wholesaler, at wholesale prices, with no intention of selling them in the shop. She will keep them for herself, although the business paid for them.

5 An employee has to struggle very hard to persuade the Inland Revenue that he or she ever lays out a penny to do his or her job better – not so the self-employed.

When I was an employee, I bought a pocket calculator in the days when they were rare and expensive. I kept it in my desk drawer and used it solely for work. The Inland Revenue refused to allow me to deduct the cost of either the machine or the batteries to run it from my salary. They argued, quite legally, that if your employer decides you *need* something, the employer will provide it.

Sally, as a self-employed person, never has this problem, because she alone decides what she needs. I remember one jeweller who decided he needed a Rolls-Royce to deliver repaired jewellery to his clients' mansions. Any lesser vehicle would have devalued his stock!

6 Many self-employed people 'live on the job'. Perhaps they run a farm, a hotel, a guest-house, a convalescent home or a pub; or they simply occupy an ordinary house with part converted into a surgery or an office. They can all claim part, and sometimes most, of the cost of their domestic electricity, heating and telephone bills as a business expense. Others claim these expenses because they do some work, perhaps writing up the books, at home.

I have known pet food claimed as pest prevention or security expenses, and children's ponies claimed as farm animals. I even heard of one farmer who claimed the cost of his swimming-pool. He pointed out the farm was isolated, and if the hay-ricks caught fire, the fire brigade would need the water to put the fire out. The Inland Revenue took him to court, but he won his case.

7 As a self-employed person, Sally can employ whom she likes. The cost of their wages is a business expense. Of course, these people should be working in the salon, but it has been known for them to do the owner's housework, mind her children or do repair jobs around her home as well.

There is nothing to stop a self-employed person paying a salary to other members of the family. How many wives reading this receive a salary according to their husband's accounts that they never even knew about, let alone received? This may apply to children too, or to Granny.

One of my pilot clients flew a crop-sprayer. He paid both his pre-teen sons to stand out in the field and be sprayed over. Although highly dangerous, it was the best way to identify the right field from the air. If he sprayed weed-killer on the lettuces growing in the next field by mistake, he would have massive compensation to pay. Alternatively, Farmer Giles might grin to see his wheat showered by Farmer Brown's expensive fertilizer, but Farmer Brown would not be so delighted.

Shunting money around the family is a common way of saving tax. Bear in mind that anyone can earn broadly £3,000 (1992 figure) before they need worry about tax and National Insurance.

These are just a few examples. Some are acceptable. Others are not. All happen regularly. I am not suggesting that you become dishonest, but simply pointing out that if employees knew what the self-employed get away with, there would be a revolution.

The Inland Revenue know. They combat it every day. Most of their disputes with the self-employed fall in one of these areas. This is why a second amount of National Insurance (called Class 4) was introduced. Only the self-employed pay it. The aim was to make things fairer compared to what employees pay. In fact, the extra is still tiny. Lump together employee's and employer's contributions, and the government claws in far more for each employee than it does from the self-employed, including the Class 4 payments. Besides, the self-employed pay NI late, at the same time as income tax.

If you find all these self-employed tricks shocking, remember that life is rarely black and white. Even the most careful record-keeper will mix up business and private expenses. One shopkeeper I knew clocked up 10,000 miles in his car in the year. He said he drove 9,000 miles on business and only 1,000 on taking the kids to school, etc. So nine-tenths of the buying and running costs of his car were claimed as a legitimate business expense. Is this reasonable? You cannot judge until you know his circumstances. That said, accountants are paid to spend much of their time negotiating favourable compromises with the Revenue on behalf of their clients.

Take Sally. How many miles a year would you expect a hairdresser to drive on business? Regular trips to the bank? To her accountant? Perhaps to her solicitor about the lease, or to a plumber to dispute his outrageous bill for stopping a leak in the salon in the small hours? Yet Sally will remember the elderly customer who fainted under the drier and whom she had to drive to hospital; the brave, house-bound woman with multiple sclerosis whom she collects from her home and returns (it does happen); the staff she had to ferry around during the transport strike. There is no hard-and-fast rule, and Sally's mileage will vary from year to year.

RECORD-KEEPING

We said that Sally must keep records, just like every self-employed person: records of how much she spends and what on, how much she receives and what for. There are several reasons why record-keeping is essential if you are self-employed:

1 To account for VAT on what you buy and sell.*

2 To account for PAYE for any employees you have.

3 To hand to an accountant to prepare your accounts. These accounts fulfil two purposes. First, you must supply a copy to the Inland Revenue to calculate your own income tax. And second, your accounts tell how you are progressing – have you made a profit and if so, how much? Are you running your business efficiently? Where could you improve?

---

*I will not go into more detail about VAT here. If you need to know, the Customs and Excise Department produce excellent booklets. And they can tell you in ten seconds over the phone whether your business needs to register. They will call in to explain all the details if you ask them, or give you a clear 'yes' or 'no' on any query. Compared to income tax and the welfare state, VAT is child's play.

GETTING STARTED

Now you have discovered the advantages of self-employment, how do you get started?

If you are an employee and fancy the benefits of 'sham' self-employment, ask around. Is anyone else who does your job self-employed? Some call themselves freelance, on contract, contractors, commission agents or consultants. If they are, ask how they arranged it. Maybe if you ask the boss, he will agree to treat you in the same way. Remember the advantages to the employer.

In draughtsmen's offices, in accountancy firms, in hairdressing salons, in computer installations, you can watch two people working side by side at the same job. Yet one is self-employed and the other is not.

If you are unemployed and want to start up a genuine new venture, the government may give you money to set up your business. Ask about it at the DSS office well before you start. Remember, there are conditions to be satisfied. You must adjust your set-up to meet them all if you want to claim the money. No one will bend the rules to suit you.

Even if you are not officially unemployed, you may persuade the government or local council to help finance your new venture. There are all sorts of grants and subsidies and the offer of low-rent or even rent-free premises available. This is especially the case if you plan to operate in a run-down area, or if your venture will provide employment for others. Hunt out the areas officially selected for special help. Sometimes moving a mile from where you planned to set up can make all the difference.

I knew one client who obtained tens of thousands – a gift, not a loan – to rescue a stately home in the heart of Wales that was falling apart and turn it into a hotel. Of course, he put up money of his own as well, and he could present a well-researched case and had a successful track record too. The money is available. It is up to you to track it down and prove your case.

Anyone who plans a real new venture, not 'sham' self-employment, will have umpteen things to find out about, consider and decide. Sally had to find the right salon in the right place and arrange a **lease**. She had to arrange a bank loan, decide what redecorations to make, choose the **stock** to buy, order headed stationery for the new business, take on staff, etc.

Before she committed herself to a penny, Sally did her sums. She worked out what she would need and how much it would cost; how much money she could scrape together from savings and borrowings; how much she would have to earn to pay back her loans; how much she would have **to** charge, how many customers she would need to earn that amount and how long it would take her to pay off her debts.

Visiting the bank manager is excellent discipline for this. We look at these sums in more detail in Chapter 11 when we consider how to borrow successfully. Even if you can finance the whole show from your piggy bank without borrowing a penny, you must do the same calculations – to protect yourself.

ACCOUNTS, ACCOUNTANTS AND PITFALLS TO AVOID

If you are hoping to buy an existing business, you should ask the present owners to let you see the last three years' accounts, in confidence of course. Perhaps the accounts will not mean very much to you. They should make more sense when you have read this and the next chapter. You definitely need to show them to your accountant for advice before you decide to buy.

Of course, like Sally, you will fizz with new ideas of your own. But these accounts at least show what receipts and outgoings are possible.

No matter how small your business, I recommend at least

one visit to an accountant. Choose one who is chartered (ACA) or certified (ACCA), because any unqualified person can still legally call themselves an accountant. Even if you intend to prepare your own accounts in future, an accountant can tell you:

- what records to keep;
- what bank accounts to open;
- many pitfalls to avoid in starting up.

This should save you far more than the £60 or so one hour's consultation will cost. (Besides, the £60 counts as a business expense.) Have a list of all your questions ready to get the most out of your consultation.

Here are just a few of the expensive pitfalls that entrap people who set up their own businesses every week of the year.

You might spend hundreds on buying a **limited company** off the shelf, because some know-all told you you needed it. 'Off the shelf' means it is brand new and has never been used.

You could spend hundreds buying an **offshore** company because some ignoramus told you wrongly you would save tax that way.

Maybe you will start off as a husband-and-wife partnership when it would have saved you money for one (on paper) to employ the other. Or perhaps you will not start off as a partnership when you should have done.

Then again, you might buy the **shares** of an existing limited company to obtain its business. I will frighten you later on with examples of this dangerous pig in a poke (see Chapter 6).

The accountant can advise you whether you would do better to work flat-out to open your doors for business on 1 April, in the old tax year, or hold fire and open after 6 April, in the new tax year.

Maybe your business has developed from a hobby that just snowballed, and for years you did it simply for fun. Perhaps you collected antiques and now you think you know enough to start trading a few. An accountant can tell you when you officially started to trade.

Your accountant can advise you what date to choose to prepare your accounts. There is no set rule. It need not be a year since starting. No card shop wants the extra burden of accounts, or stock-taking, in the Christmas rush or the week before Valentine's Day. No farmer wants to devote himself to his books when clouds may threaten his harvest or all his sheep are producing lambs.

Some of these points may appear petty. They are not. Each can make a difference of thousands of pounds to the tax you pay and when. They can threaten or boost the whole future of your venture.

The accountant can also tell you (and this is vital) how much of what you take in you must set aside, on deposit in the bank, to cover future income tax, VAT, and the like. Many newcomers gaily reinvest every penny that comes in, only to go bust when the first big unexpected tax bill arrives.

Perhaps all this seems too grand for the modest venture you have set your heart on. If you cannot think on this scale yet, go to a stationer's and buy a Simplex book to keep details in. You absolutely *must* keep all receipts. Make a note of all you spend even when you don't get a receipt. For example, when you pay the window cleaner, a little note scribbled 'Window cleaner £10, 9 June,' pushed into the till will do.

If you give credit or do your work before you send out **invoices** (bills) to clients, monitor closely the number of customers who don't pay. Don't just grind your teeth and try to forget about them.

Non-payers and late payers probably cause more new businesses to capsize than anything else. You waste time and money doing the work and then again as you try to get paid. Worse, you may be forced to borrow when they don't cough up as promised.

If you are still in business after a year (two out of three people will not be – running your own business is that demanding), I again recommend you to go to a qualified accountant and pay for them to prepare the accounts for your first year. They can set you up right.

You cannot imagine just how important this first set of accounts is. Even if it only records your trading for the first twelve months, it normally fixes how much tax you pay for the next three years. Any tax office will confirm this. In future years you can always update the accountant's figures yourself and economize that way, if need be.

ACCOUNTS – IN MORE DETAIL

Just what are these accounts, this sheet or two of paper, on which I recommend that you spend several thousand pounds?

Every business will need a **profit and loss account**. This is sometimes called an 'income statement'. Every business but the tiniest will also need a **balance sheet**; another name is a 'statement of **assets** and **liabilities**'.

The profit and loss account records what came in and what went out in the year. The difference between the two is the **profit** (or loss). Perhaps you think your bank statements already show all this. Well, they are important documents for a starting point but can never give the full picture.

You paid for many items in advance. Perhaps you paid three months' phone rental or twelve months' car insurance yesterday. Then there are other bills you know will come but you have not yet received, like the car service or an electricity bill. You paid in cheques which have not yet cleared. You bought stock but have yet to sell it. Your bank statements ignore all these factors, whereas your accounts include them.

The main question is, did you make a profit? If so, how much? Did you simply break even, in which case you worked hard for nothing? Or did you suffer a loss, in which case you are worse off now than you were before you started?

Table 1 (opposite) shows the profit and loss account for

Table 1 SALLY'S SALON, PROFIT AND LOSS ACCOUNT FOR
THE YEAR ENDED 31 DECEMBER 1999

	£	£
Takings (including £23 bank interest)		53,456
less		
Purchases (shampoo, conditioner, etc.)	5,432	
Wages (including tax, employer's and employees' NI)	16,380	
Bank interest paid	418	
Repairs (to hair driers, etc.)	567	
Motoring (including HP)	1,234	
Rent for salon	5,000	
Miscellaneous	92	
Electricity, water, gas heating	4,499	(33,622)
Profit		19,834

Sally's Salon for her first year. Accountants may set out their figures in slightly different ways, but this layout is typical. The figure of £4,499 is underlined to show that the whole column of figures is being added together. You will see that the total comes to £33,622. This is put in the next column and inside brackets to show that it is being deducted from the takings. The result gives us the profit of £19,834.

Not difficult, is it? The figures don't matter much – except to Sally – so long as you grasp the general idea. If all Sally's expenses had come to £63,456 instead of £33,622 then she would have made a loss of (£10,000). Losses are put in brackets too.

'Miscellaneous' covers all the odd small expenses, like the window cleaner and Christmas decorations, that are not worth recording separately. Another name for them is 'sundries'.

I have encountered lots of businessmen who paid for

accounts and did not even understand this much. For a start, they confused takings (sales, receipts – call them what you like) with profit. They thought that because they rang up £53,456 on the till in the year, this was the profit they made.

You may be working hard, and your shop may be full of paying customers. You may even reluctantly turn people away. But this does not mean that you are making a profit. To find out, you need accounts and you need them quickly.

The longer you delay after the end of the year before you get your accounts prepared, the less they can tell you about the health of your business. They will be like clues on a trail that you have allowed to go cold.

Perhaps you made a small loss at the end of year one. If you had known this, you would have reviewed every expense and pared it to the bone. You would never have taken on an extra assistant, for instance. Instead, because the records gathered dust untouched for ten months, by the time the accounts are prepared and you know the truth, they are ancient history, and you may be deeply in debt. Men, particularly, have the happy idea that they can 'trade themselves out of trouble' – that is, keep going regardless, and hope that things will brighten up. Nine times out of ten, they are headed for **bankruptcy**.

Look back at the entry for wages. If Sally had prepared her own accounts, she would have included there the £250 a week she took out of the business in the year. This is what she used to live on and to pay her National Insurance. It would be common sense, but it would be wrong.

The wages she paid herself, often called drawings, are not a business expense. That £250 a week did not help Sally earn profits. Drawings are a distribution of the profit that has already been made.

Sally can spend as little or as much out of the business as she fancies and the till can produce, and it has no effect on the amount of profit she has made. She did not earn £13,000 profit (250 × 52 weeks), she made £19,834.

There are certain other payments you will never find in a profit and loss account: the £3,000 Sally paid for new driers; the £1,000 she spent at the outset to lease the salon. These are capital payments.

Remember at the beginning we talked about the difference between income and capital? By and large, income payments crop up year after year, like the electricity bill. Capital payments are a one-off. They are not forgotten. Their place is the balance sheet.

If the profit and loss account is a history of what has happened in the year, the balance sheet is like a snapshot of the business. It shows you just what assets and liabilities you possess on a given day. Table 2 (overleaf) shows Sally's balance sheet.

First, what does the £8,334 represent? The surprising answer is, nothing at all. Both sides must add up to the same figure – they must balance – or else the accounts are wrong. The figure itself means nothing, so forget it.

You will have spotted that the only figure that appears in both the profit and loss account and the balance sheet is profit.

The capital account shows how much the business is worth to Sally. At the beginning of the year, because it was new, it was worth nothing. At the end, it is worth £6,834 to her. Next year £6,834 will be the starting figure. This figure does not mean very much either. The higher the better, of course, but it does not mean that Sally could go out tomorrow and sell her business for this sum.

Because both sides of the balance sheet must always balance, all the assets added together must equal the liabilities. The capital account is a liability of the business because it is what the business owes to Sally.

Looked at another way, the value to Sally of her business is the value of all the assets less the value of all the liabilities to outsiders.

Sally's only liability to outsiders is her **creditors**. Creditors are people you owe money to, in Sally's case the **hire purchase** company for her car. She arranged a small **overdraft** from the bank, but she paid it off as soon as she could, to avoid paying interest. You will notice that the £418 **interest** she did pay is

Table 2   SALLY'S SALON, BALANCE SHEET AS AT
31 DECEMBER 1999

Liabilities	£	£	Assets	£
Creditors:				
HP on car		1,500	Cash in hand	34
			Cash at bank	600
Capital account:				
Opening			Stock, towels, etc.	200
capital	0		Debtors	0
Profit	19,834		Driers	3,000
less			Car	3,500
Drawings	(13,000)	6,834	Lease	1,000
		8,334		8,334

deducted in the profit and loss account. If she still owed the bank money, it would be included among her liabilities.

Sally is lucky. With a cash-only business, she has no worries about **debtors**. These are people who owe you money, the opposite to creditors. Debtors are assets because when they pay up, this will produce extra money for the business. And if they never pay up? Then the amount of the debt is deducted in the profit and loss account, just like any other business expense.

Businesses with lots of debtors can either pay someone like a debt-collecting agency to try to collect them, or sell their debts altogether. The organization that buys them will pay very little of their original worth unless they rate their own chances of getting the money much higher.

The next chapter will show what Sally's accounts really mean and how she can use them to help run her business and plan her future. This is where the fun begins. But if you have decided by now that self-employment is not for you, and you know all you want to, skip the next chapter and turn to Chapter 7 to try your luck at getting capital.

6 UNDER-STANDING YOUR ACCOUNTS

Drawing up your accounts is one thing; interpreting them is another you can buy simple, cheap software programs for your computer which will churn out your accounts for you. Fine, provided you feed in the figures correctly.

If your accountant merely puts the accounts down in front of you, with his or her invoice on top, change your accountant. A good accountant will talk you right through the accounts, with advice and helpful suggestions.

What can Sally learn from her accounts? She made a **profit**. Great. Was it enough? If she could have earned twice that much as an employee, then the answer may be no. She has not forgotten she will now have to pay tax and the extra Class 4 **National Insurance** on her profit. On the other hand, Sally does not have to bother about the cost of running her car, because this comes out of the business.

The acid test is to take your profit and divide it by the number of hours you worked in the period. Be honest now. You might be horrified to find that you could have earned more addressing envelopes. The same is true of some employees.

Some women who claim to be self-employed are not really,

although they work hard. They don't run a business, just a disguised hobby. The **Inland Revenue** define a hobby as something you undertake for pleasure not profit. As soon as you achieve a profit (after deducting all expenses), your hobby ceases. It transforms itself into a business.

If your hobby offers a challenge, enjoy it. Just recognize that it is not only *not* making money, it is gobbling up the time you *could* spend making money. Dabblers, whose 'hubby's' money cushions the bills and bails them out, reinforce women's reputation as mere amateurs in business.

Or you could look at life the other way and admit that women still relish the right to dabble, while men have lost it.

Sally made a profit. She is satisfied with the amount. But you will not find her preening or sitting smugly on her laurels. She will be studying her accounts to ask herself: Is my business well run? How can I increase the profit? Are any of my expenses too high? How can I reduce them?

Her accountant should be able to help her because he will have prepared hundreds of accounts for similar businesses. Besides, after the first year, Sally can look back at last year's figures for a guide.

Sally enjoys one great advantage. She worked in the trade for many years before branching out on her own. Even as a trainee, then an improver, she kept her eyes open and watched how her employers ran their businesses.

You would be amazed how many couples sink their life savings into a shop without knowing the first thing about the trade. In seaside resorts and other popular retirement spots, each season brings new traders as regularly as day trippers.

Husband and wife buy the shop, full of optimism, with their retirement nest-egg. They have looked forward to their independence for years. 'Our own little shop' conjures up the second-favourite British dream after the cottage with roses around the porch. We really are a nation of shopkeepers.

But the husband has slouched for a lifetime over his desk as he pushed a pen in an office. Suddenly he must lift, carry and restock all day long. The extra hours take their toll. He overdoes the heavy work and succumbs to a heart attack.

His widow cannot carry on alone and sells off the shop. It never achieved much profit because they did not know how. She receives next to nothing for it because of the poor results. The couple's dreams and savings have gone down the drain. Agents and solicitors cheerfully sign up the next hopeful pair, confident that the little shop will find itself back on the market again in a few years' time.

How can such sad waste be avoided? Every occupation guards its own rules of thumb and short cuts. Like Sally, you will need to master yours. It is always a good idea to spend at least a few months working in the sort of business you plan to buy.

Often the seller will offer to train you before you buy and take over. Make sure the period of training starts before you pay up, so the seller cannot leave you high and dry on day one. This initiation period also shows if you can physically tackle the task. Many trades that you think will not involve great muscle turn out to demand as much brawn as brain. Take cellar-work, for example – yet many men yearn to run a pub when they retire. If you hint they are too old or weak, they think of pulling a pint and laugh.

Perhaps your results are middling and you are wondering whether they really reward the long hours and constant worry. But perhaps next year will turn out better. Why? To start with, you have more experience now, which helps. Look for other solid reasons on which to base your optimism.

A steady increase in takings month by month shows you are building up a faithful clientele. Perhaps a new employer is moving into your area and bringing their workers – potential clients for you. Perhaps you are now the only one in the district with a new and genuinely different product to sell or service to offer, and the manufacturers are launching a major advertising campaign. Perhaps your competition has shrunk. These are all genuine reasons to be optimistic, not gold-at-the-end-of-the-rainbow dreams.

Your results can look mediocre, not because your business lacks promise but because of your prices. Newcomers face the common difficulty of not knowing how much to charge. Again, each trade keeps its own rules. For instance, in catering you should reckon to charge £3 for every £1 worth of food you buy. Surprised? This is not just the rule for fancy restaurants with inflated prices.

People often create insurmountable difficulties for themselves by not charging enough. They doom themselves to fail. It is not always the cheapest who make the most profit. Especially in a prestige business or where you provide a personal service, people genuinely want to pay more. They value your product in proportion to what you charge for it.

Generally, in a new business, the crunch comes after about eighteen months. This is the make-or-break time. If you have not sorted out your teething troubles by then, you never will. You also receive your first tax bills around this time.

Had you forgotten about tax? It can eat into your hard-earned profit, leaving you with crumbs. Did you spend your takings as they came into the till on new **stock** to sell?

Your accountant should have advised you roughly how much to set aside to provide for tax. This reserve of cash should go straight into a bank or building society, earning **interest**. If, instead, you now need to borrow to get ready money to pay your tax, you are saddling your struggling business with yet another outgoing – worse still, with one that is not even an accepted business expense.

Sometimes, depending on the business, accountants only have to glance at the accounts they have prepared to see that something is wrong, although the figures balance and both accountant and proprietor have acted honestly.

If, for example, a pub bought £10,000 worth of beer in a

year, it should have sold it for far more than £12,000. So if £12,000 is the total of sales in the year, an ocean of booze or money, or both, has disappeared. There is a hole in the profits. Was it the barmaid with her fingers in the till? Or mother-in-law who lives in? Has the landlady salted the missing money into a villa in Spain or lost it on a racehorse? Is the landlord so blind drunk by nine o'clock each night that he has no notion what he or his staff are charging? Did the takings plummet when he employed a manager so he could enjoy a week's well-earned rest in the sun? I have known all these things to happen.

In her trade too, Sally must get to know what figures to expect and to hunt for the reason if they fall short. This leads us on to evasion.

TAX EVASION AND TAX AVOIDANCE

Both tax evasion and tax avoidance have the same aim: to pay less tax. Evaders break the law and risk prison doing so. As with many crimes, there are almost as many different ways to evade tax as there are evaders. Broadly, they either hide part of what they have received (the greediest ones hide it all) or invent imaginary or unacceptable expenses to claim.

For instance, one restaurant honestly recorded every meal it served in the evenings but 'forgot' that it opened its doors at lunchtime too. A carpenter's accounts included every job he did during the week but skipped those he did at weekends. On the expenses side, all sorts of things are wrongly included as 'purchases of **stock**' – even the family grocery bills from the supermarket or Dad's account with his bookmaker.

In practice, few people go to prison for tax evasion. The Inland Revenue normally agree not to prosecute, without involving the police at all, if you pay penalties plus interest on the tax lost. This usually doubles the sum you would otherwise have paid in tax. It also costs you thousands of pounds in extra accountant's fees, plus the misery of sleepless nights during an inquiry which may drag on for years. Of course, your affairs will always be closely reviewed ever afterwards.

A reputable accountant will never help you to evade. He or she risks joining you in the next cell. But accountants do use all their expertise in legal avoidance. They may suggest legitimate deductions that would not have occurred to you.

For example: a small wage to Mother for answering the phone and helping out in the shop occasionally. You don't actually pay any money over. Mother is included as a **creditor** of the business. When you tell her, she says, 'It was nothing. I was glad to help. Forget it.' This means, in accounting terms, that the debt is forgiven and the money is yours to keep.

A good accountant will use his detailed knowledge of tax law. From the dozens of options the rules permit, he will choose the one that means you pay the least tax.

Let us jokingly imagine that I receive £100,000 from sales of this book. This sum might all be taxed in one year. But if my accountant knows his stuff, he will choose to pay as though I had earned the money over three years, at £33,333 a year. This option will save me a staggering £9,000 in tax – just for a letter, and totally legal. This is tax avoidance.

SOLE TRADERS, PARTNERSHIPS AND LIMITED COMPANIES

Sally runs her business on her own. She is a **sole trader**. There are two other ways she could run it if she chose: as a **partnership** or as a **limited company**.

If she joined forces with Jenny, another talented sole trader in the next town, the two of them could form a partnership. Each of them would be a **partner**.

A 'legal person' means that the law treats it as much like a human being as possible. A limited company must be born (set up). Then it lives until it dies (is wound up). The company continues to live even though the shareholders and **directors** change and the trade finishes or a new one starts. Some have existed for centuries, running businesses that started hundreds of years before that.

Think of the company as a bus. The shareholders provide the money to buy the bus. Each owns a **share** in the bus, hence shareholders. They own it, so they decide who should drive it. The drivers are called directors. In small limited companies, the shareholders usually choose themselves; in other words, they appoint themselves directors. The shareholders, as owners, receive the profits from the passengers. The directors, as drivers, just collect the profits for them.

Why are limited companies 'limited'? If the trade fails and the company owes more money than it can find, the shareholders' loss is *limited* to their original stake – that is, to the money they put up to buy the shares in the beginning. They can wave goodbye to that, but this is the worst they have to fear. All their other **assets**, like the family home, remain safe. This is the big advantage that limited companies enjoy over partnerships and sole-trader businesses.

Directors are employees of the limited company. They usually receive a wage on which **PAYE** is operated, just like the rest of the company's employees. The company itself pays a sort of **income tax** on its profits called **corporation tax**. Then it can pay out the rest of its profits to the shareholders. The cash shareholders receive is called a **dividend**.

So shareholder-directors can earn dividends as well as a wage, and of course they can vote themselves a bonus or tax-free expenses if they wish.

Two vital questions will probably have occurred to you by now:

Why should someone who went to a lot of trouble to become

self-employed to avoid PAYE now turn himself into a director and return to being an employee again? Also, if company profits suffer corporation tax, and then shareholders' dividends suffer income tax, this makes two bites of tax out of the same income, so won't you be worse off as a result?

So anyone might expect. Reality is more complicated. It is still your business and you control the cash. You can still employ whom you like and run your company car on the business. There are all sorts of legal ways, known to any good accountant, which allow you to delay or choose which tax (corporation or income) you pay. This all makes a limited company highly attractive – but not for a beginner.

Build yourself a thriving business first. Remember, your accountant will charge you more than twice as much to prepare accounts for the tiniest limited company, because there will be far more work to do. Get a few years' good profits under your belt. Then consider buying an off-the-shelf (brand-new) limited company and transferring your business to it. You become shareholder and director, of course.

PRIVATE AND PUBLIC LIMITED COMPANIES

You recognize a **private limited company** because it has 'Ltd' (short for 'Limited') after the name. It has a small number of shareholders, usually a family.

A **public limited company** has 'PLC', 'plc' or 'Plc' after its name, like Lloyds Bank Plc. Lloyds counts its shareholders in tens of thousands. You or I can join them if we buy its shares through the **stock market**.

Once a private limited company achieves a certain size, it will almost certainly change over to become a public limited company.* This is called 'going public'. The company issues a

*There is a halfway house for companies called the Unlisted Securities Market.

lot more shares to the family. They then sell them on the stock market and can grow very rich overnight.

On the other hand, there are now hundreds of new shareholders in the new PLC. Each has a say in how the company should be run. They can attend the annual general meeting and vote. The previous shareholders, the family, may well lose control of their company to outsiders with quite different ideas.

This is a long way from Sally and her salon. She is unlikely ever to grow this big. Most hairdressers stay sole traders. Empire-building is normally a masculine dream. The few hairdressers who really hit the big time, like Vidal Sassoon, establish a chain of salons and then branch out into their own range of hair-care products.

LIMITED LIABILITY

Limited **liability** is only the name for the advantage I mentioned above. If the trade fails, your losses as a shareholder (your liability) are limited to what you paid for the shares. The rest of your assets remain safe.

In practice, limited companies go bust every day of the week. There is a special City newspaper, *The Gazette*, which lists them. Over the years, many banks that have lent money to these limited companies have often lost it. They cannot persuade the courts to seize the shareholders' personal property to sell it off, as they can with sole traders and partnerships.

So, to protect themselves, banks insist on **personal guarantees** from directors or shareholders before they make a loan. Even accountants ensure that they get their fees by insisting on such written guarantees. If you sign one, your home and all your other possessions are no safer than if you were a sole trader.

In Chapter 4 I said never buy an existing limited company just to obtain its trade. Why not?

Remember, a company is a legal person. It had a life before you bought it. Anything can come to light later on. It is like taking in a stray dog and finding out later that its previous sufferings mean you dare not trust it near your children, or that it is infected with distemper.

With a limited company, you are responsible for anything the company did in the past, even for things that happened before you ever came on the scene. Just a few examples:

- Some previous work was shoddily done and the customers claim recompense. You will have to do all the work again – for nothing.
- The accounts did not show all the debts that the limited company had incurred. Now the **creditors** are pressing for their money, and you have to pay – not personally, of course, but out of the company's money.
- The accounts show that various customers have not paid up, so you expect to receive their money. It may never come, even though when you bought the company you paid extra because of the value of those debts.
- Earlier years' tax affairs may not be settled or may be reviewed. Perhaps the old directors were on the fiddle for years. It is the company you now own that will have to pay to sort everything out, and fork out the extra tax at the end.

(Maybe you will have a case to sue the old directors or the accountants who misled you. In practice, you can forget it if they have no assets or have left the country. Besides, all the professions are adept at covering their tracks.)

Luckily, there is an easy alternative if the business you yearn to buy is run by a limited company. Make an offer for the trade – the company's assets, **lease**, etc. The sellers may insist on you buying the **debtors** and stock, perhaps even the **goodwill**, otherwise don't bother with these things. We have already warned that money owing from customers (debtors) may not come. The stock too may include old or unsellable items. You have nothing to show for buying goodwill, as explained below. Avoid buying all three if you can.

Goodwill is another of those vague, invisible assets. It covers those vital, unmeasurable things like having a faithful clientele ready-made rather than having to work hard to build one up from scratch. Goodwill may be hard to value but is still important.

When you bought its trade, that old company became an empty shell. It still belongs to the old shareholders, and they, not you, must pay to allow it to die (wind it up).

Even though you bought it from a limited company, run your new business as a sole trader or partnership until you get established. Allow yourself at least two years. Then buy your own off-the-shelf company and transfer your business into it. An accountant will do this for you. It is quick, easy and not particularly costly.

We have spent three chapters looking at money you have to work for – **income**. In the next, we consider the other sort – **capital**.

7

If you fancy your wealth in a sizeable **CAPITAL** *chunk, as* **capital***, your best hopes are to inherit it or receive it as a gift or as compensation. An outright windfall surprises most people at least once in their lifetime. If you want funds for a specific purpose, you can try to borrow the money.*

You can build up capital through savings, as we shall see in Chapter 10, or invest your capital to grow. We investigate this in Chapter 12. But you cannot really *earn* capital, even though people who looked after an elderly relative for years and were remembered in his will might feel that they deserved it.

When you receive wages from a job or **income** from an **asset** (such as rent from your spare lock-up garage), as soon as you invest the cash, it becomes capital. Maybe you put it on deposit in the bank. The interest you earn from it is income.

If you leave this new interest on deposit so that it earns its own interest, it too becomes capital. Income can transform itself into capital, but capital can never turn back into income. An apple (income) contains pips that can start a new tree (capital), but a tree can never shrivel back to an apple. It is a funny old system, but this remains the basis of all accounting, banking, finance and taxation everywhere in the free world – if only because no one can agree on a better one.

INHERITANCE

Inheritance is the most common method of self-enrichment. Even in the USA, that land of opportunity and the self-made man and woman, most millionaires are only millionaires because they were born that way. It was Pa or Grandpappy who had the brains or did the hard graft.

Most people inherit fairly late in life and from their parents. As people now live longer, children who a generation ago might have inherited in their forties now don't inherit until their fifties or sixties. By this time their hard-up years of child rearing are a vague memory, and most of their plans and dreams have been either realized or abandoned. The wealth is not as useful to them as it might have been earlier.

Most married women can expect to inherit from their husband. (On average, wives are younger than their husbands and live longer anyway.) There are wise and foolish ways for women to manage such a windfall.

Farmer Roberts, one of my clients, stinted and scrimped all his life. He boasted he never wore underwear; he did not believe in it. His neighbours said that if he rubbed a hole through one wellington boot after ten years' use, he would refuse to buy a new pair. No, he would rather wear a gumboot saved from a previous pair, on the wrong foot if necessary, until that wore out too.

Farmer Roberts showed me around his house once. Every piece of furniture dated from 1910. This was when his father had bought the house and furnished it for him. He had bought nothing since.

In his eighties, Farmer Roberts sold off several fields. I helped him to make, keep and invest many tens of thousands of pounds. Mrs Roberts looked on smiling, never offering a suggestion of her own.

When he went into hospital for his first and last visit, complete with his first-ever pyjamas, the nurses were amazed to discover that Farmer Roberts had no medical card. He had never seen a doctor in his life! He died childless, and his wife was suddenly transformed from a life of cheerful meanness to being a very wealthy widow in her sixties.

She took it all in her stride. Her solicitor and I arranged everything to provide her with ample cash day to day, far more than I earned. She built the modern house of her dreams nearby and invited her sister to keep her company. Together, they enjoyed frequent holidays, bought the best of everything and generally made up for lost time.

Mrs Roberts still found time to treat the entire old folks' club to a super tea and to support her favourite charities. She arranged that after her death as much as possible would go to the people and charities of her choice. She did not lose a single friend.

Mrs Coleman, by contrast, lost her husband suddenly in her forties. He had been a builder, moderately successful so she supposed, and she a shy little housewife. Imagine her surprise when he left her 150 building plots, each worth tens of thousands. Suddenly she found people's attitude to her transformed. Men who had never glanced in her direction before started to tell her how pretty she was. Women began to ask her opinion or advice. The bank manager invited her to dinner. In no time, she found she had attracted a live-in boyfriend.

Mrs Coleman had two daughters, both happily married with toddlers. Idolizing her grandchildren, she thought it might be fun to buy a holiday flat in Spain. Then the family could enjoy it together. 'Why settle for a flat?' the estate agent suggested. 'Why not buy the whole floor?' So she did.

When the family came on a long holiday, Mrs Coleman kept a firm grip of the purse-strings. She decided how every penny should be spent. No one could even take a taxi without her insisting she must pay for it, and everyone had to see her pay. Her sons-in-law started to resent it. They grew short with her daughters. Only in the bar, downing cheap brandy, could they swap complaints and feel free of Mother-in-law.

Mrs Coleman found it wearing, living with noisy toddlers, despite her affection for them. She meddled in their upbringing; well, everyone else was asking her advice these days. At the same time, she could not understand why her family despised her boyfriend. He had no job, never opened his mouth and spent his life cadging.

Family rows grew worse and worse. People began counting the days until they could go home. The sons-in-law hinted that next time they would prefer to come without Granny, which hurt her very much.

The Spanish investments did not yield much income, but Mrs Coleman was not bothered for the moment. This was the last thing on her mind after she answered the doorbell to a stranger one morning. The woman clutched a baby and asked for her husband back. Mrs Coleman, humiliated and ashamed, turfed out her boyfriend on the spot.

Poor Mrs Coleman. She has not exhausted her inheritance yet, but it is only a matter of time. She lives on her own again, with her family alienated. Why? Basically because she could not cope with the sudden influx of money.

If her husband had had more foresight, he would not have expected her to. He should have set up a **trust** with skilled trustees to help her. Looking back, it would have been better to leave some money, or building plots, directly to his daughters too. It might have sweetened the sons-in-law. It would certainly have sheltered family money from the taxman's clutches.

Goodness knows how much the family would lose in **inheritance tax** should Mrs Coleman die. Of course, she does not want to think about such a thing. (I will go into this in more detail in Chapter 15.)

And the moral? We are never too old to enjoy a **legacy**. Whether it turns into a blessing or a curse depends on our attitude and on how prepared we are beforehand.

GIFTS

'Wherever did you get the money to buy your house?' the tax inspector asked the pleasant young man without a penny in the world.

'Mike Brown gave it to me,' came the ready answer.

'A relative?'

'No.'

'But you must pay it back?'

'No. It was a gift.'

'Er, why?'

'We both attend the same church.'

The official spluttered. This young man expected him to swallow that! A tax inspector spends his day sorting through the truth, fibs, distortions and downright whoppers. He was inclined to file this tale among the whoppers. So he showed the fellow the door and made inquiries in every direction he could think of about the church. When the results came in, he hummed and he hawed. He asked his colleagues and his superiors. He slept on it. In the end he had to concede. The young churchgoer had told the truth.

By all accounts, this particular community of Christians really did help each other financially. One member would cheerfully give a large sum to another in need, with no strings at all attached.

The young man explained that, later on, when his family's needs grew less, he would do the same for someone else. Perhaps he would take out a **mortgage** and give the money to someone else to buy a house. Perhaps he would move out of his present home, so that a larger family could occupy it. There was nothing in writing. It was all a matter of trust. Such things do happen, even today.

For most people, gifts come from members of their family. Maybe they start off as loans, and after a while the lender says to forget it. Parents adopt this approach to help youngsters feel more independent.

Gifts in the hand are one thing, but beware of gifts with strings attached. They may not be as generous as they appear, even if the strings are of your own making.

'You can live in this house rent-free all your life. After I die I will leave it to you,' promised my great-uncle George to his nephew Bert. Bert and his bride Florrie were delighted. Few newly weds then were so fortunate, especially as Uncle George lived elsewhere. They moved in at once. George kept his promises, but he did not die until he was 97 and Bert and Florrie were in their seventies.

The couple lived in his house for fifty years. During all that time, they never changed a thing and hardly bought a thing. They never even put a coat of paint on the front door. They lived in extreme discomfort – believe it or not, no heating even in January, no inside water tap, let alone toilet or bath – while their bank balance grew and swelled.

Why? Because the house was not theirs. They were terrified that if Uncle George changed his mind, their efforts would be wasted. Their uncle's very generosity kept them chained for life, because the one thing he did not give them was security of tenure, and this devalued what he did give them.

Once upon a time, lifetime gifts did not suffer tax, but gifts on death (legacies in a will) did. So wealthy people naturally gave everything away *before* they died. Great-Grandpapa would sign away his possessions with his final gasp.

A Labour government introduced capital transfer tax to tax gifts whenever they took place. Conservative governments repeatedly weakened the rules and finally removed all taxes on lifetime gifts. The donor simply had to survive for seven years after making the gift. If he or she only survived three to seven years, there was tax payable but not so much. Some form of tax on lifetime gifts may be introduced again. The only tax on gifts on death is called inheritance tax. I look at it again in Chapter 15.

In the days when capital transfer tax was still strong, one of my colleagues saved a client £100,000 by persuading her to give her son the farm he already ran. This was the difference between the tax she would pay on the gift and the tax she would have paid if she had left him the farm in her will.

Mrs Leigh, the mother, started off reluctant but conceded, 'He might just as well take it now as when I'm gone.' So if you are trying to persuade an aged relative to give you something now, the tax saving is a good angle. Under today's rules, Mrs Leigh would have saved even more, provided she survived three years, preferably seven.

Yet she was right to hesitate. She recognized what a twit her son was. In three years he ran through the £400,000 the farm was worth and came back to ask for more.

His stupidity even hit the local newspaper when he embarked on a little illegal stubble-burning, let it flare out of hand and started a blaze. He seized the nearest thing to put it out – a cylinder of spray. The chemicals inside produced dioxin gas. Even when eleven people, mostly fire-fighters and his own labourers, had been rushed to hospital, he dismissed the scene as a fuss about nothing.

Mother-in-law and daughter-in-law did not hit it off, and this was another reason why Mrs Leigh senior had appeared reluctant to save her family a fortune. So, if you are seeking a gift, remember that the donor may be quite willing to give to *you* but reluctant to see your husband/boyfriend/associate with their paws on the money.

The last I heard, Mrs Leigh was still shelling out of her bottomless hoard. By now it was a habit; her old reluctance had yielded to resignation.

Mrs Leigh's daughter-in-law, her patience at an end, turned her back on these endless streams of new money, and sued for divorce. Luckily, her own mother sends similar top-ups from her Channel Islands **tax haven** to keep daughter and grandchildren smiling.

WINDFALLS

Some people are born great, some achieve greatness, and some have greatness thrust upon them. This saying also applies to money. Some people, without raising a finger to earn it, may suddenly find themselves rich.

Windfalls appear under every guise: a pools win, a lucky bet, a lottery ticket. Maybe you will strike lucky as a contestant on a quiz show, or write the winning slogan in a competition.

An out-of-the-blue inheritance may arrive from a relative you never knew you had. You may inherit a vast legacy like the one Mrs Coleman received, when she only expected a small sum. Even a lump-sum divorce settlement (see Chapter 14) counts. Hundreds of people receive windfalls they would rather not have – redundancy payments because their employer has cut back on staff or gone out of business.

Far more common than pools winners are people whose lump sum arises as compensation paid under an insurance policy. Suppose you were hurt in a car crash, for instance, made an insurance claim and received compensation for your injuries.

The courts too can order a lump sum to be paid to a victim. Courts decide when people have been harmed, either bodily or mentally, or their reputations damaged. They make the people responsible pay compensation.

You have to sue, of course. But suppose you are one of dozens injured in a train derailment. All the victims band together, the courts hear one test case, and your lawyers settle the amount due to you out of court. Don't expect instant riches and start spending – you may wait years. Above all, unless you are really desperate, never borrow on the strength of the compensation you *may* receive one day.

I heard of a female barrister, the friend of a friend. She was walking to court, immaculately turned out in gown and wig, briefcase under one arm, when she had to pass a road-tarring machine. As she stepped around it, the apparatus went haywire. It covered her from head to foot in hot tar. The local council coughed up her compensation at once and handsomely.

Then again, disaster funds are often set up for the victims of a public tragedy. The trustees have wide discretion what they pay out, when and to whom.

Sometimes ordinary people get caught up in events and find that the newspapers will offer a fortune for the photo they snapped on the scene, for their account of what happened. They don't even need to put pen to paper, because usually reporters do the actual writing for them.

There are as many types of windfall as there are stars in the sky, and new ones are appearing all the time. Take the man who was simply digging his garden. He forked out a weed and was about to toss it away. Then he looked again. It was clover. But there was something odd. Then he realized: every stem had four leaves. So he potted it up and watched. Sure enough, the plant only produced four-leafed clovers. Soon he developed a flourishing business selling lucky four-leafed clovers by post. Tax-free. The Inland Revenue admitted the freak plant was a pure windfall.

How often have we envied the woman who discovered that the ugly old vase her aunt left her was genuine Chinese porcelain and worth a fortune? Or the man who nearly threw a hideous old painting on the bonfire, only to notice a tiny scrawled signature in one corner which turned it into a priceless old master? Such stories cheer us all and send everyone rushing hopefully to the attic. They do happen – as sudden and rewarding as a lawnful of mushrooms.

We all know how planning permission inflates the value of a plot of land. When my local council announced a development plan for one village nearby, several of my farmer clients found themselves millionaires overnight. Their fields rocketed in value from £2,000 an acre to £70,000 an acre. The farmers were besieged with offers from building firms that wanted to construct housing estates.

Can you predict windfalls? No. Far-sighted people buy land on the outskirts of towns or which might one day provide vital access to others. Then they bide their time and hope. The biggest gain I ever came across was made by a canny farmer who bought a field for £100 in 1945 and sold it for £100,000 in 1975 when a motorway was built.

The art of managing a windfall is to recognize it for what it is: a one-off. Unlike a pop group I dealt with – they achieved one monster worldwide hit. (You would recognize the name.) They made it with the cheap guitars and drum kit they had always used. But their new agent persuaded them that they needed brand-new state-of-the-art equipment to stay at the top.

They blew all their earnings on it, including tens of thousands for a synthesizer whose banks of switches would have befuddled an airline pilot. It was so novel, they had to have it flown in from the USA. The group threw away the simple guitars that had backed the great hit. And guess what? They never managed another hit at all. Despite their huge earnings, which dribbled in for years, the group fell deeply into debt. Their agent soon pocketed his fees and the kickbacks from the instrument sellers. He left them to sort themselves out and went off in search of other mugs.

So – windfalls are wonderful. But don't expect them to keep on arriving. Even Aladdin only found one magic lamp.

Another of my clients was offered a very odd windfall but refused to accept it. Why? Because he was too greedy! He was expecting a tax bill for £30,000. When the bill came, it demanded £3,000. The bill was handwritten and legal; quite exceptionally, the clerk had made a mistake which would never be rectified. So what did my client do? Pay up and shut up you might think. Not likely.

'I'm not paying those leeches a penny yet,' he growled,

although he admitted he owed the full £30,000. So he complained. The affair was reviewed, the mistake was noticed as it was certain to be, and he received his bill for the full £30,000. Then he was satisfied.

BORROWING AND INTEREST

Most of us need to borrow at one time or another. It should always be for a specific purpose, such as to start a business or to buy a home. Never borrow just to keep going until next pay day. If you are that bad a manager (or that desperately poor), go to the Citizen's Advice Bureau. Ask for help on budgeting and ask if there are any welfare benefits you should be claiming.

If you have money but somehow seem to lurch from one crisis to another, go to your bank. You might find its budget account is just what you need. Together, you work out which big bills are likely to fall due when. You may receive a special chequebook to pay them; or alternatively the bank may allow you to pay out more than you have deposited. The bank takes its money, and **interest** on the loan, from your regular deposits.

There are many sources of loans, but even today the most common is the family. This is the only form of borrowing where you are not likely to pay interest. Organizations like banks and **finance houses** exist to make a **profit**. They earn it out of the interest they charge. It must always be higher than the interest they pay you on your deposit account. This is how they cover their expenses and pay for their plushy offices and their television advertising.

Why must you pay interest on loans, and how does it work?

Let me offer you a choice. Which would you prefer: £100 in your pocket ready to spend or £100 coming in a year's time? There is no possible reason to choose to wait, even ignoring

inflation. In a year's time someone else may have bought what you wanted or you may not be around to enjoy it. Besides, you will have had to bite your nails while you wait.

Interest is the reward you receive for not enjoying your own money now. Equally, when you borrow, interest is the price you pay for enjoying someone else's money and forcing them to wait.

Naturally, whenever you borrow, you want to do it as cheaply as possible. The main cost of borrowing is interest, so you aim to minimize the interest you must pay. For this you need to know what the real **interest rate** is.

Suppose you want to borrow £100 for a year, and the interest rate quoted is 10 per cent **per annum**. (Per cent means 'out of a hundred' and is often shown by the sign %. Percentages are explained in Chapter 20. Per annum, or p.a., just means a year.) At the end of the year, you repay the original £100 (called the **principal**) plus £10 interest. Total £110.

But suppose you agree to repay the loan and interest regularly through the year, say £9.16 a month (£9.16 × 12 instalments = £110). Then, although the interest rate is apparently 10 per cent per annum, in fact it is far higher.

Why? Well, after month 1, you only owe £91.67, because you have repaid the first instalment: £91.67 is the £100 you borrowed less £8.33 of the £9.16 you paid. The other 83p is one-twelfth of the £10 interest you are paying.

By month 11, you owe virtually nothing. But the 10 per cent was calculated as though you owed the full £100 for a full year. If you work out how much interest you pay on what you actually owe, the interest swells to a horrific 18.46 per cent.

To avoid this misunderstanding, you want the interest calculated *on the reducing balance* – that is, on £100 for one month, on £91.67 for the second month, and so on. This way, you only pay interest on the money you really owe. So there is a vast difference between a straight 10 per cent and 10 per cent on a reducing balance.

If you borrow £100 at 10 per cent on a reducing balance over a year, you actually pay £5.42 interest instead of £10: £5.42 over a year on £100 is effectively 5.42 per cent.

If you think this is impossibly muddly, so does the government. This is why they introduced the APR to help you. I explain this in Chapter 11.

All sorts of organizations will fall over each other to lend you money. They will eagerly offer you a credit card or a charge card. Many shops offer an account card which is a credit card that only covers goods in their own shop. (These are all different from a bank card or banker's card. This only guarantees that any cheque you write will not bounce. So it protects the shopkeeper.)

Other organizations entice you with hire purchase or lease purchase. (I explain these in Chapter 11.)

All lenders demand proof that you will be able to repay them. You fill in their form, giving details of your income and outgoings. Sometimes they also want extra security. The hire-purchase company, for instance, continues to own the car you have bought, and you cannot legally sell it until you have repaid the loan.

Sometimes the security takes the form of a signature by a guarantor. This person volunteers to pay up if the borrower cannot. In the past, female borrowers often had to supply a male guarantor, simply because they were female.

I knew one single woman, a long-standing civil servant in her late thirties, who had to persuade a distant male cousin to sign as guarantor so that she could buy a house. And she had to pay 15 per cent interest when the going rate was 6 per cent. Not any more: today she would be recognized as a valued customer in her own right. She might even act as guarantor herself. Many women do, like the mother of a teenage son buying a motorbike but too young to sign a hire-purchase agreement.

Where organizations don't take up references or demand

security or a guarantor, you should beware. Some newspapers carry small advertisements offering to lend money to anyone, even to pay off other debts, even for people with no job and no money. Their interest rates will be crippling – 60 per cent is not unknown.

Besides, because they are lending to the riskiest people, the men who come to collect the debts may not be too gentle. If you want to entangle yourself until your dying day, this is the way to do it.

I have said enough about borrowing for you to see why it needs Chapter 11 to itself.

OTHER WAYS TO GET CAPITAL

There is one more way to raise capital, and that is to steal it. This is not a way which would occur to many women, but you would be amazed how many men consider it, and even plan it.

Are women more honest than men? In my opinion, yes. In eleven years dealing with tax evasion, sometimes on a vast scale, I only came across one big-time female villain. I will tell you her story later.

And the proof of all this female honesty? For a start, the prisons are full of men.

'You know why that is,' scoffed one woman-hater I know. 'They ended up behind bars because they broke the law trying to please some woman!'

Most female thieves fall into the category of Marlene, who worked for the **Inland Revenue**. Her job was to send out cheques to repay people who had overpaid their tax. She thought it the easiest thing in the world to open a few files for people who did not exist. She would open bank accounts in their names, post the cheques to her own address and pocket the money. Easy.

It was so easy that many people had dreamed it up before.

Marlene knew that there would be regular Civil Service audits to check for this sort of theft. She also knew that her employers would be certain to prosecute her. She shrugged her shoulders.

The auditors knew just what to look for. Marlene ended up in prison. To crown it all, the sums concerned were paltry.

At quite the other end of the criminal scale you find the skilled male who thinks big. After a blameless career, he wants a monstrous fortune from one perfect crime. He commits it during his everyday work, using the expertise he has acquired. It may involve little more than tapping a few entries into his computer terminal. With some computer frauds, the criminal even knows he could be traced. But he covers his tracks so thoroughly that he knows it will cost his employers too much to trace through to find out whodunit.

Often too, unfair though it may seem, employers are too embarrassed to bring charges, and the criminal goes scot-free. Why? Perhaps his crime was so large-scale that the publicity of a trial would show up a yawning chasm in the firm's security. **Shareholders** would want to know why. Alternatively, his scheme might have been so profitable that the employers adopt it and continue to operate it legally.

Successful criminals do their homework, sometimes for years. They know exactly what detection they are up against and even what their chances are of being caught. They know how well a firm's records are checked. Besides, big crime often demands a large expense of capital to set it up – often from the proceeds of earlier crimes. Marlene never stood a chance.

Female criminals are rare. Much more common is the woman who, if she has any sense at all, must realize that her husband or lover or employer cannot have come by his money honestly. She looks the other way, perhaps living a life of fear and dreading every knock on the door.

Take Jill. She thought the world of her boss – he was always so pleasant towards her and well dressed. But she also thought that all businesses must involve secrecy, lies and angry customers. She loyally held the fort during his sudden dashes overseas, followed by his sly returns. How often did she phone me promising that her boss would pay our four-figure bill if I would return all his papers first? There was plenty of evidence of skulduggery. Her boss even ordered all income to be paid directly to his solicitor. This way, he did not possess as much as a bank account in his own name. Trusting Jill stuck to her post. Finally, her boss decamped from his prestige offices to hide behind her name in her flat. She thought he was just going through a bad patch and needed her support. And all the time she was running the risk of standing in the dock beside him as an accessory.

Most women realize how much easier it is to be honest – easier on the nerves, the tongue and the memory. They still need to be able to recognize the signs of dishonesty.

One last thought before we leave the subject of how to get your capital. A lot of people wave goodbye to their own money because they cannot be bothered to claim it.

Does anyone owe you money now? What are you doing about it? Sometime a simple letter from you or your solicitor can work wonders. People genuinely do forget. You have to pay for a solicitor to write. Don't ask them unless you are owed over £100. Then tell your solicitor the maximum you are prepared to pay them.

When I sold a boat, but the agent hung on to the money, I asked my solicitor what he could do for £30. The answer was, 'Quite a lot.' Just one letter from him made the agent cough up, and the selling price was higher than I had expected.

Has someone borrowed something valuable and forgotten to return it? Are you now thinking of paying to replace it rather than asking for it back?

When did you last check your Premium Bond numbers? Millions of pounds wait to be claimed, mainly because winners have forgotten to register their new address. Do you always claim refunds that are due to you – for instance, when you sell your car and you have just paid for a year's insurance?

It is amazing how much guaranteed, tax-free money people are willing to turn their backs on for the price of a postage stamp and two minutes to write a letter. Remember too, every day you delay, not only is your money worth less but you are also losing interest on it.

'I've won a hundred quid,' marvelled the man in the pub. He studied the card he had just scratched. 'Says here you have to go and claim it. Can't be bothered. Anyone buy it off me?'

'Ninety quid,' his neighbour offered, opening his wallet.

'Done. Here you are. Like a drink?'

At the other end of the social scale was the lady, a friend of my client, whose aunt died. The solicitor told her she had been left a mysterious legacy – seventy packing cases in store with Harrods. She could not even be bothered to look.

It was my client, bursting with curiosity, who persuaded her to open the cases and discover what she now possessed. The contents were revealed: beautiful antique marble statues from Italy, each one a work of art in its own right and highly valuable. The owner would have paid Harrods just to store them for years.

Then again, I have known people pay for years into a health insurance policy. Yet when they fell genuinely ill, they refused to claim. Why? They somehow worried that if they did, they would 'get into trouble'. Yet that was precisely what they had been paying for.

When you break a mirror, a sink, the loo, a window, spill red wine on your carpet or a pipe leaks, do you check your household insurance policy to see whether you can claim? If there is a no-claims bonus to lose, is it worth your while to do so?

If, heaven forbid, your house burns down, do you have a record of all you possess, in order to claim in full? People often receive far less than they should, simply because they rely on their memory. If you are reading this at home now, close your eyes and mentally list everything in the room. Now open them and look again. How much did you forget?

Sometimes the quickest way to record everything is to hire a video camera and film every room and the contents of every drawer. Place the film in the bank for safe keeping and update it every year or two.

Once you have your capital, the choice is yours. You are free as the wind. You can spend it, save it, invest it or do a little bit of each. Whatever you plan to do with it, the first essential is to *keep* it. This is what the next chapter is about.

8

KEEPING YOUR MONEY

Having achieved your fortune, you may find that it fritters away even as it lies in your pocket, or in your bank account. You never had a chance to spend it, still less enjoy it. You wonder if mice are nibbling or even a rat gnawing away the odd chunk. How can your money shrink – and how can you protect it?

The explanations vary with the nature of your wealth. Take wages. You receive your salary only after **income tax** and **National Insurance** have been deducted from it. So if you can minimize these deductions, you have more left to spend. Methods of reducing your tax bill would fill a bookshelf. The shelf would sag.

If you don't need or intend to pay an accountant, the best layperson's guide is published by the Consumers' Association. Every spring they produce a *Money Which?* tax guide. You can buy it in bookshops. Never economize with last year's copy, because the rules change every year.

The next mouse nibbling away at your earnings is **inflation** (see Chapter 17). Every price rise lowers the value of your money; it buys less for you, so it is worth less to you. If you can choose, it is better to be paid weekly or fortnightly than monthly. Your earnings have less time to lose value.

If you are paid by cheque, arrange for your salary to be paid direct into a building society or **interest**-bearing bank account. At least you will be earning interest on your money straight away.

Many 'ordinary' current accounts which you use with your chequebook also pay you interest. Or you can change from one that does not to one that does *simply by asking to*. You have to ask – the bank would rather not pay you interest if you are satisfied without any.

If you inherited your loot, you may find that what Aunt Annie left you has been immediately shrivelled by **inheritance tax**. If Aunt Annie had done her homework (unless she was stinking rich), this should never have happened. Inheritance tax resembles the sudden gulp of a shark more than the constant nibble of a mouse.

Still, not all need be lost. There is something called a **deed of family arrangement** which every solicitor should know about. Your solicitor can draw up a document to be signed by all the **beneficiaries**. These are the people who would have received money or goods under the will. They sign to agree that the will should be changed.

If this is done within two years of the date of death, the new allocation takes the place of the original will. The new split-up will aim to reduce the tax payable as much as possible. Unlike in cookery, with wills it is possible, by recutting the cake, for everyone to increase the size of their piece. We look at this again in Chapter 15.

In practice, the problem is to persuade all the beneficiaries to agree to the changes. Families grow notoriously suspicious of each other where wills are concerned. Some people would prefer everyone to receive less rather than everyone more but a few even more than others. They would happily cut off their nose to spite their face.

Even when you simply borrow your money, you may find it whittled away. Some **brokers**, banks, etc., charge **arrangement fees** for making a loan. In theory, these cover their costs of paperwork. In practice, it is often just a way to squeeze a little more money out of you.

The same thing can arise if you later rearrange your borrowings. Suppose times grow hard and you extend your house or flat **mortgage** from twenty-five years to thirty to reduce your monthly repayments. Alternatively, you may wax prosperous and want to pay off part of your loan early. Either way, you can find yourself saddled with arrangement fees to pay.

What can you do about this? At least ask at the time you borrow for full details of all the extras you will have to pay. Then they will not come as such a nasty shock.

Big organizations lay down set rules. But if your borrowing is on an individual basis, and if the lenders are keen to lend, you can sometimes persuade them to forgo their fee. Senior bank managers often have discretion and can make what terms they think fit.

Perhaps you can arrange things to avoid fees. If the fees only apply to repayment within five years of borrowing, for example, it may be worthwhile to hold back your sale until the five years have just finished.

Sometimes lenders insist on **life insurance** and offer you their own expensive policy. You may be able to avoid this. Perhaps you can persuade them to accept instead the policy you already pay into, or a cheaper one that you can arrange with a broker.

As you struggle to keep your money intact, to defend it from the mice's nibbling, don't just think in terms of black and white – of keeping your money or losing it. Half a loaf is better than none. You may not be able to avoid an expense completely, but any reduction in an inevitable bill, like tax, is worth having.

Sometimes by planning ahead you can choose between income tax and **capital gains** tax. At the time of writing, the rates are effectively identical. But the detailed rules of capital gains tax may still make it the cheaper tax to pay. For instance, inflation is taken into account, which always works to your advantage. Better still, you can make £5,500 worth of gains a year (£11,000 for a married couple; 1992 figures) and not lose a penny in tax.

This sort of planning needs professional advice and regular reviews. Not so long ago, income tax stood more than twice as high as capital gains tax. Any change of government or policy may throw your well-laid plans back into the melting-pot.

Sometimes you can save money by paying a bill early if you receive a discount for prompt payment. Alternatively, if you can put off paying a bill until later, this saves you money. This is not the same thing as refusing to pay on time. Perhaps you buy from a catalogue. If it gives you the choice between paying cash and taking interest-free credit, choose the credit. Put the money on deposit, earning you interest, until you have to pay up. Don't weaken and spend it in the meantime, and don't tie it up. If you know you will have to pay in six months' time, don't invest in the sort of building society account, for instance, where you cannot withdraw your money for a year (often called 'term accounts') or where you can but only at the cost of losing much of the interest you have already earned.

Much tax avoidance aims to delay payment. For instance, Jane sold her florist's shop on 5 April 1990. She had to pay tax on the profit she made on the sale on 1 December 1990.

Mary sold her knitwear boutique on 6 April 1990, just one day later. She did not have to pay tax on the profit she made on the sale until 1 December 1991 – a whole year later than Jane.

If Mary's tax bill was £3,000 and the building society was offering 10 per cent p.a. interest, then she could save £300 by waiting a day. She put the money to pay the tax into the building society, and it earned her £300 interest before she had to hand it over.

For tax avoidance like this, most people need the advice of

an accountant. Do tell your solicitor in writing beforehand what date you need on your document. Don't expect them automatically to do everything in your best interests. They may not know either your personal situation or the tax rules.

The same applies to anyone else you deal with. For this reason, keep your money under your own control as much as possible.

John and Sue sold their house when they moved abroad. They flew off before the sale was complete. The proceeds were paid to their solicitor, and they waited anxiously for him to send the money on. After a couple of weeks it arrived. So far so good.

At the time when the solicitor completed the sale and obtained their money, John and Sue would have received $2.90 for every £1. Two weeks later the **exchange rate** changed. Now every £1 of their money only bought $2.10.

The couple sold their house for £80,000. The solicitor's delay lost them $64,000 towards their new house ($232,000 − $168,000). This sum alone could almost have bought them a house in their new country. Yet their solicitor had done nothing wrong. It was not his job to get them a good exchange rate. And they never impressed upon him the urgency.

What should they have done? Told him to pay the £80,000 straight into their bank account in England. Then they could have phoned the manager themselves and found out every day what exchange rate the bank was offering. They could have changed their pounds to dollars on the day of their choice over the phone. If necessary, they could have waited, with their £80,000 earning them interest, not converting their pounds until the rate improved. (I will say more about exchange rates in Chapter 16.)

FORGET GAMBLING!

If you want to keep your money, forget gambling. It devours your funds − at best like a greedy mouse, at worst like a ravenous shark. By gambling I mean gambling of every sort, from roulette to bingo, from Premium Bonds to horse-racing, from the pools to draw tickets.

Gambling is a vast industry which employs thousands of people. All those wages and those glamorous casinos are paid for by gamblers. Did you know that betting shops are kept dismal by law? It is a feeble attempt to discourage punters. Otherwise they would emerge as plush as a hotel lounge.

Next time you pass a fruit machine in a pub, remember that the **profits** go one-third to the publican, one-third to the owners of the machine and one-third to the brewery. And they all do very nicely. You may even spy the landlord feeding in change until he has milked the machine of all its pay-outs for his own pocket.

Next time you spot a one-armed bandit, look for a label saying how much gambling tax that machine pays every year. Don't be surprised if the figure rises over £1,000. Now imagine how much profit that machine earns its owners. They still gain handsomely, even after tax. So why is the pub not packed out with such gold-mines? Because the tax charged on the second one is even higher.

Gambling thrives on mistaken beliefs. Here are just three:

1 *'The law of averages'.* People console themselves, 'I lost last time, so I might well win this time, and I'm certain to win next time.' Wrong. Ask any mathematician. Probability theory is the name for the branch of maths which covers chance. Perhaps you thought there was no more to it than crossing your fingers and hugging your lucky rabbit's foot!

Suppose you toss a coin. What are your chances it will come down heads? If the coin is normal they are 50:50 or, to put it another way, 1 in 2.

If you toss a coin and it comes down heads, what are the chances of it coming down heads again? You will hear all sorts of answers to this one, based on some sort of law of averages. In fact, the answer is 50:50 or 1 in 2 again. It will go on being the same, even after you have thrown the coin 1,000 times and each time it fell heads.

Why? Well, first of all you must work out all the possible outcomes and count them. With a coin this is easy; it could only fall heads or tails. This only offers you two possibilities. If it comes down heads, this is one of the outcomes, it is 1 in 2. So your chances of a normal coin coming down heads are 1 in 2.

Every time you toss, you face a new situation. You must work out the odds again. What happened in the past has no influence at all. Mind you, after 1,000 heads, anyone would begin to wonder if the coin really was normal.

Go a stage further. If you take a pack of cards, what is the chance that the first card you turn up will be a diamond? Total the possibilities. There are 52, because there are 52 different cards; but any of the 13 diamonds would do. So there are 13/52 chances or, put another way, 1 in 4.

If you do turn up a diamond and set it to one side, what are your chances of the next card being a diamond? Answer 12/51. Why? There are 51 cards left, and only 12 of those can be diamonds.

Remember, you cannot work out your odds unless you know all the possibilities beforehand. So in a lottery you cannot even start to work out your chances of winning until you know how many tickets are sold.

In the next stage of calculation, you take account not just of what could happen but of the *likelihood* of it happening. Of the ten horses dancing around at the starting post, one may have suffered an injury not long before, another may not like heavy going, a third may be ridden by the champion jockey, a fourth may carry a lead-packed saddle to handicap it, and so on. You have to find out all these things. Then you must decide how important each one is.

Professional bookies are not that much wiser than the rest of us. They set the odds based on the amounts that punters are betting on each horse. They keep adjusting the odds so that overall they cannot lose. Even then, they use a system called laying-off.

To protect themselves from their wrong bets – those where the punters win – bookies bet among themselves. If the worst comes to the worst and every favourite wins, they themselves win enough money from other bookies to pay out their customers' winnings and still come out ahead. If professionals need to hedge their bets like this, what hope do the rest of us have?

Here is the next fallacy about gambling:

2 *'For everyone who wins, someone loses.'* This is not true either. Take the **stock market**, where people gamble that the **shares** they buy today will be worth more in the future.

Perhaps you sell some British Telecom shares because yesterday the price was high at £3 a share. The day you sell, the price drops to £2.75 a share. Have you lost?

This all depends. If you bought those shares for £1.50, then you have made a nice profit of £1.25 (ignoring the brokers' fees). If you bought them for £2.90, then you have lost 15p per share. Either way, the fact that the share price was even higher yesterday is irrelevant.

What about the person who buys your shares? Have they won? Again, it depends. If they go on to sell the shares for more than £2.75, then yes, they have. If they need to flog the shares off for £1.20, then they have lost. Either way, what happens to your buyer does not concern you. In the same way, what happens on the days you don't buy or sell has nothing to do with you either, except as a general guide.

Third fallacy:

3 *'My luck must change soon.'* Why should it? Tell that to the **bankruptcy** court. Each gamble has its own odds, remember?

Bookmakers often offer you a choice. Place a bet and, if you win, you have betting tax to pay on all you win. Or place a larger bet where, if you win, there is no tax to pay. (The bookie will pay it for you.) Always choose the former. The 'choice' is simply a ploy to persuade you to bet more money. Besides, what could be more stupid than to pay for tax on a bet you did not even win? Would you pay income tax on wages you never earned?

There are people who make a living from betting. You could probably count them in Britain on the fingers of two hands. They work as hard and as long hours as people do at any other job.

You may wonder, if mathematicians know all the answers, why don't they coin it in? Several reasons. First, they realize that, even where everything is completely honest, casino rules are designed to favour the banker. The banker needs that edge, that advantage, to avoid bankruptcy. Second, consistently successful players will find themselves refused entry to casinos, or bookmakers will refuse to take their bets. The betting industry has its livelihood and profits to protect. If a punter appears with a winning 'system', the operators must change the rules or go out of business.

Having said all that, life without the odd flutter would be very dull, and for some people it would be hopeless. The remote hope of a pools win sustains them for monotonous years in the factory.

Money, well used, brightens your life. It should not fill it with penny-pinching gloom. There are a million and one ways to gamble, and some can offer great fun. Just treat gambling like a hobby. Tell yourself you enjoy it but mentally write off (forget about) the stake money as soon as you lay it down on the green baize. You have spent it, and it has vanished, just as much as if you had gone to the cinema instead. Never rely on winning to pay the bills.

DON'T OVER-TIP

One last mouse that nibbles away at your money: tipping. Women are notorious over-tippers, probably because some restaurants, hotels and hairdressers are so intimidating. I remember one four-star hotel where every member of staff pounced, hand held out, as you walked down the corridor.

Never tip more than 10 per cent. Give nothing at all if a tip is already included in the bill – they call it a 'service charge'. Remember, you are already paying VAT on the tip you have been forced to give, even if the waiter was surly and the food was cold. So how do you get good service? In my experience, what matters is your coat or jacket. It must look timelessly, unfakeably expensive. Fur – if your principles permit – or upmarket leather works wonders. And who knows if it is second-hand? You may know that your bag cost a fortune and your diamonds are real; a waiter will not. There are very few genuine female status symbols.

These are just a few ways to ensure that you keep your hard-gained money. You want it entire, to enjoy, to control, to spend, to increase. You don't want to watch it shrink and vanish like water in the desert. Money can manage other disappearing tricks too. We look at them in the next chapter and see how you can avoid them.

9

HOW (NOT) TO SQUANDER

Do we really need a chapter on squandering money? you may wonder. We can manage it without help. Yes, we all do sometimes. By squandering, I don't mean a wild spending spree, a pre-Christmas shopping orgy, a splurge. If you decide to spend your money in that way, you are free to do so and at least you should get pleasure from it.

The sort of people I have in mind simply don't realize they are squandering. They genuinely believe they are saving money. They even pride themselves on their economy and boast about it to their friends.

Here are eleven simple ideas for how to squander your money:

1 *Shove your savings under the mattress.* You run the risks of theft and fire. You tempt the family to help themselves if they know it is just lying there idle. It should be at work earning you **interest** or giving you pleasure. Besides, **inflation** is eating away at all that idle money and reducing its value.

Take Dai and Megan. They ran a butcher's shop in a small

Welsh town and did very well in a quiet way – so nicely that they thought it a shame to pay so much tax. They started hiding a little of the takings down the sides of the settee. A few years of this and they could find nowhere left to hide it. All the upholstery was padded stiff with folded banknotes.

Every member of the family knew about the hoards. Neither Dai nor his wife dared spend it. In that small community, the neighbours would have started to ask questions.

When they died, the family found that many of the banknotes had been nibbled by mice. Others were such old-style notes that the local bank refused to accept them. Dai and Megan may have saved their money, but it was the worst possible sort of saving. It gave them no pleasure, simply worry. It brought insecurity when it should have brought reassurance.

As some sage said: *you don't possess possessions; possessions possess you.*

These days the people most likely to keep large amounts of loose cash at home are pensioners. One old lady gave me a touching explanation. If she was ever burgled, she reasoned, the intruders would expect to find bundles of notes; not because she had it, but to prove they had not wasted their time. She needed to be able to produce plenty. Otherwise they would beat her senseless on the assumption she must be hiding it.

If this is your reasoning, I suggest you hide £100 right next to a miniature burglar alarm and put the rest safely in the bank. And don't flash around a wad of notes in a crowded post office.

2 *Spend your money on **depreciating assets**.* A depreciating asset is one that quickly drops in value, whether or not it is worn out, even if you paid a fortune for it. A new car plummets in value when you drive it out of the show-room. New furniture drops dramatically in worth as it crosses your threshold.

To work out how fast an asset depreciates, ask yourself how long you can expect it to last and stay reliable. The maker's guarantee may be some guide here. They will only cover the period they are sure will be trouble-free. In general, you can congratulate yourself, and your family, if household appliances or electrical goods last ten years. (In France you cannot insure appliances over ten years old. The insurance company assumes they are worn out.)

Your ten-year-old car will probably look a sad remnant of the new one you bought. By contrast, your ten-year-old house or flat will never wear out. With any luck you could sell it for far more than you paid for it. The same applies to any antiques that you have owned for ten years. These are not depreciating assets but the opposite: **appreciating** assets.

Suppose you buy a new car. At the end of four years, it will probably have covered 50,000 miles. Even if not, it certainly cannot compete with a new car. For the same performance and reliability, you need to replace it. Suppose it cost you £6,000. You work out its depreciation as follows:

Year 1	Cost £6,000
less Depreciation	£1,500
Value at end of year 1	£4,500

How did I work this out? Well, we decided that the reliable life of the car was broadly 50,000 miles or four years.* Divide the cost by 4 to get the depreciation of £1,500. This is the amount by which the car's value has dropped in the year. Deduct this from the original cost and you get the value of the car at the end of a year. Only £4,500. Depressing, isn't it?

Repeat the same process, year after year:

Value at end of year 1	£4,500
less Depreciation	£1,125
Value at end of year 2	£3,375

---

*This is rough and ready. Precise values, model by model, are printed in *Glass's Guide*, the car trade's Bible.

less Depreciation	£844
Value at end of year 3	£2,531
less Depreciation	£633
Value at end of year 4	£1,898

At the end of four years your car is not worn out. If it was, its value would have reduced to nil. In fact, it is still worth £1,898. What this all means is that over four years' use your car has lost £4,102 (£6,000 − £1,898).

Of course, if you had bought a really expensive car, it would have lost correspondingly more. So what can one do? You need a car.

Look again at the figures. You will see that the value drops furthest and fastest in the early years. Your car plummets £1,500 in the first year but only dips £633 in the fourth. If you had bought a car like yours at two years old, you would have had to pay £3,375. Each year after that, you would have lost a lot less in depreciation. Moral: buy second-hand if at all possible.

How fast things depreciate does not just depend on their useful life. Some things become worthless overnight, like last year's calendars. Ask yourself when buying, does this have a resale value? Is there a market?

Perhaps you never sat on your new three-piece suite, never slept in your put-you-up bed. You will still receive far less than you paid for it, even if you can sell it. Why? There is no market for quality second-hand furniture, until you come to antiques.

In general, try to spend as little of your money as possible on depreciating assets. Choose instead assets that will hold their value or even increase it (appreciate). This makes a tiny flat a better buy than a mobile home. An original anything keeps its value better than a copy. Compare real gems and costume jewellery, original art and copies.

3 *Pay money for advice and then ignore it.* People do this all the time. They don't want advice but reassurance. They want someone with expertise to advise them to do what they have already decided to do. Unscrupulous advisers play on this. Just like fake fortune-tellers, they find out what people want to hear and then feed it back to them.

4 *Play one expert off against another while you pay for both.* One of my clients, a brutish American, hired a firm of solicitors to buy him a British stately home. Things went wrong, so he hired another firm to look into what the first firm had done. He did not like what they told him, so he hired a third firm to check the checking of the second. All the solicitors were honest. The people who were 'selling' the mansion turned out not to own it. He spent £7,000 in legal fees and still did not buy his stately home.

He was as bad as Anne, who consults her doctor and her herbalist at the same time about the same complaint. She blithely swallows whatever either prescribes but does not tell either about the other. When she feels better, she thanks the herbalist because his potions cost more!

5 *Buy or build a brand-new house.* Even after you move in, you will find you need to shell out a fortune over the next few years: to stock, lay out and fence the garden; to put in extra power points, shelves and cupboards; perhaps, after the walls have dried, to wallpaper. With a 'second-hand' house, someone else has paid for all this, suffering the mess and inconvenience. Builders will tell you that people who extensively modify their homes often move soon afterwards. Why? The house has lost its charm. A new house will involve you in constant expense. A 'used' one at the same price works out far cheaper.

6 *Buy something you don't really like because you think it must be useful.* Surely no one can be so stupid, you might think. In fact, we all do it – perhaps a plain, dull garment that is described as a 'classic', or a 'must' for the kitchen that you never use. If you cannot whip up real enthusiasm when you buy it, before long you will want to replace it and will then have paid twice as much. Or you will hide it in a drawer until, in shame, you give it to the Oxfam shop. How many garages are stuffed with never-used DIY tools and never-attached car accessories?

7 *Buy by price alone.* Julie came back to the office from the sales, clutching a bag and looking radiant. 'It only cost £2,' she cooed, 'so it must be a bargain.' She held up a black, shapeless piece of cloth that might have been a poncho or a stole. 'Fancy buying a garment for only £2,' she marvelled. 'I must be able to wear it somehow.' In fact, she paid £2 for something she never wore. It ended up as an expensive duster.

Remember the real definition of a bargain: *A BARGAIN IS SOMETHING GOING CHEAP FOR WHICH YOU WOULD WILLINGLY HAVE PAID FULL PRICE.*

Bargains are rare but they do exist. Anything else is simply something going cheap – not a bargain – because no one else wants it.

8 *Change your lifestyle every few months.* The biggest single way to waste money is change. It may be moving house, separation, whims or fashion, refitting a kitchen or keeping up with the Joneses.

I knew of a couple who moved house seven times in twelve years, all within a town of 20,000 people. Moving house was their hobby, although of course they would never have admitted it. As soon as they had completely rearranged the new place to their taste, they hankered after the challenge of another one. Sometimes they just moved to another house in the same street. Imagine the thousands they squandered on legal, estate agents' and removal fees, and in fitted carpets, curtains and lighting, all left behind.

Worse still is change with false economizing. You want to repaper the lounge. You know it is just a whim – the existing paper is immaculate – so you salve your conscience by resolving not to spend much. Reluctantly, you cast aside the wallpaper you *really* fancy. Another adequate design is going cheap. So you buy the cheap paper.

Before long, you confess you don't really like it and fancy a change again. And so on. You may spend a fortune and never buy what you really want.

Ruth is just such a penny-pinching squanderer. She prides herself on her economy but over the years she has bought umpteen of the following and never been satisfied with any of them:

- lawn mowers, none of them good enough to tackle her half-acre lawn;
- vacuum cleaners, none of them powerful enough for her large house;
- sheepskin coats, none sufficiently figure-hugging to look smart in her view;
- cookers, all of which developed wiring faults or had gadgets that did not work or doors that warped, because Ruth expected top quality and every novelty at a cheap price;
- cars, because she never really bought the one she wanted, making do with a cheaper substitute and then regretting it.

Of course, our lives change all the time, and we have to spend to adjust to this. Sometimes we have no choice. But if you are spending just on a whim – what you own is perfectly adequate, you just fancy a change – stop for a second. Ask yourself, what will the new item actually *do* that the old one cannot? How much better or quicker will it be? Think how much the replacement will cost and then double the figure. After this, if it still seems worthwhile, go ahead.

This is not a notion I dreamed up. People in industry follow the same plan when they estimate the future cost of a new project. They call it 'allowing for contingencies'. Often they triple the starting figure.

❾ *Always be the first to buy something new.* This costs extra.

Think back over the last few years; how many goods have reduced dramatically in price? Videos, computers, colour TVs, calculators, anything electronic, long-distance travel. Sometimes just waiting a year, or even until after Christmas, can mean that you buy the same thing for a lot less. If you must always rush for tickets for the latest show, fine – just as long as you realize how much extra it is costing you and decide it is still worthwhile.

10 *Always be the last to buy something.* It may come cheaper but if it is too old-fashioned in style or technology, or too out of season to be useful, you have squandered money, not saved it. Lack of spares or of mechanics familiar with the model will shorten its life.

11 *Buy British or something with an English-sounding name out of patriotism when the foreign alternative is cheaper and better.* For a start, that English-sounding name may not really be British – like Brother, a Japanese firm.

Even if the firm is genuinely British, you may well find a little 'Made in Taiwan' sticker on the products they sell.

More and more multinational firms manufacture their products from items made in many different countries, including the UK. Perhaps the 'foreign' product is assembled here, like Japanese Sony televisions in Wales.

Most important, you are not helping British industry or preserving British jobs when you buy what you would not really have chosen otherwise. It encourages firms to continue producing the wrong thing and hastens their downfall. If customers bought elsewhere, they would have to change their ideas.

REAL ECONOMIES AND FALSE ECONOMIES

You need to know how much something really costs you to buy. Two garages may offer the same model of car, but one may quote a far higher price. Then you find the high price is the 'on-the-road' price. The cheaper garage will add on delivery charges, the costs of road fund licence and, often, a full tank of petrol. Then again, look closer at the cars. One may have a £50 radio, the other a £500 radio.

I knew two business partners who ordered identical prestige cars at the same price for 1 August. The first sported all the trimmings, expensive radial tyres from a leading manufacturer, even a monogrammed leather key-ring. The second had cheap cross-ply tyres of an obscure brand; the keys were tied together with string.

Most articles have two costs: the cost of buying them (the purchase price), and the cost of using them (running costs).

You may waver between two second-hand cars offered at the same price. One may zoom along, bigger, newer and flashier than the other. But if it only manages 15 miles to the gallon (18.75 litres per 100 kilometres) and needs Group 5 (very expensive) insurance, it will soak up an oil-well and cost a fortune to run. Now you know why the owner offers it so cheaply. He found out the hard way.

Two dresses may carry the same price tag, but if one requires dry-cleaning it will cost you much more in the long run. Anything electric that runs on batteries costs far more than a similar item that runs from the mains. And so on.

One common fallacy is that the only running cost of a car is petrol. *Motoring Which?* magazine used to consider petrol about a tenth of the full cost! Insurance, road fund licence, servicing, oil, loss of interest on the money you bought the car with, etc., make up nine-tenths.

If last year your car only clocked up a couple of thousand miles, it would be far cheaper to sell it and use taxis. (Except that in practice people refuse to use taxis. When they actually fork out the money, their extravagance shocks them. People prefer a series of little bills to one big one, even though the big one is much lower than the total of the small ones. This is another of the dangers of thinking week by week or month by month.) The break-even point arrives when you manage 8,000 miles a year. Above this a car comes cheaper than taxis. Of course, when you take passengers, you must add the miles they travel to your own.

A third factor to consider when buying is the depreciation costs we looked at before. This is what every business does. The more your car is worth to sell at the end of its usefulness to you (its trade-in value, resale value or even scrap value), the less it has really cost you.

Businesses look at all three factors: purchase price, running costs and depreciation. In a process called 'discounted cash flow', they work out every likely expense over the life of the article and when it should arise. Then they work back to calculate what the article really costs if they had to pay for everything today. They don't bother doing this before buying every nut and bolt, but if they face a choice between several new machines they will do calculations for each before deciding which to buy.

So how can you really save money when you spend it? By spending as little as possible to get what you really want. Here are four guidelines.

1 When you consider buying something you have never owned before, a dish-washer or a video camera, a gymnasium or a boat, find out if you can hire one first. The range of things for hire grows ever wider: power tools, carpet cleaners, musical instruments. Look in the Yellow Pages of the phone directory. You won't need to worry about breakdowns; and if, at the end of the shortest possible hire, you don't like it, or you found, once the novelty wore off, that the article sat abandoned, you have saved the purchase money. Where hire is not possible, buy an old one second-hand.

2 Buy second-hand rather than new. Someone else has endured the teething troubles and suffered the depreciation. My first dish-washer cost £10. It soon convinced me it was worthwhile and provided two years' service into the bargain. Second-hand books, for instance, can provide real savings. But think twice about electrical goods like heaters, in case they are no longer safe – unless you know who owned them before, or they have been reconditioned by an agent.

Dress agencies, an owner once told me, exist for three reasons: the garment was too big; the garment was too small; or the husband/boyfriend did not like it.

It can pay you to take a trip to a wealthy area where women still only wear their clothes once. Good agencies insist on dry-cleaning all garments to be sold. They also offer a rack or two of brand-new things, so you don't need to wear a wig or turn up your collar and look both ways for fear of being recognized before you step inside.

The stock may be as up to date as in ordinary shops, normally at a third of the new price. Try on everything you fancy, not just your size. Often the wrong label was stitched in originally, hence the previous owner's mistake.

3 Where possible, buy goods that have two values: the value of the article (a teaspoon) and the value of the raw material it is made from (silver). You can enjoy using it, and it should appreciate in value. One day, if the worst comes to the worst, you can always sell it, either as a spoon or to be melted down. The same goes for antique furniture. These days this covers anything pre-Second World War. It is often more robust, made of better materials and far cheaper than new. Buy things to use regularly rather than just ornaments and clutter.

Some people buy jewellery or furs with the idea (or excuse) that if they become hard up they can sell or pawn them. True, but basically they prove a poor investment over the years – although better than no investment at all.

One client of mine owned a ring worth £36,000. At 10 per cent interest, she was turning her back on **income** of £3,600 a year. She finally sold the ring because no insurance company would cover her.

One word of caution: beware of limited editions. They raise a lot of money for the artist or promoters. They would rather sell the same thing ten times over than once and for all, or even 800 or 8,000 times over. This explains those glossy offers in colour supplements for china, hand-painted thimbles, and the like. Limited editions exist for things that *might* be collected some time in the future – if they happen to catch on. If not, you will be lucky if you can resell them at all. For investment, you want things that are *already* collected and already appreciating in value.

There is a dead period – perhaps twenty years, perhaps fifty – before most new articles become collectables. People reject them as old-fashioned, then hideous. Many are thrown away. Afterwards the few left may rise in value. You want to leap-frog all that.

4 Once you have settled in your mind which item to buy, you want to pay as little as possible for it. We all know the principles of shopping around, if you can find the time and energy. We all know the dodge of buying from about-to-be-changed catalogues at a price that was set six months before.

Some well-known stores offer to refund the difference if you find something you bought from them cheaper elsewhere. These offers are genuine. You are doing their market research for them.

When you have decided precisely what you want and where you plan to buy it, ask for a discount for cash. If the shop accepts **credit cards**, it pays $2\frac{1}{2}$ per cent or more to the credit card company. So it is no worse off if it gives you $2\frac{1}{2}$ per cent discount instead. This means £2.50 for every £100 you spend. Cash no longer has to mean a fistful of battered tenners; a cheque with a **banker's card** will usually do.

Alternatively, having negotiated your cash discount, if you know the **interest rates** that your bank charges, you can decide whether it is worthwhile to arrange a short **overdraft** to get the cash. It would be very rare for your credit card to work out cheaper.

Many shops offer discounts to members of certain organizations like trade unions, student unions or motoring organizations; or to people who work for a certain employer, such as the Civil Service. Can you benefit from any of these? The organization issues to members lists of firms with which it has negotiated special deals, or you may find stickers on the shop window. Carry your membership card and remember to ask.

My twenty-year-old hard-up niece once spent far more than she needed on travelling to see me. Father insisted Rose carry her student card and told her to ask for a discount. She forgot. Rose never had the wit to ask for a return ticket instead of two singles. She could have saved on both counts. 'Why didn't anybody tell me?' Rose wailed afterwards. The answer should have been, 'You're a big girl now.'

Just one final word on squandering. Spending money is a skill. Like any other, it needs regular practice and it should give you pleasure – not necessarily selfish pleasure either. Perhaps you are spending on someone else. Or maybe you decide to treat yourself to an electronic wheelchair instead of those dreadful chariots the Red Cross provides; a special keyboard-phone to keep you in touch with your friends despite your deafness; a modified car to help you lead an independent life or even earn your living . . .

Whatever your situation, you cannot expect to spend years hoarding every penny and then not make a mistake when you do finally buy something. How many people have saved for so long they cannot remember what they are saving for? How many people eke out their last years in misery with ample in the bank or under the mattress? As some cheerful person once remarked, there are no pockets in a shroud.

This chapter has steered you around an obstacle course, helping you to avoid squandering your funds as you spend them and as you save them. The next looks at genuine ways to set aside money for your long-term needs.

10

Do I hear a wry laugh?
Perhaps you think, SAVING
fat chance I have to save money. I struggle
hard enough to rake up sufficient for day-to-
day living. Well, if cash really is that tight, see
my advice in Chapter 7. For most people, you
may be surprised to discover that you are al-
ready saving hard, whether you like it or not.
Or someone else, like your husband or the state,
is setting cash aside on your behalf.

The whole welfare state could be described as one vast savings scheme. You pay your **National Insurance** contributions while you earn and claim your old-age pension years later.

PENSION SCHEMES

It may seem daft to be thinking about your pension when you are in your twenties. But there will never be a better time.

By and large, the state pension offers a very good investment. (Except for married women lucky enough still to pay contributions at the 'reduced rate'. You are outside the state pension scheme; stay that way, girls. Resist all arguments to persuade you to change to the full rate. The extra pension you would receive one day is peanuts compared to the extra contributions you must pay now. Perhaps you are worried about not getting a pension in your own name. If so, pay the extra you would otherwise pay to the state – the difference between ordinary and 'reduced rate' – into a private pension scheme.)

Why is the state scheme good value? Because the government simply grabs all it can today from those working and hands it out to pensioners, etc. Private schemes will demand much larger contributions to provide you with the same rates of pension as the state pays.

Why? Because they must invest your personal contributions between now and your retirement to earn you the pension. They cannot simply dish out your contributions to other customers today. The pension companies must invest the bulk of your money with safe, reliable concerns. These probably pay less. (I consider safe investments in Chapter 13.)

If you are sick or registered as unemployed, the government pays your state pension contributions for you. For a full pension, you need thirty-nine qualifying years – that is, thirty-nine years when contributions were made by either you, your husband on your behalf or the government. If you only managed thirty, you will get just over three-quarters (30/39ths) of the pension, and so on.

You can easily find out how many qualifying years you have built up to date. Write to the DSS pensions department, Newcastle upon Tyne. Quote your full name (and previous names if any), address and date of birth. Allow them a month or two to reply.

Sometimes you can catch up your missing years by paying voluntary contributions. This is normally well worthwhile, because the contributions are tiny for the extra pension you receive. Again, if you ask, they will explain how.

All employees and self-employed people must join the government's DSS scheme, and employers must add hefty contributions too. But the old-age pension level falls far short of average earnings. So many employers arrange a pension scheme for their workers to bridge the gap.

If you are one of the lucky ones and your job provides an occupational pension, fine. Better still if it is non-contributory (your employer pays all the contributions). The opposite is a contributory pension where your contributions are taken out of your wages.

Luckiest of all are those who can look forward to a non-contributory inflation-linked pension, as in the Civil Service. The pension you receive is increased each year in line with the **cost of living index** (see Chapter 17 on **inflation**). In practice, this means you receive a larger pension than you otherwise would. Ever since index-linked pensions started, prices have constantly risen.

My father-in-law retired from the RAF at 55. He started to draw his RAF pension straight away. Some of his colleagues were promoted, received higher pay and continued to work until 60. Yet the pension they received then was far lower than his. Why? Because it was inflation-linked. In the extra five years the others had worked, their pay rises even after promotion had been lower than my father-in-law's increases for inflation.

So, when comparing salaries, bear in mind pension rights. A job with a lower salary can in fact pay you more when you take this into account. There are several questions that you need to ask.

EMPLOYERS' PENSION SCHEMES: SOME QUESTIONS AND ANSWERS

HOW MUCH ARE MY PENSION RIGHTS WORTH?

You know broadly how much pension you will get (say, half your salary). Ask a pension sales agent for a quotation to give you the same size of pension as this. The contributions they will quote will show you roughly the size of your 'hidden salary'.

WHAT HAPPENS TO MY PENSION IF I CHANGE JOBS, OR IF MY EMPLOYER IS TAKEN OVER?

Many people, especially women, lose out drastically on changing jobs or through company take-overs. When you leave, are your pension rights lost? If so, forget about any pension. You receive nowt. Are they frozen? If so, you will get something when you reach pension age. Keep all your documents in a safe place (like the bank), and make sure the pension people know your latest address and any change of name.

IF I RESIGN, CAN I CLAIM BACK MY OWN CONTRIBUTIONS OR ANY MADE ON MY BEHALF BY MY EMPLOYER?

Often the pension-scheme organizers will try to dissuade you from claiming back contributions. They tell you you will only receive peanuts after tax has been paid. This is rubbish. I claimed back my employer's contributions when I left teaching and again when I left the Civil Service. The tax was a mere 10 per cent – far less than the 30-odd per cent I was paying on my salary.

Claiming back your contributions gives you flexibility. A lump sum in your twenties may be far more useful to you than a tiny pension forty years on that you might even forget to claim. Alternatively, you could use the money to buy extra pension rights with your new employer's scheme. Then again, you could pay for a new private scheme of your own.

CAN I TRANSFER MY PENSION RIGHTS TO MY NEW EMPLOYER?

In the jargon, is your pension fully 'transferable' or 'portable'? In the past, people were often unwilling to move jobs to where they were needed, because they lost out so badly on their pension rights. Governments have tried to improve this in recent years. They have not yet succeeded enough for me to give any general advice. You can only find out about your own particular scheme and plan accordingly. (If you think you are still getting a raw deal, ask your union or the Citizen's Advice Bureau.)

HOW CAN I INCREASE THE VALUE OF MY PENSION?

Perhaps your job carries a pension but you have not worked there for long. Now you are approaching retirement and worried about your small pension. You can usually buy 'back-years'. This means that you volunteer to pay extra contributions now. These are called additional voluntary contributions or AVCs. When you retire, your employer calculates the amount payable to you as though you had been working for them for years longer. This way you receive a bigger pension.

Is it worthwhile? Each case differs. You need to compare what you have to pay with what extra you should receive. Then decide if instead you could do better by investing that money yourself – say, in the building society. Chances are you could not do better, because pension schemes get favourable tax treatment. They keep more of what they earn from investments. Besides, savings in a pension scheme grow 'out of reach'. You will not be tempted to spend them as you might if you knew they were sitting there in the building society.

WHY SHOULD MARRIED WOMEN BOTHER ABOUT A PENSION SCHEME AT ALL?

Married women will share their husband's state pension and any pension from his work or which he has paid into – as long as the couple are still together when they reach retirement age. Sad to say, no one can guarantee that any more.

Although lost pension rights should feature in any court's decision on how much **alimony** to award a divorced wife, they can be overlooked, undervalued or simply beyond the husband's present means to pay. Besides, many women are married to men who leave tomorrow to take care of itself. So his (and her) pension rights may be tiny or non-existent. Perhaps he has worked abroad for many years and made no contributions at all. Those years will not count for a state old-age pension.

'Why pay for a pension?' Keith argued complacently. 'You might never need it.'

'And your widow?' I persisted. He shrugged, puffed on his pipe and gazed into space. Yet he was a happily married man.

Keith lives in New Zealand where even the government scheme is optional. Like many other professionals, never mind blue-collar men, he did not bother. At 66 he found work a strain and wanted to stop, but he could not afford to. Yet he still insisted he had done the wise thing by refusing to join the pension scheme.

PRIVATE PENSION SCHEMES

If you are a self-employed person or an employee in a job with no pension scheme, you can pay for a private pension. This earns you tax relief. In other words, you pay less tax because of the pension contributions you make.

You can start to draw your pension at 60 (sometimes even earlier) and don't need to retire to do so, unlike in the state scheme. Such pensions move with you if you change jobs. This is fine unless you happen to join a firm with its own pension scheme. Then you will have to join the new scheme. Your previous contributions are not lost, but you cannot add to them. They continue to build up and will pay you a pension when you retire.

You will find hundreds of different private schemes and hundreds of insurance salesmen eager to explain them to you.

Most pension companies pay **commission** to their agents. This commission is their bread and butter. Some receive little or no other wages. Now you understand why they can pester so – no sales means no pay.

Some pension companies don't pay commissions at all. Their salesmen receive a straight salary. These are called non-commission houses. An example is NPI (National Provident Institution). Always ask which type you are faced with. Those commissions come out of the pension contributions you pay. Clearly, the more of your contributions that vanishes in commissions, the less there remains to invest to build up a pension for you and pay administration costs.

The art of saving for a pension is to start early in life. If you invest £100 in your twenties, it will earn you as much pension as £200 invested in your thirties, £400 in your forties or £800 in your fifties. In practice, very few people care about pensions before they reach 30, and many often don't have much spare cash until they attain their fifties with the family off their hands.

Incidentally, you can buy a private pension with just one large payment instead of small regular ones over many years. Again, the art is to buy it early. Use that odd £1,000 you inherit in your thirties to buy a 'single-premium' pension and it could pay you handsomely when you retire.

SAVE AS YOU EARN AND TESSAs

So far we have only looked at long-term saving through pension schemes, but there are other ways to choose. SAYE (Save As You Earn) is operated by many employers and building societies. You can arrange to have a regular amount deducted from your wages and invested. SAYE has not really caught on widely because, in my view, it does not represent good value. Bear in mind that any scheme the government offers to everyone cannot be the best that is available. There are only a limited number of bargains, and not everyone can enjoy them.

There are also TESSAs (Tax-Exempt Special Savings Accounts) offered by building societies where, at the end of five years of regular saving, you receive your interest tax-free. I mention them here for convenience, but five years is not really long-term. So you should compare the returns from SAYE and TESSAs with the investments we consider in Chapter 13 rather than with pension schemes.

OWNING YOUR OWN HOME

Another way of saving long-term is to put all your money into your home. This has many advantages. You enjoy the benefit of the money you spend on the property. The sale proceeds are tax-free. In the long term (over ten or twenty years or more), property keeps up well with inflation. Housing is a short-term investment only when house prices are rocketing. Such booms end as suddenly as they began – as sellers who bought in the late 1980s are discovering.

In practice, people change houses all the time. The average **mortgage** only lasts seven years or so. When you sell you may find that, as an investment, many of your improvements did not pay. Fancy kitchens, lavish redecorating, landscaped garden, sauna, anything mildly eccentric like an aviary – none of them increase the price you receive by as much as you paid for the improvement. A swimming-pool can actually reduce the value of your house. Why? It is hard work and expensive to maintain.

If you have worked hard to make your house by far the smartest in the area, you will probably be disappointed when you come to sell. The price reflects the area too. This is why some people object bitterly to anything that might possibly 'lower the tone' of a neighbourhood.

What counts with a house is size. Extensions, conversions, a room in the attic, an extra garage – these all pay handsomely, at least at the lower end of the range. Or they provide you with a bigger home without the expense of moving. Up-market, your extension must look original to add value – that is, it must match your house exactly in materials and style.

The main drawback with investing long-term in your home comes when you have to give it up. This can be a problem partly because you love it so much but also because, beyond a certain age, you can no longer bear the strain and upheaval of moving. There is one way you can obtain income from your home without lodgers and still live in it. I look at this when I cover retirement in Chapter 15.

LIFE ASSURANCE (AND LIFE INSURANCE)

As well as pensions, savings schemes and your home, you may choose to make your long-term saving through **life assurance** policies. First, we must separate life assurance from **life insurance**.

You pay into a life insurance scheme year by year. If you die in that time, your dependants receive a sum of money. If you survive, what you paid is lost. What you bought was a year's security and peace of mind for yourself and your dependants – vital but not a financial investment.

By contrast, a life assurance scheme covers a fixed period, perhaps from now until you reach 60. Again, you pay regularly every year. If you die during this time, your dependants receive a sum of money. If you survive, the policy finishes (matures) and *you* receive a sum of money. So it is 'heads you win, tails you don't lose'.

There are umpteen assurance schemes available and they are so long-term that it is difficult (perhaps downright impossible) to compare them to predict which will provide the biggest lump sum.

Some schemes are also linked in with a mortgage. (I look at these again in Chapter 13.) Personally, I am a bit suspicious of schemes that try to cover everything. Basically, if you are insuring your life that is one thing. Buying your home is another. If you are trying to save and invest using life assurance, that is yet another. I prefer to keep these separate and get the best terms on each. Yet a joint scheme is still far better than nothing.

Saving is like spending; it is a habit. Practice makes perfect. Remember the old saying: *if you can't save on a little, you can't save on a lot.* The younger you learn the saving habit, the easier it grows.

Saving also has its own pleasures. I have known clients derive great satisfaction from gloating over the balance in their building society account. Just reading out the figures gives them pleasure. Others like physically to stash up and count their cash. They bask in glorious indecision as to what to spend it on. The choice overwhelms them. In their minds they savour each purchase in turn. They relish the bun and the penny too.

Others go too far, aiming to be the richest person in the graveyard. They scan the newspaper columns to read what others have left and foolishly snort that is less than they expected. Little do they realize the careful tax planning which created that low figure, carrying out the deceased's wishes while minimizing **inheritance tax**.

So far, we have just touched on a few ways of saving. We will make a detailed review of many more – building societies, **stocks and shares**, etc. – in Chapter 13. But enough of long-term planning, dull pensions and death-bed scheming. In the here and now, you nourish ideas, plans, projects, dreams. To succeed, many of them involve borrowing. This is where the next chapter can help.

11

'Who goes **BORROWING** aborrowing goes asorrowing,' threatens the old saying. 'Better go to bed supperless than rise in debt.'

Nowadays, we flourish our **credit cards** and laugh.

Those warnings arose in the days when prison doors yawned open for **debtors**. Most of our prisons were built, not for murderers and rapists (they suffered different punishments), but for unfortunates who fell into debt.

And if you puzzle how anyone can possibly haul themselves out of debt again while languishing in prison, the law at last agrees with you. No judge condemns you to gaol for debt nowadays – at least not in Britain.

The wheel has turned full circle. Our whole economy is based on the assumption that people *will* borrow. If everyone decided to repay tomorrow and resolved never to borrow again, the dole queues would stretch to the coast. Besides, borrowing marries up people with plans and people with cash; it joins the inventive, the progressive and the dynamic with those who just want a quiet life and some extra income.

Like everything else, there are ways to borrow and ways not to. (The prospect of credit cards for children, which they already use in the USA, terrifies me.) A life of debt is no picnic. Lending also demands skill, so you will find a hint or two on that at the end of the chapter.

We touched on borrowing in Chapter 7 – when you should consider borrowing and when not. We looked a little at **interest**, what it is and how to calculate it. Then we mentioned plastic money (credit cards, and the like) and **hire purchase**. Finally, we said most lenders demand **security** and perhaps even **a guarantor**.

Here we take a quick peep at borrowing generally to fill in the background you need. Then we consider how to borrow successfully. Next we investigate borrowing for the most popular reason of all – to buy a house or flat – with a few hints on successful buying and selling. Finally, there's a word on how to lend money.

BORROWING GENERALLY

If you try to borrow, say, to start a business or to buy a car, the first thing that will surprise you is how many sources of borrowing you can choose from.

WHO ARE THE LENDERS?

You might approach your family, friends or workmates. Some employers operate loan schemes. If you are a member of the Afro-Caribbean community, you will probably know about the flourishing credit unions that exist to link up savers with borrowers. These are **mutual** concerns. This means that only members can lend and only members can borrow. The face-to-face commitment makes borrowers try harder not to let their lending friends down.

Further afield, you can pick and choose between banks galore. Many building societies offer second **mortgages**. They attract people who are well on the way to buying their home outright and can now afford to increase their borrowings. That is, their incomes have risen so much, they can now repay a second mortgage without straining their budget. More and more, the building societies place no limits on how you choose to spend the second loan.

Open a newspaper, and advertisements entice you to borrow. Step inside a shop or show-room, and the sellers will hasten to arrange a credit sale with their associate credit company. You can even carry your tiara to the pawn-shop for a loan.

The next surprise is how widely lenders vary in the conditions of borrowing and the **interest** they demand. Conditions and interest vary not just from one lender to another but even with the same lender, depending when you ask for the loan. Why is this?

The difference between one lender and another often depends on what they think of you – not as a human being but as a potential borrower. If they expect you to run into difficulties and not be able to repay them, they will refuse to lend at all. Or if they do lend, they will demand more interest and security.

WHAT CAN I USE AS SECURITY?

A valuable back-up as security may be the **deeds** of your house if you don't have a mortgage. Remember, though, that if you cannot repay the loan as agreed, your house may be seized and sold. The lender may require references, like a letter from your bank to confirm that you are a reliable customer, or from your employer. Sometimes they may ask for evidence that you have orders lined up for your new business venture. Or the letter offering a fortune for your masterpiece will serve as security.

You can use other odd things as security for a loan from certain lenders. You can borrow 'on expectations' if you know someone is leaving you money or goods in their will. Or you can borrow on the strength of a **life assurance** policy (see Chapter 10). This is guaranteed money, but expectations are risky. Uncle Albert may change his mind and his will, or live to be 110. So the interest rates will be higher. If Uncle Albert does cut you out, you are saddled with debts and no prospect of paying them.

Lenders who suspect that you are a high-**risk** borrower may insist on a guarantor, and the **interest rate** will be high. So the better the impression you can make on the lender, and the more firmly you can convince them you will succeed, the cheaper it will be for you to borrow. We look at this again below.

A lender who was enthusiastic to lend three months ago may act coldly when you visit him again. Don't take this personally. Market conditions change.

When interest rates rise, people grow keener to lend, even to more risky customers. They stand to make high **profits**. Besides, fewer people come forward to borrow because the cost is so high.

When interest rates are low, the opposite happens. Lots of people want to borrow, but lending earns less profit. Lenders can pick and choose, so of course they choose the safest. This is the rules of **supply and demand** at work again.

DIFFERENT WAYS OF BORROWING FROM YOUR BANK

Suppose your lender is the bank and you ask to borrow money to install a jacuzzi or an exercise bench. The bank manager might be unwilling to lend through an **overdraft** or bank loan. He might be keener to steer you to an associated hire-purchase company or give you a credit card to use instead. Why? Because they will squeeze more money out of you that way. So *how* you want to borrow will influence the bank's response too.

WHAT IS THE REAL INTEREST RATE YOU PAY?

Interest rates used to be simple. Everyone quoted the yearly rate, say 12 per cent **p.a.**, and you paid back your borrowings at the end of the loan. If you borrowed £100 on 1 January at 12 per cent p.a., you repaid £100 capital and £12 interest, total £112, on New Year's Eve.

But then lenders suggested regular repayment by instalments and started quoting monthly or quarterly interest rates, because these appeared lower and so more attractive than annual ones.

You might expect 2 per cent a quarter to equal 8 per cent p.a., because there are four quarters in a year. In fact, it works out at 8.25 per cent, rather higher.

Many credit cards demand 2 per cent a month. If you tried to work it out, you might expect it to total a horrific 24 per cent p.a., because there are twelve months in a year. You would rarely consider accepting that rate if the bank suggested it to you. In fact, the true figure looms even worse – 26.8 per cent. It means that you pay more than a quarter of what you borrow in interest, every year. Four years like that and you have paid as much in interest as you borrowed in the first place.

THE ANNUAL PERCENTAGE RATE (APR)

So many confusing rates befuddled and misled people that the government stepped in. It laid down a method of calculation and insisted that all advertisements must also show clearly a second rate (**APR**) which is always calculated the same way. Always look for the APR and use it to compare one lender's terms with another. It exists to help you. In the example I gave in Chapter 7, the APR would have warned you that an apparent 10 per cent really worked out at 18.46 per cent.

Another trick of lenders is not to tell you the interest rate at all. They simply say how much you have to repay each week or month. This way, not even a maths genius can work out how high the interest rate is. It is quite impossible. You need to know how many instalments you have to pay as well.

Many people, sadly the poorest and worst-informed, just consider the amount, decide they can afford it and forget they will be stuck with paying it for years, perhaps for ever. If the weekly or monthly repayment figure screams at you first from the advertisement, beware. The interest rate is probably gigantic.

Broadly speaking, if you can borrow from your bank, they will offer you the cheapest deal. Why? Because they know your history, so you appear less of a risk to them – especially if they already receive your salary every month. They will also offer advice and not let you borrow beyond any hope of repayment.

Money-lenders feel no responsibility for the difficulties you land yourself in. They may well seize your goods because you fall behind with payments.

EXISTING DEBTS – AND REARRANGING THEM

The warning against loan-sharks above applies more than ever if you are already floundering in a sea of debts and want to 'rearrange' them. That is, instead of writing out and posting separate cheques on different dates for the stereo, the TV set, the car and all the other debts you have run up, you pay one regular sum which covers the lot. You are likely to pay far less if you set up this 'rearrangement' with your bank than if you do it with any other organization.

BANK LOANS AND OVERDRAFTS

Bank loans are cheaper than hire purchase and **lease purchase** (both explained below). However, banks are often reluctant to lend money to buy cars. They have no security. If you borrow from a hire-purchase company, it owns the car. If the worst comes to the worst, and you cannot repay, it takes the car away (repossesses it). Then it sells it to pay off your debt.

Bank overdraft facilities come even cheaper than bank loans. You must agree an overdraft with your bank in advance. The manager allows you to withdraw or pay out more money than you actually have in your account, up to a certain limit. This can turn out cheaper than a loan, because you don't start paying interest until you actually spend the money. Then, you only pay interest on what you actually owe at the time. With a loan, you pay interest from day one on the full amount, whether you have spent it or not.

Sometimes you can agree, later on, to extend your overdraft. The manager will increase your overdraft limit to allow you to draw out more, should you need it.

CREDIT CARDS

People like to use **credit cards** and **charge cards** because they are easy and convenient, especially when you are travelling in the UK or abroad. Besides, you don't need to ask anyone's permission to borrow.

You pay high interest, plus in some cases an annual standard charge. You can run up large debts regardless of your means and can suffer a shock if someone steals your card and uses it. Credit-card thefts abound, and frauds are rife. Professional thieves would often rather filch your credit card than your cash.

PAWNBROKERS

Borrowing from pawnbrokers carries one big advantage. They will lend on the sort of securities other organizations refuse to touch – jewellery, watches, a stereo, even golf-clubs. I heard of one man who repeatedly pawned the spare wheel of his Rolls-Royce! Not surprisingly, pawnbrokers' loans turn out expensive, and you run the risk of losing your cherished pledge.

Two final words of warning on borrowing in general:

Never borrow to invest. (This is a male failing – women usually have more sense.) Why? The opportunities where you can really borrow here at 10 per cent and invest there at 11 per cent, making an instant profit using someone else's money, are few and far between – especially for the amateur. You will usually discover too late that you have misread the small print and end up out of pocket. For instance, the 10 per cent may be fixed but the 11 per cent is variable. Tomorrow it may plummet to 7 per cent.

Above all, *never borrow short to lend long.* Never borrow money you must repay in a year's time and lend it out to someone else for two years. When the year comes around, you have no funds to use to repay your debt. Obvious? Yes, but men fall for it every day. It still causes many a downfall and **bankruptcy**.

HOW TO BORROW MONEY SUCCESSFULLY

'People even pop up on Christmas Eve. No warning. They want to borrow money to splurge over Christmas. No thought of repayment. They must think I'm daft. Of course, they never get a penny. Mostly women, too.' The pompous young bank manager smirked down at his audience. My class of twenty-year-old secretarial students swallowed hard. They glared back at him with loathing. I veiled my delight. He brought a cold breath of the real world to the classroom. He also showed them what not to do.

Banking remains a male domain. Don't let the flock of girls behind the counter fool you. Bankers remain highly suspicious of lending a woman money – unless they know that her husband has means. Where they do lend, she may well pay extra.

To get a banker on your side, you must be thorough, business-like and never frivolous. You have to sell both yourself and your scheme.

Take Shona, who lives by the sea. Now in her thirties, she did a clerical job before she married Michael. For some years her time has been devoted to her children. Now she has found she has time to spare. Shona wants another interest and some extra income of her own.

One day recently, inspiration suddenly struck – a creaking sign outside a nearby house: 'BED AND BREAKFAST. H & C ALL ROOMS'. Why not build an extension to their large house and offer bed and breakfast too? Shona puzzled, planned, discussed her idea with Michael. He hesitated, pointing out how often his job as a sales representative takes him away from home. This meant that the idea will be Shona's baby from start to finish.

Long before Shona approaches the bank manager, her idea has swelled and taken definite shape. She knows that his first question will be, as Michael's was, 'How much money do you need?' So she has obtained a couple of free quotations from builders. Over and above this she will have to buy new beds and bedding, furnishings, crockery, etc. Then expenses will arise like advertising in the newspaper, a sign by the gate, repairs when guests cause damage, replacements as bedding wears out more quickly.

Here, chats with friends and neighbours already in the trade prove invaluable. They raise important points – like keeping your family separate from your guests, and the discipline this imposes on all – and fill in gaps that Shona would never have thought of.

When the day comes, Shona can go to her appointment with the bank manager clutching a folder of precise figures backed up by evidence. Everything will be neatly typed, with a copy for him to keep. At the sight of this, Shona will immediately overcome the banker's first prejudice against women – that they are too vague. Also, she will overcome his second – that they are frivolous – by arriving as formally dressed as he is and looking every inch a professional, the sort of person he would be happy to employ. With meticulous attention to detail, she will even make up her eyebrows knowing that delicate female arches radiate uncertainty.

Shona's preparations go far beyond estimates of costs. She knows that the bank manager will be certain to ask how she proposes to pay back the loan. The general answer is, out of her earnings, of course; but she has to be more specific than that.

First she needs to know roughly how much interest he will charge her if he agrees to lend. Her starting point is to find out the going interest rate. This always depends on the **base lending rate**.

Shona can find this by phoning up or visiting any bank. Or she can read it any day in the heavier newspapers. She realizes this is only a guide and must expect to pay several per cent more than base rate (another name for base lending rate).

How much more she will have to pay depends on the nature of the loan and how she impresses the manager. She has to overcome the fact that she has never personally borrowed before. Lenders look with a kinder eye at people with a successful record behind them.

If Michael were in her shoes, he could point out that he has been repaying the mortgage satisfactorily for years. So Shona must not be too dismayed (outwardly) if she is asked why Michael is not seeking the loan instead of her – and whether this means that her husband is dead set against the whole venture.

Bankers like borrowers to provide some of their own funds for the business venture as well. This shows they are prepared to risk losing their own money, not just the bank's. In Shona's case the manager will ask if she has any savings. If she can only answer 'no', her morale will plummet.

In fact, Shona's reply, which boosts her self-confidence at least, will be that the house stands in joint names. So she owns half, and the value has risen £10,000 above what they paid for it five years ago. This is not strictly relevant – neither Shona nor Michael wants to sell the house – but it stops her feeling a penniless dependant and encourages her to continue her request.

For this type of loan, Shona absolutely must convince the manager that her venture is soundly based. How much profit can she expect to make?

She has all these estimates ready to hand him. She knows how much she can charge; how long the season lasts; what her likely occupancy rate will be. The local chamber of commerce and the tourist information office were able to help her with these facts and figures.

What about the competition? If last year's summer had alternated drizzle and gales, but all the street sported 'No Vacancies' signs, Shona would surely be backing a certain winner. If no signs had appeared, even at the crest of the summer heat wave, she should think again. In fact, judging by the competition, her prospects are fair.

When Shona has worked out the most she can hope to take in, she also needs to estimate her expenses. How much will it cost her to provide breakfast – not just the bacon and eggs, but the electricity for the cooker and the materials for cleaning it? Will she need to buy a tumble drier to cope with the laundry? Will she have to take on someone to help out, and if so how much will she have to pay?

You have realized, of course, that Shona is producing a **profit and loss account**, just like Sally did for her salon in Chapter 5. The difference is that Shona's uses guesswork while Sally's recorded the facts. Both exercises are just variations on how you balance the household budget.

Taking expenses away from receipts shows Shona the maximum profit she can hope to earn. If this sum is not enough to meet the loan repayments, or is only just above it, she can forget the whole project. She would be working for nothing.

The manager will take his copies of all these details and may ask for time to study them more closely. This is reasonable.

Shona is not so foolish as to expect a snap decision when so much is at stake. The manager has his career to think of. He cannot afford too many lame ducks.

In the meantime, Shona will have other queries to raise about the loan. She will not trust to her memory in the stress of the moment. She makes a note of all these queries in advance and will scribble down his answers. Over what period might he be willing to lend? Would he consider an overdraft instead? Can she 'top up' by borrowing a further sum later if she needs to?

Shona must expect objections. She has tried to anticipate ones like 'You have two small children, Mrs Morris. How are you going to cope with them? Your husband works for a nationwide company. What happens if he gets transferred?' She may want to snap back annoyed, 'This has nothing to do with my husband.' But she wants that loan so she will answer with a calm smile, even if it is a tight one.

The manager's questions may be perfectly reasonable or they may be downright rude. ('How are you going to get your husband's dinner ready on time if you are running around doing bed and breakfast?'). The point is, Shona has an answer ready. If the question is offensive, she will force herself to bite her tongue, smile to show she is in control, then assure him she has discussed everything fully with her husband. She can count on his full support in the venture.

Shona may be sitting there, tense as a ramrod, only to find the manager suddenly relax. He has been testing her by needling, but she has passed the test. Women, being 'queer cattle' as far as the world of finance is concerned, have to undergo these little niggles all the time. Once you realize what they are, they lose much of their force. It helps Shona too to think of the dozens of people who have wasted the manager's time and strained his temper with badly thought through requests in the past.

Shona must school herself not to worry if the manager floors her with something she has never even thought of. She will calmly make a note of his query and promise to find out. After all, he may have just saved her a lot of money and future anxiety by pinpointing a weakness in her plans.

Shona must keep reminding herself that basically the man behind the desk wants to lend money. This is how banks make profits. Also, by starting so well prepared, she will have greatly improved her own chances.

She knows, even if he says yes straight away, she will not just ask one bank. A rival may offer her a better deal. On the other hand, if he finally refuses, even though the meeting itself went well, this should encourage her to tackle other managers for her loan.

So at the end of the day, does Shona get her loan, build the extension and start the next season? It all depends on the figures, and on the other people with schemes of their own who are competing with her for the bank's limited money. But generally, if Shona has successfully done that much spadework beforehand, there is no reason why not.

Besides, although you must be serious, there is no need to be solemn. I know one enterprising group of women who offered to immortalize their helpful bank manager in return for a loan – by naming their new restaurant after him. It flourished.

HIRE PURCHASE AND LEASE PURCHASE

Compared to Shona's ordeal at the bank, getting hire purchase (HP) or lease purchase is far more impersonal. You simply fill in a form to prove you have the means to repay. At the same time, hire purchase costs you more. No one looks coolly at your project or gives you any advice.

Hire purchase and lease purchase cover specific assets (Shona's new tumble drier or bedroom suite) rather than money to spend generally in the business. When you buy something outright (even with a bank loan), you own it at once and can resell it if you want to. Normally, you pay the full cost at the start.

With hire purchase, you only pay a deposit before the goods arrive. They don't belong to you until you have paid the very last instalment. Until you have repaid a third, the finance company can seize the goods back if you fall behind with payments. You are not totally safe from losing your goods until you have paid half. You cannot sell them until you own them outright.

Lease purchase covers umpteen variations of buying by instalments. Some involve a big payment at the start or at the end. Other contracts make you sell the item – often a car – at the end of the period for a set price. Sometimes they give you the option to buy it back again immediately.

The advantage with hire and lease purchase is that you need not find so much money at the outset. You can buy what you cannot afford and pay as you go. The disadvantages are the high interest rates you pay and the fact that buying this way is too easy.

If you sign an agreement and then get cold feet, you will find details of your legal right to cancel on the form itself. Normally you have more protection – that is, a longer period to change your mind – if you agreed and signed at home than in a shop or show-room.

Many people tie themselves up with too many commitments. Some even borrow from the bank and then use the money to pay deposits on umpteen hire-purchase deals. They forget they are paying interest on the bank's money they use to pay their HP interest with. Many slide into a muddle and gradually realize that they have used up all their purchasing power for years to come. Treat hire purchase like champagne: very nice, in moderation.

BORROWING TO BUY A HOUSE OR FLAT

Gavin and Debbie are a typical young married couple, fed up with living in grotty rented accommodation with other people's cast-off furniture. When they decide to buy a house, they immediately think, like most people in Britain, of their local building society. These are the most popular, although not the only, source of mortgage money. Besides, building societies show themselves more sympathetic to personal hardship than other lenders (as they did during the 1984–5 miners' strike, for example) and willing to wait for their money or allow borrowers to continue as tenants. At present, the scheme they have agreed with the government helps hundreds to keep their homes.

To avoid painful repossessions, building societies place restrictions on lending in the first place. Their guidelines have stood the test of time. Normally they refuse to lend more than $2\frac{1}{2}$ years' worth of joint **gross** earnings. (That is, what you earn on paper, not what appears in your wage packet after tax, etc.)

They may refuse to include Gavin's overtime **income**, as he cannot guarantee that it will continue. Gavin earns £10,000 a year and Debbie £8,000 a year, so the most they can hope to borrow is £45,000 (£10,000 plus £8,000 multiplied by $2\frac{1}{2}$).

At the same time, the society considers the repayments to which Gavin and Debbie will commit themselves. These must not eat up more than one-quarter of their joint gross salary, here £4,500 (£10,000 plus £8,000 divided by 4). Practice has shown that people cannot manage to keep up repayments at a higher level than this without great strain on their finances, temper and possibly marriage.

At first, Gavin and Debbie think this is unreasonable – until they remember that they will also have to find tax and **National Insurance** out of their joint £18,000, together with all their other living expenses, including those of the new house.

Most societies, unless they are suddenly swamped with lots

of spare money to lend, insist that you save regularly with them first before you can borrow. Our couple foresaw this and opened an account six months ago. They have been paying in a small amount regularly by **standing order** towards a house deposit.

Building societies usually offer a straightforward **repayment mortgage**. This is the most popular sort and it usually works out cheapest in the long run. Suppose Gavin and Debbie succeed in borrowing the £45,000 maximum on a 25-year mortgage. By the end of that time, they will have repaid all the £45,000 capital plus all the interest due. They will owe nothing, and the house will be theirs, free of all debts.

Their repayments will be lightened by tax relief on much of the interest they pay. Either they will pay less tax or they will pay less interest under the MIRAS (Mortgage Interest Relief At Source) scheme.

Although repayment mortgages usually work out cheapest, you need a high income to start with. Neither Gavin nor Debbie could have borrowed enough on their own. Alternatively, you need **capital** of your own to supplement the amount your income enables you to borrow. The two together may build up to enough to buy you a property. Both fall hard on a young couple, so there are alternatives.

Some builders offer schemes where you buy a share in your home rather than buying it outright. Often they give you the option (choice) to buy the rest after a few years when you should have found your feet financially.

These schemes mean that you need a smaller deposit or a smaller mortgage. The drawback can come when you sell. If you still only own part, you have to share the profit you make with the builder, but the builder does not share the selling costs with you. You pay the lot. Remember that, in practice, most mortgages only last seven years. People sell their home and pay off their mortgages early for many reasons: a job move, divorce, death, increase in family size, loss of employment.

These builders' schemes help low earners to get started. They also help builders to sell houses. Gavin might prefer this if he is afraid of the burden of a large loan, especially if Debbie is keen to start a family, leaving him to shoulder it alone as sole bread-winner. If you can afford it, stick to outright purchase; it is cheaper and more profitable in the long run.

Building societies are not the only organizations to offer loans to buy homes. Others, like insurance companies and banks, may offer **interest-only mortgages**, where you repay only the interest due as you go along. You may repay the capital by selling the property either at the end of the period or at any time when you want to move.

If the value of the house or flat should tumble, so you can only sell it for less than you paid for it, you will have to scratch around for more money. That is highly unlikely over twenty-five years but quite possible over two or three, especially including selling costs. Property prices rise and dip, but the underlying trend on our crowded island is up and up. Interest-only mortgages help you budget in the early years while you are still unsure of your future.

For this reason, interest-only mortgages are often offered by insurance companies and linked with a life assurance policy or even a pension scheme. The policy or pension scheme is designed to mature at the same time as the mortgage ceases. You use the lump sum from it to pay off the capital you owe on the mortgage. This way, you keep your home and own it outright. There is no guarantee that the lump sum will have grown enough, although it usually does and with money to spare.

These schemes (called **endowment-linked**) turn out more expensive. They can be useful for an unconventional property. Perhaps Debbie has set her heart on a houseboat which the building society may not be keen to lend on. Or the house she wants may be in an area – run-down inner city – where building societies are unwilling ever to lend; or it may even have been built using ultra-modern construction techniques with steel, wood or plastic that the societies are suspicious of. In general, Gavin and Debbie should still stick to a repayment mortgage if they can get one.

People, especially older and more affluent people, can buy their home on a straightforward bank loan. This may cover five years or ten, or the bank may offer a full-blown 25-year mortgage. Banks often prove more adventurous in their lending than building societies.

Beginners like Gavin and Debbie usually find bank finance more expensive than a building society mortgage. The banks have burned their fingers and so are more reluctant to lend than before. This may well change again. In business simply to make a profit, they are less sympathetic than building societies when things go wrong, less willing to wait for their money.

A recent development is the **foreign currency mortgage**. Suppose the interest rate in Britain stands at 15 per cent but the rate in Germany is only 5 per cent. Instead of borrowing in pounds, you borrow the equivalent amount in Deutschmarks (the German currency) and repay in Deutschmarks. This way you pay 5 per cent interest instead of 15 per cent. This sounds neat, but beware!

The **exchange rate** between the British pound **sterling** and any other country's currency changes every day, and did so even when Britain belonged to the European Exchange Rate Mechanism. The rate can turn against you. (I give an example in the glossary, Chapter 21.) So, after years of repayments, you can still face debts of more than you borrowed in the first place. Foreign currency mortgages are a wild gamble.

Perhaps the amount the building society offers Gavin and Debbie is not as much as they need, even when they add on the amount of deposit they have saved. So they hunt around for someone else – a bank or solicitor perhaps – to offer them a **top-up mortgage** (second mortgage) as well.

This will prove more expensive than the first, because the lender faces a greater risk. Debbie and Gavin have already reached their limit according to building society rules. Besides, the building society will keep the property deeds as security and take first bite at the proceeds if the house has to be sold up. The second lender comes next, if there is enough, and finally Debbie and Gavin can keep any cash left.

There may also be strings attached to the second loan. Perhaps they have to use a certain solicitor to do the **conveyancing**. This is the legal work to buy the house.

A few years later on, Gavin and Debbie may be well established in their new home with mortgage repayments under control. Then Debbie may get a windfall or Gavin promotion. So they can consider repaying all or part of their mortgage early. To their dismay, they discover they have to pay *extra* to do this.

The 'reason' is that the society or bank cannot charge you so much interest because you are borrowing less or for a shorter time. The penalty you pay consoles them for this loss of interest. Many mortgages contain a clause along these lines. People often find it cheaper to continue to pay the mortgage and put their spare money on deposit, perhaps even with the same building society, crazy though it appears.

HOW TO BUY A HOUSE OR FLAT

Not so long ago, building societies would only lend to married couples. If they included any of the wife's earnings in deciding how much to lend, this was emphatically a favour.

Even then, most houses and flats and hence mortgages stood in the husband's name only. A solicitor friend told me that he counselled each new husband client separately. Be absolutely sure your marriage has worked out, he would advise, before you even think of including your wife's name in anything.

All married women should try at the outset to get property and mortgages in joint names or to get them changed now.

There is no need for a wife to be earning for this to apply. This makes it easier for a wife to establish her rights in case of divorce, separation or widowhood and can reduce **inheritance tax** later on (see Chapter 15).

Nowadays, unmarried couples can borrow. So can single women, either on their own or a couple together. Single men have never suffered any difficulties.

The joint purchase of a home on a mortgage by an unmarried couple can still cause problems. These arise either when the couple split up or when one of them dies. Normally, it is not the mortgage that causes the tangle but who owns the home.

Building societies insist that each earner takes out **mortgage protection insurance**. That said, they sometimes forget or disregard married women even now. The policy pays the survivor the amount still owing (outstanding) on the mortgage. He or she can pay it off and keep the home. With a married couple this is straightforward. With an unmarried couple, who inherits the deceased's share of the property?

The division of property between married couples stands clearly defined in law. This is still a cast-iron reason to coax and cajole any reluctant bridegroom to the altar!

With unmarried couples, life is a free-for-all. Especially if there is no will, it is unwise for a live-in girlfriend of many years' standing to assume that she will inherit. The so-called rights of the 'common-law wife' are another fallacy that many women find out about the hard way.

Where two friends share a home, unless one wills his or her share to the other, it goes to the relatives of the deceased. They can insist on immediate sale, which can leave the surviving friend homeless. She or he will receive their share of the proceeds, less their share of the mortgage, but this may not be enough to buy another place.

Similarly, when an unmarried couple split up, if one wants to sell but the other does not, the one who does can insist on the sale, leaving the other without a home.

These are all things to bear in mind, given your particular circumstances. A solicitor can tell you what legal safeguards exist, if any, or can be arranged to protect you. Obviously, you will have to pay for any documents the solicitor draws up, and you may need the written agreement of your co-purchaser. Gavin and Debbie have agreed straight off that their home will be in joint names, and so will the mortgage.

Next they jiggled a few figures before settling down to the pleasant task of house-hunting. They know the level of their income and the building society's rules of thumb. From this it is easy for them to work out how much they can hope to borrow. Then, bearing in mind any other capital they can scrape together, and also the costs of furnishing, they can decide how much they can afford. Their other capital is the money they have saved with the society, a few thousands that Debbie's mother will chip in and the proceeds from a scrambling bike that Gavin is willing to part with.

Now they must be firm with themselves. They must only look at houses in that price range. To look beyond is to court disappointment.

Many people fall in love with a house and then call on the building society, only to discover they cannot afford it. Not only are they bitterly disappointed but it puts them off the properties they can afford. Not surprisingly, cheaper houses appear poky or bare by comparison or situated in a dismal area.

Gavin and Debbie collect sheaves of estate agents' details. They find that some houses are described as freehold, others as leasehold.

FREEHOLD AND LEASEHOLD

When you buy a freehold house, you and your heirs own it outright for ever. When you 'buy' a leasehold property, you rent it for a set period. This may appear a long time, and many leases last ninety-nine years. You may start off with a new lease or step into the shoes of someone else (the present lessee), with a lease of perhaps just sixty years left to run.

To 'buy' a leasehold property, you pay a sum called a **premium**. This is what you need the mortgage for. Every year after this you pay an amount of rent. It may be tiny – just a few pounds – or significant, perhaps thousands.

The lease will also lay down the conditions of your occupation: what you *must* do, like paint the property regularly inside and out, what you *can* and *cannot* do to the house or flat and even what you can use it for. It may forbid you to run a business from it.

Later on, if you want to, you can assign your lease and move out. That is, you sell the right to rent to someone else for however much remains of the original number of years.

Given a choice, Debbie and Gavin will be wise to buy freehold. Leasehold property carries only disadvantages. As the end of the lease draws near, the value of it falls, so you will get much less if you try to sell it. Don't be deceived even if the house or flat or similar ones are rocketing in value. You are not selling the property itself, only the right to rent it for a time. The right to rent for five years is worth much less than the right to rent for ten.

On the other hand, you may still make a profit on a leasehold property. Suppose you bought a thirty-year lease in 1975 for £10,000. Ten years later even a twenty-year lease might have been worth far more than this because of the rise in all property values.

At the end of the lease, you must either leave or negotiate a new lease, usually at a much higher rent. You leave behind any improvements you have made, normally without compensation.

Maybe instead your landlord (the lessor) will offer to sell you the freehold. In other words, you cease to own a lease and buy the property itself freehold.

If your landlord makes this offer not at the end but in the

middle of a long lease, expect to pay at least seven years' worth of lease rent for the freehold.

If you are considering buying a flat, you will have to buy leasehold. Building societies will only lend on leasehold flats. Builders erecting a block of flats will set up a management company and transfer the freehold to it. Then, as they sell the leasehold of each flat, they also sell a share in the management company to the purchaser. This way all the tenants jointly own the freehold. They run the company together, paying in enough to ensure the proper upkeep of the whole building.

Without this, flat-owners can run into horrible problems when the roof leaks and threatens the whole building and the top flat-owner refuses to repair it. Similarly, the cellar may flood and cause damp. With a management company, all occupants jointly own the freehold and so have an interest in maintaining their investments and their homes.

I have only skimmed the surface of this subject. A solicitor, Consumers' Association publications or any up-to-date specialist book can tell you far more. You now appreciate that leasehold property is messy.

On the other hand, selling leasehold, especially converted flats in city centres, offers owners a lovely way to milk more money out of their property over the years. They rake in premiums and rent from a succession of leases. At any time they can sell their freehold interest, the outright ownership. The lessee has no say in this – the landlord can change overnight. (You should bear all this in mind for the next chapter when we look at investments.) If you are the hapless buyers and you want the flat, you will have to knuckle down to the landlord's terms.

HOW TO SELL A HOUSE OR FLAT

People agonize over which house or flat to buy and enjoy themselves doing it. Often they pursue another myth: the

Perfect House. It does not exist and never can. But for people seeking a standard, easily resellable three-bed semi, the choice is vast. Once that decision is settled, the actual buying is easy. It is selling a property that is difficult, or jiggling the two together.

With our creaking, slow English system, people can let you down even while your furniture van is being loaded. Or you can get shackled up in a 'chain' in which your sale depends on a hundred others going through. Moral: NEVER BUY BEFORE YOU HAVE SOLD.

If necessary, and unless you are hampered by a young family and an old English sheepdog, consider selling with nowhere else to go. Move into bed-and-breakfast accommodation or stay with relatives, with your furniture in store, until you find the right house.

You will be amazed how many problems fall away once sellers discover you have cash in hand from the sale of your old place. You may even arrange a discount for a quick or cash sale. With luck, the interest you earn meantime more than compensates you for the inconvenience and expense of dislocation. And you are not saddled with any old house that you snatched at because you felt desperate for a roof over your head.

HOW TO LEND

'Neither a borrower nor a lender be,' counselled Shakespeare. And why? 'For loan oft loses both itself and friend.' He was quite right. Yet most loans take place within the family and among friends. Could you steel yourself to sue your family to get your money back? Even if you could bear the unpleasantness, the permanent estrangement, it is a waste of family money to give it to lawyers. Besides, the chances are you put nothing in writing, so you have no grounds to sue.

If you want to help family or friends, give your money

outright. You may call it a 'loan' to make them think they are independent; but mentally be prepared to forget capital and interest in a few years' time. So don't lend money if you are really likely to need it for yourself.

Besides, whatever they say in public, people never forget a penny they lent which was not repaid. Unspoken grudges like this can sour relationships for ever, often over a fiver.

As the saying goes: *lend your money and lose your friend.*

Keep your real lending on an arm's-length, impersonal and properly documented business footing. I will offer you umpteen exciting alternatives in the next chapter, because you are now ready for the fun side of money – making it grow; in other words, investment.

12

By hook or by crook, you **INVESTING** *have gathered up your wealth. You are keeping it intact, guarding it from nibblers. It sits comfortably on deposit awaiting your decision. How can you increase it, make it blossom and grow? Where do you start?*

Financial advisers spring up like mushrooms – or rather, like toadstools, because they pop up in all shapes and sizes. Your family, your solicitor, your bank, not to mention the building societies: they all poach on each other's preserves, claiming to offer one-stop shopping for your financial needs. Sales agents call you up or knock on your door. Other advisers, like investment brokers, sit in plush offices all day while investors flock to them and pay for their recommendations.

These advisers – all of them, in my experience, men – will act as though they were your favourite uncle or your favourite nephew depending on your age. They are not the least deterred by the fact that they possess no money themselves or have squandered what they did inherit. You will find no females; aunt/niece play-acting does not carry the same authority.

Incidentally, steer clear of investment schemes 'designed for women'. This is invariably just a selling ploy. They are not one jot better than conventional ones.

So the first thing to tackle is:

HOW TO COPE WITH ADVISERS

People selling investment schemes, or insurance or pension schemes dressed up as investments, spout fountains of jargon. They produce wonderful tables, graphs and figures to convince you that theirs is the best scheme. Or it was last year – or over the past ten years. Or it will be in the future.

Keep a clear head. Make them keep repeating and explaining. If you cannot write down in your own words what they have just said, you did not really grasp it.

Once you have listened to a couple, you will realize that they have little notion what the competition can offer. Many have been drilled like parrots that their own scheme is simply the best. They pile on the jargon to cover their own ignorance, and to earn their living.

Never commit yourself to buy on a first visit, even though they promise that you can change your mind and cancel within a few days. If you do cancel, you will be ashamed to see them again and feel a dithering fool. Remember, every salesman is taught to pressurize you into committing yourself on the spot. This is part of basic selling technique, regardless of the quality of the product. Once you realize this, you can recognize the push coming and brace yourself against it.

The best advisers want to know your personal situation to the last detail. They channel you into deciding for yourself what you want your money to do for you. Then they should have a wide range of alternatives to offer to achieve just what you need. Few salesmen with only two or three schemes to offer, based on how much you can afford, can match this.

Remember the old saying: *Free advice is worth exactly what you paid for it.* Of course, it does not apply if you borrowed this book from the public library. Otherwise, it contains a nugget of truth.

Remember too, if you do decide to pay an investment

broker for advice, that if financial advisers could predict the future, few would still be working. They would lie stretched out on their yacht in the Bahamas enjoying early retirement on the proceeds of following their own advice.

Where good advisers stand ahead of you is in their understanding of the system, having followed the markets very closely for a long time. So they can recognize the trends. Beyond this, it is informed guesswork.

While you weigh up where to invest, make sure your money sits in the bank earning **interest**. If the amount is large enough, say £20,000 or more, tell the bank to 'put it on the money market'. This means they deposit it in a special account day by day. So you keep **instant access**. You can get at your money whenever you want without losing interest. The rate of interest on the money market varies from day to day. It will always be higher than normal bank deposit interest but remain as safe as a bank deposit account.

With smaller sums, don't forget that any bank usually offers several different deposit accounts. Choose the one that offers the best combination of interest and access for your amount. Otherwise the bank clerk will automatically slip it into the account bearing the lowest interest. It is cheaper for them.

Do the same thing – money market or deposit account – if you are ever lucky enough to receive a big cheque through the post unexpectedly. Bank it that very day. Put the money on deposit and tell the senders you have received it. If it turns out that there was a mistake, say a computer error, and the money is not yours, of course you must return it. But the interest remains yours to keep. Many fortunes are based on using other people's money.

DO I NEED AN ADVISER AT ALL?

Whether you need an adviser depends on the size of the sum concerned, how complicated your affairs are and your own ability. We look at this again in later chapters.

HOW DO I FIND A GOOD ADVISER?

How you find a good adviser is the $64,000 question. This area is a minefield. It is hard enough to find out whether you are dealing with an independent adviser or a sales representative. The first will be self-employed, the latter an employee, you may think. Not necessarily. There are hundreds of 'sham' self-employed consultants living on the **commissions** of one company, or several.

Even while you are paying for investment advice, the adviser may get commissions from the organizations with whom he has persuaded you to invest. So how do you know whether he is suggesting the best policy for you or the one that pays him the most commission?

The government has tried to protect investors by passing laws. Advisers must now be members of **FIMBRA**,* which has strict rules on commissions. You are entitled to ask any broker or adviser what commission they receive and they have to give you an answer. But how do you check this answer?

Some organizations make a feature of the fact that they pay no commissions. (I have referred to them already in Chapter 10.) Others point out that what matters is how much **income** the organization achieves for the investors. It is quite possible for a well-managed organization that pays commissions to earn far more income for its investors than a badly managed one that does not. True. The fact remains that organizations that don't pay commissions have a head start because they keep more of a client's money to invest from the outset.

All I can say with certainty is: never make your cheque out to the individual salesman, always to the **limited company** with which you are investing.

---

* FIMBRA, Hertsmere House, Marsh Wall, London E14 9RW (071-538 8860). The UK Securities and Investments Board will supply a guide to spotting bad investment advisers. Phone 071-638 1240.

In passing, it may surprise you just how many organizations pay commissions. Most building societies and banks pay 1 per cent. If you personally walk into a branch and announce you have £50,000 to invest, they will not pay you £500 commission (1 per cent). But if you pay your money to an adviser or accountant who then deposits it with the society in your name, the society will pay the adviser the £500. (This does not contradict what I said above. You are protected by the rules of a professional body – solicitors, accountants, and the like, regularly handle clients' money. Your solicitor collected your cash when you sold your house, remember?)

In the case of banks and building societies, don't worry. This commission does not come directly out of your money. Your full £50,000 is invested, pays you income and will be returned to you in due course.

Some advisers or accountants reap more money out of commissions than they earn from clients. If you know about the commission – and remember, you are entitled to ask – many advisers are willing to share it with you, £250 each. But they will not mention it unless you do. Remember that commissions are income and so taxable.

HOW DO I KNOW IF THE ADVICE WAS GOOD?

It is difficult to be sure if you have received good advice. Years may elapse before your investments come to fruition. Many financial problems have a whole range of acceptable solutions. There is an element of luck, never mind the crystal ball. If your investments turn out winners, great; but don't expect it. Be satisfied with achieving a good average. Too many people waste time and energy looking back, with the benefit of hindsight, and grumbling, 'If only . . .'

WHAT DO I WANT MY MONEY TO DO FOR ME?

Basically when investing, you have three choices.

1 You can choose income. That is, you invest so that your capital earns you as much income as possible. A bank account offers an example of this sort of investment. It yields income – the interest it pays you – but your capital stays unchanged. It does not grow.

2 You can choose capital growth. This way your capital, while not paying you any income, itself grows as fast as possible. You buy a gold bar, silver bullion or a valuable painting. They all sit in a bank vault and don't earn you a penny. But every day they themselves increase in value (you hope), so that, when you decide to sell them, you have greatly increased your capital.

3 Or you can compromise and aim for some income and some capital growth at the same time, but less of both than if you went all-out for either. If you buy a house to rent out, you hope for income from the rent you receive and for capital growth so that you can sell it one day at a profit.

WHICH SHOULD I CHOOSE?

Take Elsie. She is 75 and struggles by on a small pension. When her sister Dolly leaves her a **legacy** she may say to herself, 'I don't want to sit back for twenty years and watch that money grow. I want to enjoy it now, while I still can.' So she will invest for income.

Equally, she might argue, 'I have all I need. I'm too frail to enjoy gadding about now. The more I can leave the Donkey Sanctuary the better.' So she invests for capital growth.

Yet again, she might reason, 'I don't need a lot, but a few extra comforts would be very welcome. After all, Dolly would want me to enjoy it. And if I can leave a nice nest-egg to Laura – she always was Dolly's favourite niece – so much the better.' So Elsie invests for mixed income and capital growth.

Moral: how you invest depends on your existing situation but also on your personality.

Look at Mary, in her thirties and happily married to Dan, who is a highly paid diver on an oil rig in the North Sea. She wants for nothing. But she worries. Her husband's job is dangerous, and his age will force him to give it up before too long. She is anxious that when this happens, and even more so when they retire, their standard of living will fall.

When her lucky number comes up, Mary will want to invest her winnings for capital growth. This way, as large a sum as possible will be waiting when Dan has to abandon diving.

Equally, she might argue, 'Dan's money covers essentials. I would rather use this windfall now, while my children need it, to send them to private schools.' She will invest for the highest possible income to cover school fees.

Yet again, she might reason, 'A little extra income now would pay for an au pair girl. I could go back to college. This will help the time to pass while Dan is away too. The course will train me how to help Dan in the business he wants to start when he has to leave diving. And if I can provide a little extra capital then, so much the better.' Mary will invest for combined income and capital growth.

Or again, take Julie. She has just turned 50. Her husband is in a reasonable job, and she works too. They live comfortably but not luxuriously, with the future provided for. When Julie wins a cash prize in a competition, she has no immediate plans how to spend it.

Of course, it would be nice to have a little more to spend as she wants to. It would also be pleasant to think there was a little something she could leave her grandsons when she goes. She considers a compromise – to invest in something which gives her income now but also offers capital growth. This is what you might expect.

It overlooks Julie's gambling instincts. Her prize has whetted her appetite. Now she wants to increase her wealth as fast as possible, regardless of risk. This means investing for capital growth.

At the same time, Julie has always suffered under the snipes of her ambitious sister who married money. Julie only married Fred, a plodder. Julie would love to show her sister that she too can regularly afford luxuries. So she needs to invest for income.

Poor Julie, torn this way and that. She will toss through many a sleepless night before she makes up her mind.

Three women, three classic situations: one would predict pensioner Elsie would choose income, young Mary capital growth and in-between Julie a compromise. Yet each woman's decision could surprise you. Any investment adviser who tries to push you into a stereotyped mould is a bad adviser.

SO WHAT IS THE RIGHT STRATEGY FOR YOU?

You start with a thorough review of your present and future means and needs. This should not just be about you as an individual – unless you keep all your money quite separately to everyone else, and there is no one whose future you care about – but about you as a financial unit, which usually means a family.

Do you really need anyone to advise you? A proper financial adviser will guide you through an exhaustive check-list, asking hundreds of questions. You may find some rather personal.

His notes afterwards might include snippets like:

'Dislikes daughter-in-law and suspects she drinks.'

'Is afraid of father and son ganging up on daughter after she is gone.'

This is not mere spiteful gossip. Such facts are important

considerations in trying to provide a client with what she wants.

You must struggle to be absolutely honest. If you only tell your adviser what you think he will approve of – 'I love all my children equally; I intend to support my aged parents' – you are asking for the wrong advice. Just like a patient who goes to the doctor and only reveals her 'respectable' symptoms: she must not be surprised if the doctor diagnoses wrongly and the pills do not cure her 'embarrassing itch'.

A good adviser uses this detailed probing to build up a full picture of his client's present and future position and desires. A bad one looks her up and down twice and assesses all he needs from that – her age and wealth.

A good adviser then sifts through the hundreds of possibilities. He recommends those that should enable his client to use her money to achieve her goals.

Can you do this for yourself? You can if (1) you know the right questions to ask, and (2) you know about all the different schemes on the market.

Here are a few questions you might not have considered.

How much cash do you really need to keep in your purse/ in the house/readily available in the bank? Women and old people are notorious squirrels, and the banks make fat profits out of their hoardings.

Like Zoe, who prided herself she never wasted a penny, yet kept £5,000 in her current account for twenty years: it never earned her a penny of interest. She rarely touched the money and wasted at least £500 *a year*! A classic case of that old fallacy, 'You look after the pennies and the pounds will take care of themselves' – just not true.

Many women who seek advice have never managed their own money before. A husband or parent always stepped forward to shoulder all the decisions. Others, who have struggled through on their own for years, still could not answer the first vital question: Just how much do you need each year to live as you have been living? Don't guess. Look at old bills.

Now you realize why I keep stressing that you should look beyond the next pay cheque. To plan, you *must* look at the whole year together. Bills come in hiccups; a pile may fall together in one month – perhaps November, when you pay for a winter's coal or oil, or February, when Christmas and New Year overspending makes them seem much worse.

Then there are emergencies. Don't ignore any sudden expense because it was a one-off and can never happen again. You can assure yourself that something else equally expensive will.

Once you know the total that you spent last year, remember **inflation** and add on more for the future. Just how much to add on is one of the biggest problems of planning. Financial advisers abound in horror stories of how much you will need even to post a letter in a few years' time. (On inflation, see Chapter 17.)

What are the likely rainy days in your life? How much will they cost? When I was first married, had a job to keep and a mortgage to pay, I always kept £200 in the bank for an abortion – just in case the pill should fail and the doctor not be sympathetic. Fortunately I never had to use it.

How many of your worries could be taken care of by insurance rather than keeping a lump sum on hand? Are you frightened your husband might die and you might not be able to keep up the **mortgage** and lose your home? Take out **mortgage protection insurance**. Most building societies insist on it anyway, so maybe your fear has already been provided for.

Are you scared that your husband's death would leave you and the children destitute? You can take out **life insurance** on his life if he refuses to do it for himself. Some policies don't insist on a medical.

Do you worry that if he suddenly became too ill to work, you would become poor? You can buy permanent health insurance. It pays out a 'salary' for the rest of his life where there is permanent disability.

People worry about all sorts of problems, most of which can be insured against. Some complain that insurance is a year-by-year drain on their income. True. But they are the same people who buy a fire extinguisher and then complain they never needed to use it.

Perhaps your worry is genuinely insoluble, like that of my client Valerie, whose husband risks his uninsurable life every day as a steeplejack. She can only invest to aim for capital growth. His high-risk occupation brings its own high income.

When do you think you will need more money? On retirement? In widowhood? In extreme old age, when you can no longer look after yourself? Are you likely to need an operation shortly and would rather pay to go private than wait in pain?

What projects do you cherish for which you need funds (anything from a world cruise to the aim to go freelance in five years' time)? Perhaps one of your children shows a special talent, say, ballet, for which grants are not available at an early enough age; or you would like to set a child up in business. Do you aim to buy a holiday cottage, pay to educate your children, take a year or two off work to follow the art course you always hankered after, even leave your husband as soon as the children are safely off your hands? Some people fret for years that they might not leave enough money to pay for their own funeral. Whatever your project, your money should be invested towards making it possible. And a good adviser will have heard it all before, so don't worry about shocking him.

When you have worked through all these questions, including everyone whose future you care about, and written down your answers, you are some way along the road to decide what you want your investments to do for you. You also know a lot more about yourself. The next step is to investigate the sorts of investments that are available and what they can offer you. I have given them a chapter to themselves.

13

YOUR CHOICE OF INVESTMENTS

Whichever type of investor you are — a safe Sue, a prudent Polly or a reckless Rita — you must settle down to a little reading. Once you have waded through the blurb for a few investments, a lot of questions will spring to your mind. Here are just four.

WHY DO DIFFERENT ORGANIZATIONS OFFER DIFFERENT RATES OF INTEREST?

There are umpteen reasons for different interest rates, but here are the four main ones.

1 Risk. By this I mean *the risk of losing the money you put in, your original capital*. This is over and above the risk of never getting the **interest** you should have received.

The higher the risk you take, the higher the **interest rate** you will demand to make it worthwhile. Now you meet the big difference between male and female investors: a man thinks of the money he might gain; a woman thinks of the money she might lose.

Basically, women like to play safe.* So which are the safest investments? We will look at them in detail when we advise safe Sue.

2 The second thing that affects the rate of interest is *the length of time your money is tied up.* The longer you have to wait before you can get at your money, the more interest you demand to compensate. This delay could be one week, one month, six months, five or even ten years. If you need the money urgently you can often get it but you will forfeit some of the interest you have already earned. You sometimes have to pay a cancellation fee.

Jilly put £10,000 in a five-year investment on Monday. On Friday she changed her mind and asked for her money back. Although the investors had had her money for four days, she received back less than she put in because of the cancellation fee.

Normally an organization releases all money free of all penalties if the investor dies. The rules on this will be stated on the investment.

3 Another factor that influences the interest rate is *the size of the sum you invest.* The more you can scrape together, the higher the interest you can squeeze out of borrowers.

Some organizations have founded their business on this fact. They take in little sums from many small investors and deposit them in large amounts with big safe banks at a higher rate of interest. Then they pass on this extra interest after deducting their management costs to the small investors. Such firms will not be household names: Tyndalls, for instance. But it is a sound idea and long established.

4 A fourth factor is *expectations.* I will explain this below when I answer the third question which has probably occurred to you.

* Not always. Queen Isabella of Castile (Spain) changed the history of the world when she invested in Christopher Columbus's wild venture. Her husband Ferdinand laughed. Luckily, she kept her treasure separate.

WHY DOES THE SAME ORGANIZATION OFFER DIFFERENT ACCOUNTS WITH DIFFERENT RATES OF INTEREST?

If you look closely at the rules you will find that you earn more interest the more you deposit, the longer you are prepared to leave it and the more interest you are prepared to lose if you withdraw your money early. The organization – bank, building society or whatever it may be – wants to attract as many different investors as possible. It wants big and small, those who need their money on demand and those who can wait for it.

Look also at the intervals of payment. When comparing an account that pays yearly with one that pays every six months, add an extra half a per cent to the latter. Add a bit more still if it pays out monthly. Why? If you are paid early, this money can be reinvested and earn you more.*

The official rate to look at when investing, which must always be calculated in the same way, is called the **CAR** (compound annual rate). You will find this on all advertisements, so you can compare them. It is there to help you as a lender, just as the **APR** helps borrowers.

WHY MIGHT THE SAME ORGANIZATION OFFER A ONE-YEAR FIXED DEPOSIT ACCOUNT AT 10 PER CENT AND A TWO-YEAR FIXED DEPOSIT ACCOUNT AT 9 PER CENT?

I thought you said the longer you left your money, the more you earned? True, but remember expectations. If the firm expects interest rates to fall, then it will offer a higher rate short-term than long-term. It needs to offer the going high rate now to attract any investors. But in a year's time, when it

---

*Remember when we said that borrowing 2 per cent a quarter was not 8 per cent a year but 8.25 per cent (Chapter 11)? Now you see the same thing from the lender's point of view.

repays the 10 per cent people, it will expect the going rate to have fallen below 9 per cent. If so, this is all it will have to offer to replace the money it has just paid out.

Can it ever be worth anyone's while to accept 9 per cent for two years instead of 10 per cent for one year? Yes, if you think that interest rates are going to fall even lower; 9 per cent for two years is better than 10 per cent for one year and 5 per cent for the second year. It would give you £118.81 at the end of the period instead of £115.50 on every £100 invested.

This is the idea of 'locking in'. You are delighted with the high rate you are getting and you want to spin it out and make it last as long as possible.

If, on the other hand, you think interest rates will rise next year, you will take the 10 per cent for one year and look around for something even better next year.

How do you know whether interest rates will rise or fall? Any financial adviser who can answer this would not waste his time looking after other people's money — he would be too busy counting his own.

WHY DO SOME INVESTMENTS TELL YOU EXACTLY HOW MUCH YOU WILL EARN AND OTHERS NOT?

With a fixed-interest investment, you agree to lend and they to borrow, and the terms are fixed. Generally you agree to receive less in return for more security. You trade off (swap) some of your interest for a guaranteed payment.

If you buy **shares** in a **limited company**, you become part of their venture. If it prospers, you will receive handsome **dividends**. If it falters, you may receive nothing for one year, then benefit from a large pay-out the next year. No one can predict this in advance.

INVESTMENT CHOICE: SAFETY, PRUDENCE OR RECKLESSNESS?

INVESTING FOR SAFETY

Meet safe Sue, our first type of investor. She wants her capital to remain absolutely safe. She wants to know in advance how much interest she will earn.

This does not mean that Sue is a coward. If her capital is small or she is investing for something really vital, like her retirement, she dare not take risks. Even the ultra-rich, who can afford to gamble, usually shelter part of their fortune in rock-solid investments.

Sue still faces a wide choice of fixed-interest safe investments. These are investments with the safest organizations. Some even carry a guarantee – like the banks.

The last British bank crashed over a hundred years ago. American banks, by contrast, are local and much smaller, and a few crash every decade. Foreign banks with branches based in the UK also have to meet high standards here before they are allowed to trade. (It will be scant comfort to those of you who lost money in the BCCI collapse that it was the British authorities who first blew the whistle. This bank continued trading in some other countries.)

Most British banks now run subsidiary banks based **offshore**, for instance in the Channel Islands, the Isle of Man, Gibraltar or Malta. These only have to follow the local laws, which may not be so strict, so they are slightly more doubtful. In practice, the British parent company is unlikely to let its 'children' fail and will bail them out if need arises.

Other offshore banks are more doubtful still. Think hard and long before investing in the Transglobal International Universal Worldwide Bank based in Panama (if there is such an organization). Governments in places like Panama exercise no supervision of banks or any other businesses. I could set one up myself tomorrow for £100, over the telephone, persuade a few mugs to invest and disappear the day after with their money. No one would raise an eyebrow in Panama, and I would never have been nearer than Land's End.

Building societies offer safe investments. Most are members of their association. This guarantees that, if one fails, the rest of the members will club together and reimburse investors and borrowers, so that none will lose their money or their home. The only society to fail in modern times – Grays – was not even an association member, but the other societies still bailed it out.

The umpteen societies each offer a range of accounts. As already outlined, the interest varies with the minimum amount you must invest, how often you must invest, how long your money is tied up and how frequently you receive your interest. Some offer chequebooks or will send you an interest cheque each month. Some of the most profitable are small societies with few branches which operate by post. If you are lucky, you can also benefit from extra cash share-outs when they are taken over. The *Daily Telegraph* publishes a 'league table' on Saturdays.

The household-name British insurance companies still rank among the best, therefore the safest, in the world. For safety, invest in their **onshore** branches. Before now, they have sat back with eyes averted while their offshore subsidiaries in Gibraltar, Malta, etc., went smash and British people, among others, lost money.

Onshore means based in England, Wales, Scotland, Northern Ireland or any of the British islands except the Channel Islands or the Isle of Man. All onshore organizations are ruled by British laws. These are much stricter and better policed than those of most of the world, so the investor is better protected.

Offshore means based anywhere else. You can tell where a company is based by the address of its registered office. This must appear on its stationery and advertisements.

Investments linked with the government – like **gilt-edged securities** (also called 'gilts') – are all safe. So are those with local authorities, like bonds with Manchester council. The same applies to investments with official bodies, like accounts with the Post Office. You are highly unlikely to lose your money, although governments have been known, especially in wartime, to put off the dates of repayment.

On the other hand, once an organization is privatized – like British Telecom and the water companies – it ceases to have government support. Investment in it is just as risky as any other share.

Don't imagine that other governments offer equally safe investments, especially in countries where the national sport is staging revolutions. The new president may decide overnight to keep all your money.

Safe Sue may also consider **debentures**. A debenture is a loan to a **public limited company**, say Marks & Spencer or Boots. She can buy or sell her debentures quickly and easily on the **stock market**. A debenture entitles her to a fixed amount of interest which must be paid. Unlike **shareholders**, debenture holders have no say in the running of the company. They cannot vote at meetings and don't share in the profits. Debentures are safer than shares, but both rely at the end of the day on the strength of the limited company which issued them.

Gilts are the same sort of thing, but Sue would be lending to the government. Many local authorities issue fixed-interest bonds along the same lines.

Gilts can be bought and sold on the stock market. Sometimes they are called **consols** or **consolidated stock**. Details of prices appear in the quality newspapers.

Sue may notice a gilt or consol called '1999 3%' and wonder how anyone could invest for such a low return, even if it is safe – especially when they could buy a gilt called '1999 15%'. I give a full explanation in the glossary, Chapter 21, under 'consols'. Overall, Sue will find that one gilt yields (gives her) just the same return as another. The difference between them is whether she wants her money as income or as capital gain and when she wants what. But all are safe.

Whatever reliable investments she chooses, Sue must make sure she knows precisely what income she will be entitled to. Some salesmen dress up projected future rates – that is, guesses – as though they were fact.

INVESTING FOR PRUDENCE

Prudent Polly now appears as our second type of investor. She has more capital available to invest, relative to her needs, than Sue. So she can afford to take more chances. Polly owns enough capital to be able to split it into two and treat each part differently.

The first part of her capital – it may be a quarter, a half or even three-quarters of the total – she wants to keep absolutely safe, but she is willing to take a gamble on the amount of income she earns.

Polly considers the sorts of organizations Sue looked at, knowing that many of them also offer accounts where the interest payable is not fixed in advance. Polly knows that with fixed-interest investments the borrower is committed to pay out whatever happens. So, to be safe, borrowers usually promise a bit less.

Polly is prepared to risk the remainder of her capital, but she still wants to keep the risks as low as possible.

She may be able to invest profitably through a solicitor – not necessarily her own solicitor – who has some clients with spare funds and others who need to borrow. Perhaps one of these people needs a **top-up mortgage**. This may appear slightly more risky to Polly than putting her money into the building society, but she should earn a higher return.

In practice, because solicitors control clients' money (the money from every property sale actually passes through their hands) they are in a position to protect their lenders too. Their professional association protects the public against fraudulent solicitors.

Polly can also consider investing in **stocks and shares**. In Chapter 6 I explained what a share is. The shareholder, as Polly will become if she buys some, owns part of a **limited company**, has a say in running it and receives her share of the **profits** as dividends. 'Stock' is simply an out-of-date name for a lot of shares. Sometimes stocks and shares are referred to as **equities**.

Prudent Polly remembers, if she buys shares, the risks she is running. The amount of income she receives (from dividends) is uncertain, and she may not receive any. Her capital is at risk, because if the company goes bankrupt she loses that too. On the other hand, she has seen many people earn high income from their shares for years. Besides, they can sell them easily on the stock market through a **broker**. If they make a profit, they have increased their capital too.

The safest shares are sometimes called 'blue-chip' shares. Examples are shares in oil companies like BP, in banks, in ICI and in well-known shops like Marks & Spencer. Foreign 'blue-chip' giants include Nestlé of Switzerland, Shell (part British, part Dutch), American Esso and Honda, Sony and Mitsubishi of Japan. Polly should not lose much sleep if she has money invested in any of these.

She might also expect to be relatively secure buying shares in the sorts of organizations called 'utilities'. These provide everyday things that people will always need, such as a water company or British Gas.

If she wants to protect herself a bit more, she can buy preference shares. If a limited company is in trouble, it must pay its debenture holders first. Next come the preference share-holders and finally the ordinary shareholders. So, if the money has run out by then, the ordinary shareholders will not be repaid. Polly can buy herself a better place in the queue. Some preference shares entitle her to a regular fixed dividend as well.

Some investors choose huge well-known giant companies because they are established. Being big they should be safer and able to ride out storms which destroy smaller companies. Others choose small, unknown companies. Why? When they do well, small companies grow faster than big ones, so the shares are likely to increase in value faster.

Incidentally, some shares offer 'freebies' to shareholders over and above the usual dividends. A shipping line may give reduced fares on its cross-Channel ferries, for instance. Others send Christmas hampers of the products they manufacture. Lists of companies and the perks they offer shareholders are published and available through libraries.*

These benefits could make it worthwhile to buy a few shares if Polly knew she would use the service often. Otherwise, she looks on the freebies as a gimmick, although a nice one because they come tax-free. Alone, they would not sway her to buy shares.

Really, all investment reflects your personality, like the clothes you wear. You choose between the practical and the glamorous. Polly is famed for her prudence, so instead of buying stocks and shares she may prefer **unit trusts**.

A unit trust is an organization which allows a lot of small investors to invest in a wide range of shares at the same time. It takes in their money and gives them a number of 'units' in return. The trust employs experts to use this money to buy shares in different companies. These shares will yield dividends and also capital profits when the different shares are sold. This income is handed on to the investors, less the management expenses of the trust.

---

*They are listed in *Concessionary Discounts Available to Shareholders in UK Companies*. The book costs £5.00 and can be ordered from Seymour Pierce Butterfield, 24 Chiswell Street, London EC1 4TY.

There are hundreds of different unit trusts. Some arrange things so that investors receive a regular income from them. Others don't pay investors any income but hand on the profits by giving investors additional units, which they can sell when they want to. Others again give neither income nor extra units; instead they increase the value of existing units, so that when Polly sells one, she gets more for it.

The quality newspapers publish unit trust details every week. They give two prices. The lower one is the price at which the trust managers will buy back your units on request. The higher one is the price at which they will sell you new units. So Polly can easily check what her investment is worth.

Some unit trusts only invest in British companies, or only in Japanese; others cover a broad spread. Some even invest only in companies with a good record on protecting the environment.

This so-called 'ethical investment' is too new and too small-scale to justify any conclusions. One would expect that, as with all principles, you must pay for them. If you deliberately limit the profit-making opportunities of the firms with which you invest, you should expect them to make less profit and your unit trust to receive lower dividends.

The unit trust may invest in a company which makes a wonderful new device for purifying filth from factory chimneys – something in great demand and so potentially a profit-earner. Or it may decide not to because that factory itself produces vast pollution locally. Ethical investment is difficult to monitor. Even the Vatican found it had shares in a contraceptive company after a take-over.

The idea behind unit trusts is that they should be safer for the small investor because they 'spread the risk'. In other words, Polly does not put so many eggs in one basket. If she buys £1,000 worth of shares in the Doesn't-Stand-A-Hope Company and it goes bankrupt, she has lost £1,000. If she buys £1,000 worth of unit trusts, this money will be invested by experts in dozens of companies. It is wildly unlikely they will all go bad and lose all Polly's money.

Does it work? Well, Polly must remember that there are management fees to be taken out of her profit before she sees it. She would not pay these if she invested for herself. Management fees also account for the difference between the two prices quoted in the papers.

Experts can be wrong – how many foresaw the 1987 crash? – and because the investment is based on shares, they can make losses as well as profits. Also, if the whole economy is declining (as happened after the 1973 oil crisis), all shares drop in value. Unit trusts cannot protect Polly from that.

On average, unit trusts will claim they earn more for you than if you put the same money into the building society. This does not mean every unit trust does better, just on average (see Chapter 20 for averages). Even then, they usually compare a five-year period, not just year by year.

There is another alternative which professionals always recommend: an **investment trust**. This is a limited company set up to invest in the shares of other companies. Members receive shares. They have only recently been allowed to advertise.*

Polly may not fancy shares but prefer to put her money in bricks and mortar. She might try a **property trust**. This works like a unit trust but it uses investors' money to buy property, often office blocks or factory premises. Income comes from rents received and profits from the sale of premises. Again, Polly will find umpteen different property trusts to choose from.

She might also be tempted to buy a house to rent out. (Remember, back in Chapter 11, we considered the advantages

* The Association of Investment Trust Companies will send a list of investment trusts and an information pack. Write to The Association of Investment Trust Companies, Park House 6th Floor, 16 Finsbury Circus, London EC2M 7JJ (071-588 5347).

of leasehold property for the landlord?) This would offer her income from the rent and capital growth when she sells the house for a profit. It will also give her many headaches and expenses, depending on the condition of the property, how careful her tenants are and whether she can get them out of the house if need be.

Despite all the work Polly may put in, the **Inland Revenue** will never let her treat renting out a house as a business. (This is the law; any accountant or tax office will confirm it.) Polly must remember too, unlike with shares or units in a trust, she cannot sell a house in a hurry if she needs cash. The Conservative government has changed many rules in favour of the landlord to encourage people to rent out. Different government policies could tilt the balance to favour the tenant again.

On the plus side, Polly always owns the house. This makes it a relatively safe investment – 'as safe as houses'. Over the years, it is likely to mount in value. It is not her family home, so there would be capital gains tax to consider on the profits from a sale. The detailed rules allow many generous concessions to reduce the tax where a property has been rented out.

Sometimes people can buy a property cheaply because there is a sitting tenant. The tenant (often an elderly couple) enjoys the right to occupy the house, sometimes at the current ridiculously low rent, for the rest of their life.

In this case, Polly would basically be gambling how long her tenants would live. If they soon pass on, or go into care, she has just bought a bargain. If they flourish for another twenty years, her investment only produces the tiny income from the rent. If she wants to sell the house again, she cannot ask as much for it as if it were vacant. Of course, she can offer her tenants a lump sum to give up their tenancy rights. If they have any sense, they will refuse.

Already overwhelmed with choice, Polly may go on to consider investments linked with **life insurance**. These have always been very popular but don't necessarily provide good value. They are popular because most people realize the advantages of life insurance. So the insurance agent already has a foot in the door.

With a typical policy, Polly would pay regularly over a number of years. Only a small part of what she pays is set aside to buy her insurance cover. The rest is invested by the insurance company in various things like equities, gilts and unit trusts.

Polly must not forget the agent's commissions, which may continue year after year, or the management fees the company charges to buy, sell and monitor the investments.

Some firms stress as a selling point that when she has invested enough and her nest-egg has grown, they would give Polly a loan, using the policy as **security**. Of course, they charge her interest for the loan, even though it is her own money she is borrowing.

If later Polly decides to stop payments and cash in what she has ('surrender her policy'), what she will receive is not fixed in advance. It may not be as much as she could have earned if she had put the same amount every year in the building society or bank.

It is a well-kept secret that, instead of surrendering some policies, you can auction them. Someone else steps into your shoes, continues with the payments and receives the lump sum. If you can auction your policy – one firm specializing in this is Foster & Cranfield – you should receive far more than the insurance company will pay you.

One further possibility for Polly is a **personal equity plan** (or **PEP**). These are new. They started in 1987 and have proved very popular. The government allows an individual to invest up to £9,000 a year (£18,000 for a married couple) in such a plan. The money is invested in equities, either directly or through unit or investment trusts. The generous tax treatment means that gains and dividends accumulate tax-free. The investor can draw some of her money out from the very first year if she wishes. Management charges are relatively low. PEPs can only be arranged by people authorized under the Financial Services Act, members of FIMBRA.

With so many alternatives available, Polly may think it wise to seek and pay for professional advice from a broker. However, if she decides to invest for herself, she must still remember not to put all her eggs in one basket – unless it is a very strong basket (a really reliable organization) and the sums concerned are small. It is better to fill several baskets, even if they are different accounts with the same organization. Some can be short-term investments (say, up to a year), others long-term. This way Polly keeps cash available to take advantage of special offers. She can change her investments at will.

Prudent Polly is famed for her cool head. She needs it. She must watch out for and avoid the latest scare. Sales agents stampede thousands every year into 'beat-the-Budget', 'last-chance', 'now-or-never' investments. Panic buying reaches its peak between Budget Day and 5 April.

Most of the time, nobody knows what the Chancellor is going to announce, so the 'last chances' are just a sales ploy. If Polly is considering this type of investment anyway, fine; but she must not let herself be herded into it.

RECKLESSNESS

Reckless Rita, our last type of investor, has one thought in her head. 'I want to be rich – as soon as possible.' She cares nothing about her present means or future needs, enjoys taking risks and maintains total faith in herself and her judgement. She wakes each morning certain that today is her lucky day.

Rita knows that the most profitable investments are usually those that carry the greatest risk, so she scornfully rejects any chosen by safe Sue. As for Polly's selection, Rita is only interested in those based on equities – the smaller, more obscure and adventurous the limited company, the better.

Reckless Rita has her own range of investments, all of which have made a fortunate few people very wealthy in the past. They are very risky indeed, and sometimes very profitable. Personally I would need to be a millionaire already before I touched them, and then only for the fun of it. Rita's choice:

1 Become an 'angel' and lend your money to back a theatre show. For every Lloyd-Webber, there are hundreds that flop.

2 Invest in an existing limited company to run a business (see Chapters 5 and 6).

3 Invest in a venture to find deep-sea treasure from sunken Spanish galleons, the lost city of Eldorado, a Nazi hoard stashed in the cellars of Berlin or at the bottom of a lake in Switzerland, or to publish a hitherto unknown play by Shakespeare, etc.: wonderful, romantic ways to wave goodbye to your money.

4 Invest in any scheme that promises to double your money in a year (or two or three).

5 Invest in paintings, coins, medals, postage stamps, Eastern carpets, uncut gems. If you are an expert, fine. Remember, this sort of investment never gives you a penny of income. On the contrary, you will pay heavily for insurance and security systems. You may enjoy enormous pleasure and prestige but, for a profit, you rely solely on capital appreciation.

The possibility (probability) of losing both income and capital may not be adventurous enough for Rita. Lured by big-time quick money, she might consider investments which entail high running costs as well:

6 Buy a racehorse and pay to train and run it. Read Dick Francis's marvellous thrillers. Discover all the things that can stop it winning and turn your potential Derby-winner into expensive dog meat.

7 Buy and sell **foreign currencies** for profit. This is based on the wildest guesswork, or a crystal ball. The same goes for the foreign currency unit trusts you can buy units in.

When these schemes grow tame, Rita might be attracted to the sort of investment where, having forgone any income and lost all her capital, she can find herself – double or quits – incurring vast losses and forking out more capital still:

8 Invest in the **futures market** or in any unit trust based on the futures market.

Many crops like coffee and cocoa and metals like copper are bought and sold in huge quantities in markets in London. People can buy or sell before the crop has even been harvested or the metal mined. There is not a coffee bean in sight; these are simply paper transactions. The markets are called the **commodity markets**.

Investors can buy or sell for some future date without actually spending a penny at the time. Anything can change the price of a commodity: a bad harvest, a war, a change of government.

If things go wrong, *not only can you lose all your capital – forget about income, there is none with this sort of buying and selling – but, far worse, you may have to spend more on top to cover your debts.* This makes betting on horses look safe.

Suppose Rita thinks the coffee crop will be poor, so beans will be scarce and their price will rise.

On 1 January the price of beans stands at £3 per sack. Rita signs a **forward contract**. She agrees to sell 1,000 sacks of beans for £5 each to be delivered on 1 April. Rita does not actually own any coffee beans at all. She plans to buy them just before she has to, at the end of March. She expects that each sack will cost about £3.50 then.

By 1 March everyone knows the harvest has been catastrophic. The price of scarce beans has rocketed to £7 a sack. Rita knows she will have to pay this to buy the beans she must provide on 1 April. But prices change every day. Perhaps something will happen to lower them again, like a government releasing vast stocks of stored beans for sale. Rita, the optimist, waits and worries.

On 31 March she can wait no longer. Beans cost £8 a sack. She must buy them, even at this price, to sell them the day after for £5 as she agreed.

What went wrong? Rita was right that the price of coffee beans would rise. What she did not know was how much or when. If she had actually bought them on 1 January, she would have made a profit. But she would have had to pay for them then and find somewhere to store them.

Rita thought she was investing £3,500 and would get back £5,000, a profit of £1,500. Instead, she had to pay out £8,000 and only got back £5,000, a loss of £3,000. If she had to borrow to find the £8,000, her loss would have been even greater.

If risks of this magnitude set your hair bristling out of your scalp, you are not alone. Perhaps you are even wondering what the difference is between investment and gambling. It is difficult to answer.

All one can say is, a gamble can never be an investment, even if a bookmaker does try to style himself a turf accountant. On the other hand, an investment may have a hint of a gamble in it. The hint mushrooms in size as the risk increases, until eventually there is little to choose between a punter studying form in the *Racing World* and an investor reading the latest prices on world markets.

People like reckless Rita are never satisfied. What she gains today, she will happily put at risk again tomorrow. What she enjoys is the excitement of the risk. There is only one thing wrong – women like Rita don't exist.

I have met dozens of safe Sues, plenty of prudent Pollys, umpteen reckless Richards, but never a reckless Rita. Why not? Women with the means and craving to take risks do it in a more glamorous, more public way.

You will admire Rita's boldness at the casino, Royal Ascot, even the bingo hall, but you will never spy her shuffling bits of paper with her broker. She will publicly cash in her winning chips with pride. Privately swapping contract notes or share certificates, even though they represent just as much wealth, strikes our Rita as downright dull. She must be *seen* to win.

So why waste your time describing a woman who does not

exist? Because the investments do exist, and women buy them – the safe Sues and prudent Pollys who have no idea, until too late, just what risks they have been running. They never saw themselves as reckless Ritas.

Whatever sort of investor you are, you need to ask yourself about the future. Once you are satisfied your money is well invested, leave it alone. Don't make the mistake of rushing after every new scheme. It costs you money to change. (Remember what we said in Chapter 9?) Arrangement fees, brokers' fees, lost interest while your money switches from one investment to another: all bite into your profit.

Review your investments every year. The sensible time to do it is in April. Why? Because this is when you complete your **tax return**, so you need to collect much of the information anyway. Of course, you could review at the end of the year, but who wants to bother at Christmas?

DEALING WITH PROFITS AND LOSSES

WHAT SHOULD I DO WHEN I HAVE MADE A PROFIT?

The shares you bought at £5 each now stand at £10. Should you sell? Some people will say stay with the same investment, keep your shares and don't realize your profit. Others will insist you should sell at once and turn your paper profit into cash as soon as you can.

One famous multi-millionaire explained how he achieved his riches by saying, 'I sold too soon.' He satisfied himself with a quick small profit rather than waiting for a bigger one which never came. As the saying goes: *small profits, quick returns.*

It all depends on your feelings, luck and what other opportunities for investment you can find on offer at the time. After all, you have to find somewhere new and tempting to invest if you do sell.

Just remember, until you have turned your profit into cash, you have not made a profit at all. Perhaps you bought shares at £3 and the stock market price today is £6. Unless you sell today, you have not made a profit. Perhaps tomorrow the stock market price will tumble to £2.50. Again, unless you sell, you have not made a loss.

WHAT DO I DO IF A LOSS LOOMS?

Perhaps you risked buying some shares at £4 and week after week groan as the stock market price falls to £3.50, £3, £2.75. Or you run a business and the profits drop year after year. Should you sell? Anyone who knows the answer to this one must peer into a crystal ball.

Some people say sell. Don't throw good money after bad. Others say stick with it. Make the best of a bad bargain. It all depends what you think will happen in the future, and what other people (the market) think.

But remember, nobody ever made a fortune by doing the same as every other investor. Speculators (the genuine reckless Richards) are people who buy when everyone else is selling and sell when others want to buy.

The blow falls when you *have* to sell, regardless of price, because you need the money – desperately. If this is your situation, and you have already insured against the normal risks which turn people suddenly desperate for money, you should not be investing in anything risky at all. Only venture money over and above what you need for everyday living. Aim for a guaranteed income first.

INVEST IN YOURSELF

There is one last investment area you may not have considered. It should appeal equally to safe Sue, prudent Polly or reckless Rita: invest in yourself.

Perhaps your money would be best spent on training. Some organizations, like universities and teacher training colleges, will take students who don't have the necessary entrance qualifications, if they pay for their tuition, regardless of their age.

Better still, get someone else to pay for your training. Many organizations will sponsor you at university and pay you a good wage while you are learning (the Civil Service, the army and many large employers do this). Or they will give you valuable on-the-job training or **day-release training** while you earn.

Women still need to be better qualified on paper than men to be considered for the same jobs. Besides, with the rate at which the world is changing, you cannot carry too many strings to your bow.

Investments in your health (regular check-ups, a convalescent home or a preventive operation) may also be money well spent. On the contrary, investment in your looks (plastic surgery, cosmetic dentistry, health farms, etc.), unless you are already so near-perfect that you can earn your living with them, are, let's be honest, not really an investment at all – just one of many luxurious ways to spend the fruits of your investments.

This chapter probably led you into much unfamiliar territory. The next will be easier. We look at the turning points of many women's lives – marriage and divorce or separation.

14

MARRIAGE AND AFTER

'Is it worth our getting married?' the girl asked, hope shining in her eyes. *'Or are we better off living together?'* She meant from a tax point of view: a simple question, a far from simple answer. She and her boyfriend, both teachers in their late twenties, had lived together for five years and seemed a happy couple.

They were not regular clients. They came to see me a few years ago just to settle this one question. I talked on for half an hour. 'As far as this tax is concerned, you are better off married. The rules of that one favour single people. As for the other tax ...' I tried to keep it simple. I stuck strictly to their circumstances and plans for the future. They stood up to leave more muddled than they had come in.

In the end I could only advise they took a broader view. There is more to life than avoiding tax. Would their future children thank them for saving a few quid at the price of labelling them bastards?

The couple shuffled out, vaguely disappointed. I think they expected a firm yes or no.

If I were to advise them today, I would come down much more strongly in favour of marriage. The legal rules are far clearer on property and inheritance for both spouses and children. Each new tax law recognizes more and more the independence of married women from their husbands. So marriage can give you the advantages of status and security of position without some of the humiliating dependency.

On the other hand, the male tax dodger will still find a willing girlfriend a more useful accomplice than a wife. Why? Legally, a girlfriend, even after twenty years' residence, remains an outsider. Laws are framed to catch dubious deals between insiders – like husbands, wives and relatives.

The drawback for the tax dodger is that he must trust his girlfriend not to decamp with the proceeds. If she is a wife in all but name, this is not too difficult.

DIVORCE

Melissa celebrated the end of eighteen months of misery as a drudge. She spent every penny of her half of the house proceeds on a mink coat and a holiday in the Caribbean to hunt for a new husband. But she only brought back a tan.

Marnie used her American know-how to divorce three times, ending up after each richer than before. 'She's an asset stripper,' her latest victim growled at me, 'but she marries them first.'*

'Phew,' moaned Phillip, a tall debonair accountant, as we left the lecture room. We had just spent the day listening to a series of lectures on divorce. 'I'm going straight to the florist to buy my wife some flowers. If she divorced me I'd be skint. I never knew she could claim so much of what *I'd* worked for.'

*Asset strippers are people who buy up **limited companies**, not to run them but to close the factory, put everyone out of work, sell off everything the company possesses and dish out the proceeds to the **shareholders** – mostly themselves.

'Why should I pay any maintenance?' whined Roger, a client. 'It's like buying oats for a dead horse.'

'She bleeds me white,' howled another client. I glanced down at his file, poker-faced. He had to pay his wife and two children £1,000 a year between the lot of them. I suspected he was robbing his own night-club, despite all our efforts – we reckoned probably to the tune of £20,000 every year.

'I gave him the house,' said Angela, 'and some money. He's already squandered most of my savings, without consulting me, even. But it was worth it just to get rid of him.'

In my office I signed a letter. It was addressed to the court to justify Felicity's demand for more maintenance to get by on. Her detailed expenses included £5,000 a year for a month's holiday, another large sum for ponies for the children and a groom to look after them. 'Each of her children already gets £10,000 a year,' moaned Nigel, the clerk who had written the letter, a pleasant young man in his mid-twenties. 'That's more than I earn – **gross**.'

There is no doubt about it: every divorce is different. Judges need the wisdom of Solomon to try to be fair. As everyone knows, the amount of **alimony** the court awards a wife is determined by the husband's **income** and **capital** and by everyone's needs. But few men can maintain two households as well as they could maintain one.

Also, few women, especially older women, even without children, could go out and earn enough to be truly independent. If you don't believe me, just compare average male and female earnings.

When it comes to divorce, many women are torn apart, and not just on the emotional level. They want to take care of themselves, own their own home, pay their own bills. Now they have the chance, they want to show they can be independent. At the same time, they are afraid of missing out on 'their rights', especially if the person who benefits is someone who has just hurt them badly.

Perhaps for the first time, the cold figures drive home to many women just how financially dependent they have been on their husband – as dependent as the cat when he queues at the fridge every morning for his Whiskas. This deals another and often fatal blow to their self-esteem.

So often the wish to be financially independent goes out of the window, especially where there are children to consider or to justify their change of heart. Most women after a divorce still end up being maintained by their ex-husband, perhaps helped by the state.

A couple may start off wanting a simple, quick, amicable settlement. Once both lawyers have explained what they *should* be entitled to and the cheese-paring of the other party (as advised by the other lawyer), attitudes harden. Things rarely work out so simply.

The basic rule is that the judge aims to allocate a wife half the family income and one-third of the family capital. This is very generous in theory, but solicitors rarely find out all a husband's income or **assets**. I have heard both clients and colleagues boast to me of the secret reserves they kept out of the clutches of 'that greedy bitch'.

Take income. A husband will produce his pay-slips as an employee. Fine. What about the value of his perks – like the company car, the expense account, the pension contributions made by his employer for a pension that his divorced wife will no longer share in, private medical care for all the family? What about his **National Insurance** contributions? They will count towards a pension for his ex-wife only until the date of divorce. From then on, she must make her own contributions.

If the husband is self-employed or the **director** of his own **limited company**, searching out his income poses even more problems. Perhaps he has hidden his full earnings from the **Inland Revenue** for twenty years. If so, he will have no difficulty hiding them from a court, not one member of which knows one set of **accounts** from another.

Take Bert. He carved gravestones but preferred to style himself as a self-employed monumental mason. 'Monumental liar' would have done as well. Bert was as tricky as a bag of monkeys. When his wife sued for divorce, the court demanded to see his latest accounts to decide on the alimony.

It was not until after he had them drawn up that the penny dropped for Bert. He realized that the more **profit** they showed, the more alimony he would have to fork out. So Bert visited another accountant, gave him part of the original papers and received a second set of accounts, for the same year, showing far less profit.

This was crafty, except that Bert overdid it. The accounts showed so little profit that the court decided he would have to sell his house to provide money for Mrs Bert to live on. Bert was outraged. He called on yet another accountant with another selection of papers and obtained another set of accounts to wave under the judge's nose.

Believe it or not, Bert finally produced in court six sets of different accounts for the same year. When he had to show all six to the tax inspector, there was uproar. I sat in the tax court and watched goggle-eyed as Bert threatened the silver-haired presiding tax commissioner with a punch up the throat. Of course, Bert fooled the divorce court judges. He kept his house and paid far less alimony than he should have.

Hidden income may cause a discarded or departing wife to be torn two ways. Perhaps she benefited for years from, and turned a blind eye to, income she suspected was illicit. If she wants to continue to get her share rather than watch it being lavished on his new wife, she has to shop her husband. Not only must she prove him a cheat in the divorce court, but the Inland Revenue may produce that court's evidence to investigate his affairs in earlier years. If they suspect fraud, they can dig right back to 1945.

If a wife finds it difficult to unearth her husband's full income, his capital may prove even worse. Her husband may have spent his hidden income from earlier years accumulating assets all round the world – for instance, a numbered Swiss bank account, a yacht anchored in a Majorcan marina, a villa in the south of France or assets held in a false name or in his mistress's name.

In a situation like this, a wife will find it impossible to prove what really belongs to her husband. I had one client with six adult children. They provided the perfect smokescreen for Dad. Although he ran several companies, his name never appeared on any document. On paper, he did not own a bean.

There may be other assets her husband possesses which the court never hears about. Why? Because it does not occur to anyone – at least not to his wife, and he keeps quiet – that they could be valuable. Does his old car have a cherished number-plate? Does he hold rugby **debentures** for a seat at Cardiff Arms Park? A stamp collection? An asset is basically anything you can resell. What she nearly sent to the jumble sale and he created such a fuss about may be worth tens of thousands.

Of course, in court, the husband produces the evidence of his income and capital. It is up to the wife, relying perhaps on memory, to say if the evidence is incomplete. That assumes she knew everything in the first place.

You may decide, come hell or high water, to insist on your share of everything, and let your husband take the consequences. If so, don't make the mistake of many women bent on revenge. An anonymous letter to the Inspector of Taxes gets you nowhere.

Your solicitor, the court or the Inland Revenue (or **Customs and Excise** or the **DSS** if he has been fiddling either, and you don't care if he ends up in prison) needs facts. This means documentary evidence, even if only photocopies to start with, to show precise dates and amounts. Otherwise your victim can pass off your letter as spite. Every male in the place will agree and sympathize with him, even the most hardened tax inspector.

Take Wanda, a willowy, elegant, aloof sort of woman, married to a jeweller. For years she lived in luxury and never questioned how he ran his business. When she saw herself replaced by a younger model, her conscience tingled.

She told the court at length that he fiddled his accounts. Her passion on the subject startled even her solicitor. Much of the jewellery he bought and sold never went through the books. He spent the hidden profits on the horses or flying off with her on exotic holidays. He kept a huge collection of gold sovereigns hidden.

No doubt this was all true, but Wanda could not prove a word of it. Even his passport was not stamped when they went to Las Vegas on a gambling spree. I had the job of defending her husband when the Inspector of Taxes received a copy of the court statements. It was easy.

Lucy, by contrast, was married to a doctor, a general practitioner. Faced with divorce and a beggarly settlement, she reacted with her usual energy. Lucy produced a sheaf of papers to show how her husband had hidden income of £5,000 a year. This was a large sum in the early 1970s. Income from private patients, private prescriptions, kickbacks from drug companies, certificates of death, crematorium fees: it was all there. Her husband did not have a leg to stand on.

He had run his practice for ten years. The authorities immediately assumed he had fiddled a similar amount each year. They charged him tax, then **interest** on the tax, then penalties on the lot. Lucy received maintenance based on the full amount of her husband's earnings.

The difference between Wanda and Lucy was that Lucy could show *how*.

Many women reading this will have experienced how slow, humiliating and expensive it can prove to get one's promised alimony; then, every few years, to have to drag yourself back to the court to ask for more. This is one reason why the courts are turning more and more to lump-sum settlements. The wife gets one large sum of money and that is final. There is a clean break. She can sink or swim.

It is at this point that most women desperately need advice. At a time of great stress, they may be having to cope with a reduced standard of living, returning to work or even starting **self-employment** – never mind deciding how to invest their lump sum.

We have looked at employment income in Chapters 3 and 4, then at self-employment in Chapters 5 and 6. As for investment, everything I said in Chapters 12 and 13 applies here. You have to know your living expenses and likely future means. Then you must decide whether you need to invest what is left for income, capital growth or a mixture of both.

Take Fenella. When she divorced Hector, the judge ordered a once-and-for-all payment for Fenella of £150,000 and regular payments for the children to be reviewed every two years. She was 50, an up-market lady who had never worked. The sum was generous then; it represented perhaps fifteen years of my gross earnings. It had to last Fenella (plus some state retirement pension at 60) for the rest of her life.

Her investment **broker** found out in detail what she needed to live on and then set aside £50,000 to buy her a modest home. Some of the remainder he deposited with a solicitor to lend out as second **mortgages**. This earned Fenella a safe and high rate of interest. Some he put into **unit trusts** aimed to produce income, some into trusts aiming for capital growth.

He chose well, and Fenella's investments prospered. She was sitting pretty. She received ample for her day-to-day needs, did not have to work and knew that her capital was either growing or safely invested. Of course, the broker reviewed the position every year.

Unfortunately, her very success went to Fenella's head. She began to ask herself, 'Why must I make do with a small house? Hector and I had a mansion.'

Without telling her advisers, she sold her house and bought a more expensive one, selling some of her best investments to make up the price. Selling, buying and moving proved expensive. So did redecorating.

The money tied up in the house was 'dead money' as far as Fenella was concerned. Apart from the joy of living there, it could not earn a penny. The only way to get at it would have been to sell her house, which was the last thing she wanted. The house needed more maintenance and more heating, and in those days she had to pay more rates. She lived alone apart from during the school holidays. Her three children attended boarding schools, paid for by Hector. Having sold some of her best investments, Fenella discovered that less income was coming in. To fill the gap, she made her second mistake.

Without telling anyone, Fenella decided to go into business. She borrowed from the bank at exorbitant rates because she had never tried to borrow before. She tried a venture in which she had no experience and which was not viable.

Putting together her talent for flower arranging and her wide social contacts, she contracted to arrange the flowers for society weddings. Before long, despite hard work, the venture folded. The bank made her sell her house and the rest of her investments to meet her borrowings.

Poor Fenella, at 55 none of her lump-sum settlement remained.

Moral (if there is one):

1 No matter how much income and capital you may obtain, if you don't know how to invest it, or ignore the advice you have paid for, you will soon lose it.

2 Professional people spend a lot of time on, and earn much of their money from, other people's divorces.

Another common decision of the courts is to leave the wife in the family home until the children grow up. The husband meanwhile continues to pay the mortgage. As soon as the youngest child starts to earn, the house must be sold. Former husband and wife split the proceeds. Again, this is a point at which most women badly need professional advice.

In this chapter we have looked at marriage and divorce. A widow, or a woman legally separated, can find herself in the same financial tangle. Your best protection is to keep abreast of the world around you. Even if your partner controls all the major outgoings, you should at least know broadly what he must spend, when and where to keep your household afloat. If he refuses to share this information, point out that he is leaving the family terribly vulnerable if anything — a short-term illness is enough — happens to him. Besides, even if you don't earn a penny, you should expect a share in financial decision-making.

15 RETIREMENT AND THE GENERATION TO FOLLOW

Many males complain how unfair it is that women can claim their state pensions at 60 while men must wait until 65, especially as women live longer. Many women look sheepish and hasten to change the subject. Yet when the scheme was introduced, it was designed, like most things, for the convenience of men.

At the time, the average husband was four years older than his wife. How could he retire without someone at home to provide his pipe and slippers? The retiring age for a woman was arranged to allow her a few months to put the home to rights after years of skimped housework. Then her spouse could join her in their perfectly run home. His wife would remain on hand to provide his domestic comforts.

Of course, no one forces you to retire at 60 or 65 if you can still find someone to employ you. In my last employment, I worked alongside a vigorous 80-year-old whose legal knowledge commanded wide respect.

If you put off claiming your state pension, you will earn a

higher pension when you actually do decide to collect it. This is generally a bad bargain, despite the fact that people are living longer. Generally, people who retire late die first – sometimes because they dreaded retirement so much that they made no plans for it, and sometimes because they are simply worn out.

Retirement is no longer a couple of brief years of well-earned rest punctuated by ever more debilitating illness. A woman can expect to draw her pension for over twenty years. For the majority of this time, she will enjoy full health and vigour. This is probably longer than she spent raising her family. So how is such a long period to be financed? We have touched on this already in Chapter 10.

PENSIONS AND ANNUITIES

Many people, single or married, can look forward to several pensions. First, the **National Insurance** one they contributed to: this might be a single pension to the husband to include an amount for his wife, or it might be two pensions, the wife having earned one by her own contributions.

Then, either could claim a pension from an employment – or several if they changed jobs and the pension was frozen.* In addition, they could receive pensions from private pension schemes either of them paid into.

Some employers' schemes (also called 'occupational pensions') pay out both a pension from age 60 – for both men and women – and a lump sum at that date. They often offer you the choice. You can select a larger lump sum and a smaller pension, or forgo some of your lump sum in return for a higher

---

*This means that you stop making contributions. You cannot claim back the money you have paid in up to now. It stays invested with the pension company and continues to grow. When you retire, you receive a pension.

pension. Before you decide which to opt for, you should know that there is a third choice open to you. You could use your lump sum to buy yourself an **annuity**.

An annuity is a fixed amount of **income** that you receive every year as long as you live. Obviously, the older you are, the more your lump sum will buy you because you will probably be around for a shorter time to collect your money.

To find out whether the annuity choice is worthwhile, go to an insurance **broker**. Find out how much annuity your lump sum from the pension would buy you. The broker's **quotation** (the amount of the annuity they offer for your money) will be free but it will vary from day to day. Even if you are not interested in an annuity, this gives you a guide as to whether to sacrifice part of your lump sum from your occupational pension in favour of a bigger pension or not.

That said, an annuity stays the same for ever. Be wary of comparing it with a pension, which is **inflation**-linked and should increase year by year.

A pension, or an annuity, usually only lasts as long as you do. If you die the day after you start to draw your pension or annuity, your investment is lost. Many pensions provide for a reduced sum to be paid to a named dependant. Working women have often lost out here. The insurance company would agree to pay a widow say one-third of her husband's pension but refuse to consider a widower as a dependant, or the dear friend (male or female) the woman lived with for thirty years and to whom she has left everything she possessed.

The woman paid the same contributions as a man but, even if she lived longer, she did not get at all the same value out of the scheme. Always check, when taking out a policy, who the pension company will accept as a dependant. Some companies are more flexible than others.

Annuities never pay reduced amounts to dependants. On the other hand, many schemes provide that a few years' worth of annuity will be paid regardless of the date of death. (So do some pension schemes nowadays.) Check on this beforehand too. Of course, the money goes to the **estate** of the annuitant (the person who benefited from the annuity). It will pass on to whoever you name in your will, or to your relatives if you made no will.

If your pension package includes a lump sum, no one forces you to use it to buy an annuity. You can invest or spend it in any way you fancy. The original idea was to provide a sum to pay off your **mortgage**. Everyone should aim to enjoy a debt-free retirement.

If you paid into a private pension scheme, you may face even more choices when you retire. First, as with an occupational pension, you can choose between a bigger lump sum and a smaller pension or the opposite.

Then, you may have the choice between a higher but unchanging pension for life and a lower, 'with-**profit**' pension. This latter is linked in with the profits the pension company makes year by year. You share in these profits, if they make them, so they pay you a little more pension a year. Of course, there is no way of knowing how much in advance.

As if this were not enough choice, you can transfer your pension entitlement (called your 'fund' or your 'pool') lock, stock and barrel to another pension company if it offers you a better deal than the company you saved with. The first company must tell you how much your pool is worth. You tell this to any other company you fancy and ask how much lump sum and pension they will offer you for it.

Not many people work through all this. They are usually too flummoxed – like a country cousin dazzled by her first visit to Oxford Street.

ANNUITIES BASED ON PROPERTY VALUES

If, when you know your full retirement income, you think it will not provide enough to live on and you have exhausted any possibilities of state aid, then you should consider your home. Should you move to a smaller house or flat to release some of its value, or split a floor into flats and sell them off?

Many elderly people scrape along in poverty in a house far too big for them, difficult and expensive to maintain, out of sentiment. Many even choose a retirement home on the basis that it could sleep all the children and grandchildren at Christmas – and then they never come, or not all at once.

There are schemes around that offer you an annuity based on the value of your home. You continue to occupy it, in complete security, for the rest of your life. Some schemes even allow you to enjoy the annuity and then hand on the property, or part of the value of it, to your children.

Basically, don't consider these schemes at all until you reach 70. The payers are gambling on the length of your life. They know that people live longer and longer, so they have to offer you a poor return to protect themselves. Above 70, such schemes can provide a useful arrangement.

WIDOWS AND INHERITANCE

In the normal course of events, married women can expect to be left widows. Some husbands will have taken care of everything, made a will, reduced the **inheritance tax** payable as much as possible and perhaps set up a **trust** for their dependants. Others will have shrugged their shoulders and done nothing, or at best left a will leaving everything to 'the wife'.

This is a popular arrangement, but it carries a hidden snag. True, there may be no tax to pay on the death of the husband. What he left to his wife is ignored when calculating the size of his estate and working out the inheritance tax to pay. But when *she* dies her estate will be so swollen that the tax may be enormous – far more than if a little had been paid on the first death and a little on the second.

Twenty years may pass before she joins him in the family vault. On the other hand, the two may go together – perhaps in a car crash. In this case, the law assumes that the elder, usually the husband, dies first. His wife inherits with her dying breath and leaves a large estate, a major chunk of which will be gobbled by inheritance tax.

Even if the wife is the elder and they go together, if all the **assets** stood in her husband's name, the same huge tax bill will loom. He can only leave assets to people who are themselves alive, so the husband-and-wife exemption cannot apply. This may not leave much to go to the children.

So what? you may think. The children will be lucky to get a bean. But suppose there is a family business or a family farm, and that some of the children, or even grandchildren, work in or on it? If it has to be sold off, cheaply and in a hurry, to pay the tax, the children will not appear so lucky. They will lose their livelihood and the product of many years of work, in exchange for some loose cash.

PROVIDING FOR THE NEXT GENERATION

A widow needs help and professional advice. Unless she pays for it, her solicitor will do no more than follow the terms of the will and dish out the money. The ideal person to help would be an accountant experienced in tax planning. He would liaise with her solicitor and stockbroker if she has one. Depending on the widow's age, she normally faces the following dilemma.

She wants to give everything to her children but she is afraid that, if she does so, she will leave herself short – if not now, then in ten years' time.

Most women in this position don't seek professional advice. They compromise by drawing up a will leaving everything to the kids on their death, and inheritance tax takes its heavy toll.

Besides, with modern life expectancy, by the time Mother

dies at 85, her children may have already reached their sixties and retired. They may themselves be affluent and established, with all the difficult years of child rearing behind them. A little money which could have made all the difference twenty years before may mean far less to them today.

So how can you provide for the next generation?

The problem should have been tackled years ago, but many men refuse to consider it. 'Never!' many have snapped back at me when I suggested the classic remedy. 'If I give her any of my possessions, she'll take off tomorrow with the milkman.'

Inheritance tax, like capital transfer tax which preceded it, is calculated on the size of an estate. This is the value of everything a person owns on his or her death, including the family home, furniture, car, etc. The bigger an estate, the more tax you pay.

One valuable asset that is not included in a person's estate is the pay-out from a **life insurance** or **life assurance** policy. Why not? The deceased did not own it. It was only after – in fact, *because of* – death that the pay-out arose. This fact can make an investment based on life insurance or assurance more attractive. The pay-out goes directly to the named person (who need not be family at all) free of any taxes.

Each individual possesses his or her own estate. So, if the husband owns everything and the wife nothing, his estate will be enormous and hers tiny. If they own half each or everything jointly, both estates may be small enough to fall below the inheritance tax limit (currently around £150,000).* This way both escape tax altogether. If one or both still exceeds the limit, they will at least only suffer tax on a smaller amount.

Naturally, if the husband transfers his building society account, say, or the country cottage to his wife's name, she can do what she likes with it, including selling it. Many men will not risk this, especially if their marriage is at all shaky. Who

*This is the 1992 figure.

can blame them? They may have promised during the wedding service, 'With all my worldly goods I thee endow (provide),' but they did not really mean it.

Some men do make transfers but keep quiet about them – like Sid, a carefree man in his fifties, jaunty and optimistic. He had a trick of patting his back pocket meaningfully if asked an awkward question. Sid ran a timber business but did not bother to insure his stacked yard against fire.

'Waste of good money,' he would snort year after year. 'It'll never happen.' He felt the same about wills, pensions and the future in general. If I sent him pension details, he tore them up neatly and posted the bits back to me. Then one day Sid shuffled into the office a different man.

'I give in,' he sighed. 'Do your worst.'

'Why?' I could not help gasping.

'Had to go to the doctor,' he mumbled. 'He says I've got this heart.'

So I set to work as fast as possible, liaising with Sid's solicitor, who, as staggered as me, drew up Sid's will.

Sid's son Phil had worked for his dad right from school. The daughter-in-law worked for Sid too and was much brighter than her husband. Mrs Sid held some **shares** in the **limited company** and so did her daughter, but Sid wanted Phil alone to step into his shoes.

So we transferred company shares from father to son – not all at once, or there would have been heavy tax to pay. It took several years. Sid worked on as before, knowing he could go any time. Only his attitude had changed.

One day Sid's daughter-in-law delivered some signed share transfer forms back to me. At the doorway, she hesitated. Then she tilted her head and launched herself. 'I don't understand. What does all this mean?'

'Your husband owns the business,' I explained. 'Now he controls more shares than your father-in-law.'

'So?'

'He has the final say. He makes the decisions. He's in charge.'

Her face clouded, then brightened. 'That old devil. He never told us. He'd have kept the reins on tight until his dying day. Now we'll see. Thank you very much indeed.' She marched out, her head held high.

So, you may own things you never even knew about. The only way to find out for sure is to look at the original documents.

If you are widowed and your husband was one of the 'I'll be gone, so why worry?' school, all may not be lost. Remember the **deed of family arrangement** I mentioned in Chapter 8? If all the **beneficiaries** agree – and if everything went to the widow, she will be the only one – the will can be rewritten to reduce the tax payable.

One common solution is to rewrite the husband's will to leave the children and/or grandchildren the first tax-free £150,000. Then the remainder is used to set up a trust, often the sort of trust called an 'accumulation and maintenance trust'.

WHAT IS A TRUST?

A trust is a legal arrangement, set up by a solicitor, whereby one person looks after another's assets. For instance, baby Joanne was orphaned when both her parents died in a plane crash. She inherited all their possessions but clearly cannot make any decisions about them.

The people who manage the trust for her are called trustees, perhaps her uncle Bill, her grandmother and her parents' solicitor. They control everything until Joanne comes of age. When this happens, the trust will be broken. In other words, it comes to an end and everything left is handed over directly to Joanne as beneficiary.

Some of Joanne's inheritance will have been spent on her in the meantime, for her maintenance, education, holidays, clothes and even pocket-money. How much can be spent and on what depends on the terms of the trust. Some trusts lay down strict rules; others give the trustees wide discretion to act as they think best at the time.

Some trusts last a lifetime – perhaps the beneficiary is insane.

Originally designed to protect the weak, trusts are now widely used in tax planning. Many wealthy families set up one or several trusts. One may be based in Britain, another abroad. You don't have to die before a trust can be set up. If you wanted to, you could set one up tomorrow. The person who sets up the trust and puts his or her assets into it is called the **settlor**. A settlor can also be a trustee.

Take the case of Eleanor, who was recently widowed in her sixties and found that her husband had left far more than she ever dreamed of, and all to her. When she goes for advice, she has to give details of her three children, four grandchildren and their likely futures. Then, just as in any investment planning, Eleanor must spell out in detail how much she thinks she needs to live on and her own future plans.

The adviser may recommend first that she changes her husband's will by deed of family arrangement. Perhaps she should leave some money directly to her son who wants to expand his business, and to her daughter who intends to marry shortly; maybe some money directly to her talented young granddaughter to send her to ballet school. Obviously the decisions and reasons are Eleanor's, but the adviser can ensure that minimal tax is paid, now and in the long term.

Next, the adviser will insist that Eleanor keep enough capital in her own hands to ensure she can live comfortably from the income it generates. She need not own her own home (see below).

With the rest, the adviser may suggest she set up an accumulation and maintenance trust. Eleanor chooses the beneficiaries: her children, her grandchildren and perhaps her disabled sister Mary, who is very hard up.

Eleanor also chooses the trustees. These are of course people whose judgement she feels she can rely on. One of them will be her own solicitor, accountant or other adviser. Another will be Eleanor herself, so she has a continuing say in how her trust – the Eleanor Rose Spenser Family Trust – uses its money.

Trusts are as flexible as acrobats. For example, Eleanor may put her family home into it, reserving a life interest for herself. This means she keeps the right to live there for as long as she wants to. But, as the property belongs to the trust, the trust pays for its upkeep.

Trusts are rather like limited liability companies – the law looks on them as persons in their own right. Trusts pay their own low tax. They may continue to exist long after the original settlor, trustees and beneficiaries are all gone.

In general, a trust allows you to set aside, invest and use your own money, as you like, for the benefit of the people you choose, legally beyond the clutches of the **Inland Revenue** – even after you have died.

It also gives a family the weapon to act together to stop one reckless idiot dissipating the family fortune, even if he was born the eldest son. It means that a widow can both spend her money for the benefit of her family and ensure she will never go without for the rest of her life.

Too good to be true? There are drawbacks, but these are minor. It will cost you to set up a trust and to pay for accounts to be prepared for it each year. It is broadly worthwhile where the total capital is over £250,000. Bear in mind that this figure includes the family home, the husband's business and absolutely everything else. It could be worthwhile at a lower figure if the widow really has no clue and does not want any worry, but simply wants an assured **income** and a chance to help her children.

Elderly people are often very reluctant to hand over ownership of assets. They look on their possessions as their last hold on power, their last chance to have a say. They are frightened that apparently loving children will turn cold as soon as the loot, or the house, is safely theirs. Mother fears that, having suddenly become a nuisance, she will find herself packed off to a distant 'home'.

And, quite frankly, it happens.

Sometimes a trust can offer a happy compromise. Mother knows she has a say, and professional people will continue to watch over her interests. She is also reassured to know that if she goes suddenly, the family will not be plunged into financial chaos.

Like all parents, Eleanor may still be plagued with the perennial problem:

How can I treat all my children fairly?

This is another question that needs the wisdom of Solomon, especially when the children's circumstances, needs and desires are widely different and changing. And is fair treatment always equal treatment?

Not in the view of one old farmer client I dealt with. 'I treat my six childer just the same,' he croaked at me. 'Double portions for my sons and single portions for my daughters. That's fair.'

16

Thousands of OVERSEAS *women, of all* ages *and incomes, travel overseas every day. Some just jet off to an island in the sun for a few weeks' holiday. Others go from concrete city to concrete city as part of their job or to extend their education.*

Still others disembark in the most inhospitable trouble-spots where they may work for years. We will look here at travelling abroad for recreation or for short-term working visits.

FOREIGN CURRENCY

As holiday-maker or working visitor, you need to buy and use **foreign currency** – that is, the notes and coins used in the country you are visiting. You can buy them in Britain in a bank, travel agent or some building societies. Sometimes, in Britain or abroad, the office where you can change currency is called a 'bureau de change'.

How many pounds you have to pay for your foreign currency depends on the **exchange rate**. So does the number of pounds you receive when you change back what you did not spend. These rates vary every day. Why? **Supply and demand**. The more British sun-seekers want Spanish pesetas, the more they will have to pay for them – just like at an auction. It is easy to get muddled with exchange rates. Here is a quick way to decide if the rate offered is good or bad for you.

Perhaps the bank will offer you 210 pesetas to the pound and the travel agent 200. Which is better for you? It depends whether you are buying or selling pesetas. Call the pesetas 'apples'.

Suppose you are buying. Which would you rather get, 210 apples for your pound or 200? Easy. You want 210. So that is the better rate for you.

If you are selling your apples, would you rather part with 210 for a pound or 200? Easy. You want to part with as few as possible. So 200 is the better rate for you.

Carry some foreign cash for immediate use, like a taxi or phone call from the airport. But take the bulk of your money in another form, like **traveller's cheques**. You buy these before you leave Britain and can cash them in when you return if you don't spend them.

Each traveller's cheque is for a fixed amount. You sign it in advance. Then you sign it again when you cash the cheque – that is, exchange it for local currency in the foreign bank or bureau de change or your hotel. Cashing traveller's cheques at your hotel or a local shop always works out more expensive. You pay for the convenience.

If you lose your traveller's cheques or they are stolen, you can claim your money back from the organization (like Thomas Cook or American Express) that issued them. So traveller's cheques are safer than cash. The book they come with normally contains a page for you to note their numbers and tear out to keep separately from the cheques themselves. You quote the numbers in order to report their loss or theft immediately. A good idea is to put the cheques in your handbag and the list in your luggage; or split cheques and numbers between husband and wife.

Some traveller's cheques are valued in **sterling** (British pounds and pence). Each one will state on it the value, e.g. £10 or £1,000. This means that you don't know how much local currency you will get for each until the day you decide to cash it.

If you prefer, you can choose cheques valued in the currency of your destination. Your cheques might specify 2,000 pesetas or 200,000 pesetas. You have already done the currency exchange on the day you bought your cheques. Depending on how the exchange rate changes between the day you buy traveller's cheques and the day you cash them, you may do better or worse than if you had bought pound traveller's cheques.

One advantage of using local currency traveller's cheques is that not just banks but hotels and restaurants will accept them.

When you return home, you will find that the bank offers two different rates to change your surplus pesetas back into useful pounds. The better rate is the one at which they will change back foreign currency traveller's cheques. The other is the rate at which they will change banknotes; this will always be the lower of the two because foreign banknotes are a nuisance to the bank.

You don't need to buy traveller's cheques in either pounds or the currency of your favourite sun-spot. You could buy US dollar cheques or even cheques in Swiss francs. Here you change twice: once from pounds to dollars/francs when you buy the cheques; then from dollars/francs to pesetas when you cash them. If the pound is strong against the dollar when you buy, you get a lot of dollars for your pound. If the dollar is strong against the peseta when you exchange, you get a lot of pesetas for your dollar. So it is a gamble.

Wise adventurers watch how the currencies are changing (printed in the newspapers or posted up in the banks) for a few weeks before they decide, if the amount is large enough to matter. Never buy your traveller's cheques before you need to, despite what the travel agent says. They are 'dead money' as far as you are concerned. I have never found any problems getting cheques in a hurry. Travel companies make a tidy pile out of travellers who pay for cheques months before they intend to use them.

Normally, you must pay 1 per cent commission to the organization that sells you your traveller's cheques. Some organizations supply them without commission, like a building society selling to its members. So it can be worth your while to ask around.

An alternative to traveller's cheques is Eurocheques. Your British bank supplies a special chequebook and a card with 'EC' on it. When abroad, you write a cheque just as you would at home, except that you write the sum in foreign currency not pounds. Your bank converts this back into pounds, and it reduces the balance in your bank account just as it would for an ordinary cheque. You pay a small amount for each cheque you write, and there is a limit on how much each cheque can be for.

More and more globe-trotters are abandoning traveller's cheques in favour of **credit cards** like Barclaycard and Access or **charge cards** like Amex (American Express). You don't need to tie up lots of cash in advance to protect yourself against running out of money.

Most banks issue and accept these cards, and with luck you can even use them in 'holes in the wall' in your ideal ski resort, with computers that 'speak' English. Careful, though: if you forget your number or the machine swallows your card and this was your only source of money, your holiday may be ruined.

Credit cards should be safer than plain cash because of the security number, although frauds are still so rife that people sometimes have to produce two cards to prove their identity, not just one.

Credit card currency changes are calculated at the interbank rate. So are Eurocheque ones. This is a rate private to the banks. It is usually more favourable than you will be offered elsewhere. The transfers can take a while to appear on your statement. A few years ago this could involve a six-month delay, which was effectively a six months' interest-free loan to you. Now the organizations react much more quickly except in really backward spots.

The inter-bank rate of exchange used is that of the day the transaction was recorded, not the one that prevailed on the day you got your cash. It might prove better or worse for you. There is no way of telling.

If you plan to travel to the USA, you *must* use either dollars or credit cards. American banks are so local that they will sometimes refuse to change even traveller's cheques issued in the USA by another branch of the same bank! Similarly, Barclays' New York branch has refused to change Barclays' own sterling traveller's cheques before now. A trip almost anywhere aboard will make you appreciate your British bank, however much you complained about it in the past.

BARGAINS ABROAD

For many women, one of the pleasures of a holiday is to hunt for foreign bargains. Forget duty-free shops at airports and harbours. They are a worldwide swizz. You just get panicked or bored into buying a bit more cheaply than you could at home. You will probably find a wider choice of wines, perfumes, etc., and at better prices in your seaside supermarket.

So where do you find the bargains? At the risk of sounding a killjoy, I must say that they are few and far between. There are novelties by the million, but not so many bargains, especially if you include customs duties.

When the holiday mood has worn off, you will put that cute native blouse in a drawer, grimace at its shoddy quality and admit that it looks wrong with everything else you own. It will find its way to the next jumble sale.

Some staple items are genuinely far cheaper and nicer abroad – coffee beans and drinking chocolate in France, for instance.

If you are taking your car you can bring back this sort of thing easily. But it is not exactly thrilling. Remember, experts scour the world all year round for novelties to sell in your local gift shop.

To get something worthwhile, be prepared to pay a good price in the country of origin. Sorrento in Italy produces beautiful inlaid furniture and jewel caskets. If you pay £200 for one in Sorrento, you will spot its twin in a top British department store for £1,000.

Jewellery (real jewellery, not costume) can be a bargain or a con. The rules to protect the customer, and how well they are enforced, vary from country to country. Your best safeguard is where you find dozens of sellers together.

The underground jewellery market in Istanbul in Turkey, for example, boasts a hundred jewellers' shops side by side. You will marvel at gems beyond the dreams of avarice, rings as impressive as brooches and *parures* (matching sets of tiara, ear-rings, necklace, bracelets, etc.) fit for a queen. No tasteful window displays here – every shelf is crammed chock-a-block with gold. The sapphire brooch I fell for was immediately valued back in Britain at three times the sum I had paid.

By contrast, a relative brought me back a 'silver' necklace and bracelet from Africa. It turned out to be a thin film of silver over copper, which vanished as soon as I tried to polish it.

Bargaining is hard work and slow. We Westerners stand at a disadvantage because we hate it. Besides, the locals are easily insulted if we try to bargain in the wrong place. Or they despise us as suckers if we assume that the 'guide' price is fixed and pay up without haggling.

If the seller allows you to walk away then you really have hit their bottom price. Sometimes it works if you take out your money (only show the amount you want to pay) and proffer it. Sellers can rarely resist the lure of real cash.

Shoppers' paradises? If you want a purely personal recommendation from the twenty-two countries I have visited, it is Singapore, followed by Hong Kong and Bangkok (Thailand).

Some people enjoy their foreign holidays so much, they want to prolong the experience. This may mean either they seek to buy a villa in their special Shangri-La or they apply for a post abroad. Advice on living and working overseas demands a book to itself. In the meantime, back home with a bump, we look at that old bogy – **inflation**.

17

I have in- INFLATION *cluded a few*
snippets on **inflation** because more uninformed
opinions are given on this subject than on almost
any other.

WHAT IS INFLATION?

When many prices rise over a short period, people complain
about inflation. It is as vague as that.

WHAT CAUSES INFLATION?

Each economist and every politician conjures up their own
explanation for inflation like a rabbit from a top hat. Some
blame too much money, ready for the asking, with **credit
cards** and the like. If everyone wants and can afford a fixed
number of goodies, the price goes up. Everyone outbids everyone else, just as at an auction sale. The fancy name for this is
'demand-pull inflation'.

Others blame increases in the cost of raw materials which
manufacturers have to hand on to customers. Suppose all the
deposits of tin which are easy to mine have been used up.
Miners then tunnel deeper or further under the sea. So the
cost of producing tin will rise. Any goods with tin in them
(your fluoride toothpaste, for instance) will increase in price.
This is called 'cost-push inflation'.

Where the raw materials are imported from abroad and the foreign producers increase their price, people talk about 'imported inflation'.

These different forces can tug the price in various directions at the same time. Increased wages in Sri Lanka may yank up the cost of your morning cuppa. Improved packing machinery in Britain may reduce it – and so will the fact that more and more people prefer coffee.

HOW DO YOU MEASURE INFLATION?

Governments produce the retail price index, which is sometimes called the **cost of living index** or the consumer price index. How? They make detailed surveys every month of how much things cost. Governments have been collecting similar figures for years. Then they choose a 'base year', say 1970. All the prices in 1970 are taken as 100.

Suppose that sugar cost 50p a bag in 1970 and 55p a bag in 1971. This is an increase of $\frac{1}{10}$ or 10 per cent (55p the new price minus 50p the old price, all divided by 50p the old price: $5 \div 50 = \frac{1}{10}$). The 1971 index will then be 110 (the old 100 plus $\frac{1}{10}$ of 100, which is 10).

If sugar cost 59p in 1972, this is an increase of 18 per cent over the 1970 base price, so the 1972 index will be 118. And so on.

The figures are collected and processed by the government. The lower that inflation appears, the happier we voters will be. There are dozens of ways in which these accurate figures can still mislead. They don't reflect how *you* live or what *you* pay.

For a start, every price is an average over the year. Yet you know that the price demanded for, say, your Sunday roast beef varies from one shop to another, from town to town, from week to week. So does its quality, which is impossible to measure.

Which base year do you choose? Some calamity like an oil crisis or a war may have erupted in 1970, making it untypical.

Which items do you look at? A non-smoker does not give a hoot for any changes in the prices of cigarettes, cigarette lighters, pipe tobacco or cigars, let alone ashtrays, pipe-cleaners or cigarette paper.

No one bought a video in 1970; they did not exist then. So you cannot compare their prices. Many things that were popular are no longer so widely used – like manual calculators, paraffin heaters, hair-nets and carbon paper. Who cares what they cost now?

The government picks what it thinks the average household spends its money on. Then it decides how much of its **income** the family spends on each item. If most goes on food and only a pittance on entertainment, an increase in the price of potatoes will hit the family far harder than a rise in the cost of cinema tickets.

But the government can fix certain prices, like bread and milk. So it may include both as though they are overwhelmingly important. This way, it can keep the overall increase looking as low as possible.

I think I have said enough for you to take inflation figures with some suspicion. If British ones are suspect, even when accurately and honestly collected, foreign ones are far more so.

INFLATION FALLACIES

Here are two great fallacies about inflation:

1 It was caused by introducing decimal currency. Rubbish. There is nothing new about inflation. People complained about it in the 1500s when all the galleons sailed back to Spain laden with gold from the New World. The Spaniards spent so freely, they forced up prices all over Europe.

2 If the rate of inflation falls, so will prices. Rubbish. Inflation is a measurement just like that given by the speedometer in your car. If you are cruising at fifty miles an hour and you ease back to forty, you don't expect to drive backwards. You expect to go forwards more slowly. In the same way, if the rate of inflation falls, prices continue to increase, but more slowly.

When you drive backwards, when prices really fall, it is called **deflation**. This does happen. It happened in the 1930s when the prices of houses and the cost of living fell, and every civil servant was forced to accept less pay. Deflation is associated with depression, unemployment and poverty. So, if you like worrying, you can worry just as much over deflation as over inflation. Now you see why economics is called 'the dismal science'.

SHOULD I WORRY ABOUT INFLATION?

If inflation becomes hyperinflation, you should worry. That is when people carry a suitcase full of banknotes to the bakery for a loaf of bread. It has never happened in Britain.

CAN I PROTECT MYSELF AGAINST INFLATION?

You can protect yourself a little against inflation. Everything I have recommended in Chapter 8 to help you keep your money also helps you fight inflation at the same time. Then remember the hints in Chapter 9 on how not to squander it.

An inflation-linked pension helps. Some private pension schemes offer a form of inflation linking too. But it costs a lot more, and there is no guarantee it will be enough.

What you spend your money on and your choice of investments can help. Some **assets** increase in value as inflation increases – like houses, antiques, art. Guard against buying things that **depreciate** wildly – anything with a short life and no chance of reselling it; inflation makes them lose value even more quickly.

Remember, even inflation has advantages. During inflation is a good time to borrow. The £1,000 you borrow today will buy you a lot more than the £1,000 you repay in a year's time. So, in buying terms, you are not repaying as much. You are repaying even less if the inflation rate is higher than the interest rate you pay.

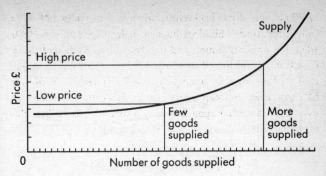

Figure 2 Supply

SUPPLY AND DEMAND

Finally, because I have referred to it several times, just a bit of **economics**. 'Economics is easy,' somebody once jibed. 'A parrot could learn it. Just keep mouthing "**supply and demand**".'

The basic ideas are quite simple.

When we talk about the 'supply' of a service, we mean the number of people willing to provide it at a given price. Clearly, the higher the price, the greater the supply there will be. If typists earned £100 an hour, we would all rush to join them. If they only scraped up 10p an hour, who would want to be a typist?

The same goes for the supply of goods. This is the amount of the goods that people would produce in factories or farms at a given price.

Economists draw a graph to show this. The supply line curves upwards left to right. It simply links up the dots which show the size of the supply at each price – see Figure 2.

As far as demand is concerned, when champagne costs £20 a bottle, most of us leave it on the supermarket shelves. If it fell to 50p a bottle, we would be queueing up outside the shop.

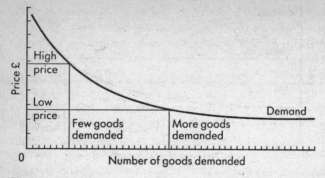

Figure 3 Demand

Demand – the number of us who want to and can afford to buy – increases as the price falls.

Economists show this on the same sort of graph. The demand line curves downwards from left to right. As the price rises, fewer and fewer of us want or can afford to buy – see Figure 3.

Where the supply line and the demand line meet is the price that buyer and seller agree on: the **market** price – see Figure 4.

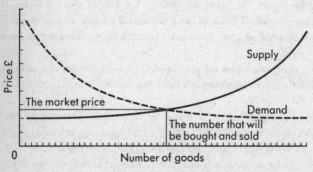

Figure 4 Market price: where supply meets demand

So far so good. Of course, the real world is far more complicated. You may prefer Spanish fizz at half the price of champagne – or cider, lemonade or even Perrier water. After a health scare, the government may ban its sale, or the French government its export. Then there are items, like cigarettes, where some people feel they must have them and would buy their thirty a day even if the price rocketed.

While you know broadly what price you would or would not pay, or what wage you would or would not accept, you don't sit down and draw a graph. Economic theory explains broadly how money makes the world go round, but for help with day-to-day living, forget it. Business people do.

It may console you to remember the old joke about economists. If every one in the world were laid end to end, they still would not reach a conclusion.

18

Con men, cheats, swindlers, rogues, rip-off merchants, fraudsters, all aim to get between you and your FRAUD *money. It draws them like doughnuts attract wasps.*

Wherever there is money, you find cheats. The fool and his/her money are soon parted, but some very clever people have been swindled out of their money too. There is a snowball effect; once a fraud develops beyond a certain size, people are more easy to deceive. This is why modern scandals – the BCCI crash, the Maxwell Group's disappearing millions – reach mammoth, worldwide proportions.

Fraud means telling lies, or abusing your position, to get your hands on other people's money – like the wicked uncle **trustee** who helps himself to his infant nephew's inheritance. Lies can be written down, perhaps in a **prospectus**. This is the glossy brochure which invites people to invest in a new **limited company**.

HOW TO PROTECT YOURSELF AGAINST FRAUD

First, you should know what return it is reasonable to expect on your money. This way, the promises of fraudsters stand out. Basically, fraudsters build up your greed and then play on it. Once you start seeing pound note signs, they have hooked you.

Beware of people who promise impossibly high returns, like investing in **gilts** for a return of 25 per cent **p.a.** No government (no safe government) pays 25 per cent **interest** to borrow money. Investments in **equities** should pay more than gilts, but you would be foolish to expect 25 per cent even from them.

What is unrealistic? This varies with the **base lending rate**. I suggest the following crude guidelines.

If the base lending rate stands at 7 per cent, you should be able to find interest of 7 per cent gross on a good, safe investment. If you are lucky, have a large sum to invest and are prepared to take a certain amount of **risk**, 10 per cent is possible. Fifteen per cent or above is wildly unlikely.

Similarly, if base lending rate is 13 per cent, hope for 13 per cent on a safe investment, 15 per cent on a risky one. Twenty per cent or above is very suspicious.

Beware of 'double-your-money' schemes. How long do they promise before it doubles? Over seven years, money doubles at 10 per cent interest. So anyone who promises to double your money over seven years is only promising 10 per cent but tying up your money for seven years.

Beware of investments with a charitable link-up. Sometimes fraudsters 'borrow' the name of a popular charity to attract potential investors, and the charity will see very little of the profits.

'My client contributed £15,000 to the Spastics Society,' declared the solicitor proudly in court.

'Wow, that's a fortune,' whispered my student next to me. 'Why ever was he arrested?'

'Hush.'

'What proportion of the bingo money was handed to the society?' asked the magistrate.

'One per cent.'

My student whipped out his calculator. He turned it to me to show that the rogue held on to £1,485,000 from people who thought they were helping spastics! The magistrate could do his sums too. He sent the bingo organizer to prison.

The next way to protect yourself is to deal only with large, well-known organizations. Stick to qualified lawyers and independent brokers who are members of **FIMBRA**. Their professional organizations insist that they carry heavy **professional indemnity insurance**. If a partner or an employee makes a mistake or is dishonest as a result of which the client loses money, the insurance company reimburses the client. Most professions, like chartered accountants, insist all members carry such insurance. The sum covered may run into millions.

When investing, write your cheque directly to the organization with which you are investing – never to the man who collects it, or your money may travel no further than his bank account.

Never do business with unqualified relations, or with people you only meet in pubs, at a party or over the garden fence. Insist that all agreements are drawn up by a lawyer, not just made by word of mouth. Men are much more gullible than women, because they always expect to make money, whereas women are afraid of losing it.

HOW CAN YOU TELL IF YOU ARE BEING CHEATED?

Some crooks carry on cheating the same victims year after year until they have extracted every last penny. They just produce a new 'It can't fail, forget about the last one' scheme. Some of their most profitable ploys are the oldest – like pyramid selling, chain letters and bills for goods you never ordered.

Warning signs can be:

- no documentation;
- they insist on cash, not cheques;
- repeated delays in supplying whatever goods/documents they promised;
- constant fobbing off;

- the person is never available to see you (contrast the time they allot you now compared to when they were persuading you to invest);
- their phone number becomes unobtainable (cut off?).

The signs may still appear too late to save your money.

Bill was just one of many who discover that people who mess you about can cause you just as much harm as out-and-out cheats. This is how Bill blew £150,000, his retirement lump sum, in a single year.

He met a man in a pub. They agreed to go into **partnership**. There was nothing in writing. Bill did not consult any professionals at all. He signed a lease for prestige offices in the middle of town for the new business. The lease was for several years in Bill's personal name.

Bill himself bought the headed paper, took on a secretary, even bought a **limited company**. He wasted time as well as cash on the new venture. The friend never appeared. Bill was saddled with rent and the other outgoings for a venture that never even started.

Where was the fraud? This is the infuriating thing, there was none. His pub 'friend' never took a penny. Bill lost much of his lump sum, but there was no one he could sue, no one to blame but himself.

Bill shrugged his shoulders; he still had plenty left. Not deterred, he discovered another road to riches. He bought a container lorry that he planned to drive himself.

Just then the newspapers trumpeted the complaints of out-of-work lorry drivers and haulage firms going broke because the market had shrunk. Bill soon discovered this for himself. No one wanted his services, and the smart new lorry sat outside his house – a white elephant. No one would even buy it from him.

Of course Bill threw all the blame on the man in the pub and the lorry salesman – never on his own lack of care or foresight. If he had pinned down the friend at the outset by dragging him off to a solicitor to draw up a formal agreement, his friend would probably have cried off at that stage.

Bill should never have swallowed the claims of the slick lorry salesman without a little research of his own. It only needed a phone call or two to hauliers to find out if they would be interested in hiring his lorry. Their sharp reaction down the line would have convinced him to think again.

Suffering from stupidity or blatant fraud is one side of the coin. People can also often find themselves *committing* fraud without any dishonest intention, and laying themselves open to the consequences if they are found out. How honest women can find themselves in this pickle we look at in the next chapter.

19

THE OTHER SIDE OF FRAUD

The more women work and the more senior the positions they achieve, the more they discover the extent to which downright lies, sharp practice, covering up what really happened and non-payment of debts are considered quite normal in business. The most honest and pleasant-seeming men accept all these goings-on. Many even trot out the fact that they have a wife and children to provide for to justify them cheating the other man before he cheats them.

This attitude sets up another hidden barrier to women's advancement. We are generally unused to and shocked by dishonesty. It hits us unawares. Our reaction reminds our male colleagues how they probably felt when they first encountered the same thing – before they smothered their scruples in the interests of their career and 'being a real man'. They don't like to be reminded that they have changed.

Women in senior positions offer a threat to any organization's existing practices. This provides another reason to exclude them.

Unfair to men? Too black and white? What is your reaction to the following, for instance?

Client Fred is just leaving. His hand grips the door handle. He says to his accountant over his shoulder, 'I'm off to my broker Joe now. I've decided to invest £100,000 in XYZ Trusts.'

The accountant watches the door shut, grabs his phone and calls Joe.

'I'm sending Fred to see you,' he smirks. 'I've recommended him to buy XYZ Trusts and I expect my **commission**.'

'Sure,' replies the broker, and the accountant has just earned himself £1,000.

Quick thinking? Smart opportunism? A downright lie? When the boss boasts of it to you (forgetting in his pride that you are a woman) how do you respond? Would you have thought to try it yourself? Will you risk it next time?

Or how about this:

'Add £1,000 on the **invoice** and hand it to the client when he calls in,' orders the boss. 'If he pays up, fine. If he quibbles, refer him to me. I'll say you made a mistake, call you into my office and give you a bloody good telling-off in front of him. OK? Then we'll change the invoice back.'

A man can tell another man about his 'fiddle' with a laugh over a pint. He gets embarrassed when he tells a woman. You can bet that if an organization is up to anything really shady, senior women (if there are any) or even bright juniors are kept well away from it. The time-honoured excuse is, 'Women cannot keep a secret.' The truth is that men fear women's disapproval. These are basically decent, respectable men, remember, not mafiosi.

As women advance up the career ladder, this exclusion becomes more difficult. Besides, a court might let off a secretary on the grounds that she did not know what she was a party to. It would not excuse a company director or trained accountant just because she happened to be female. So senior women are vulnerable.

'I'd never work for anyone dishonest, or take them as a client,' Patrick preached at me after I had told him a tale or two. Patrick was an accountant and nobody's fool, but he had never worked outside the **Civil Service**.

'You don't understand,' I explained. 'They don't creep into your office with a stocking over their heads, a jemmy sticking out of one pocket and a bag marked "swag" over one shoulder. They are charming and persuasive, apparently very affluent and on the point of hitting the big time. It is not until the second or third meeting that you discover they have just come out of prison. By then you have spent hours working on their next project. So they owe you money. How will you ever get paid if you throw them out then and there? And what if they are really trying to go straight?'

Any practising solicitor or accountant has to deal with, try to help and justify the activities of people he or she does not like, trust or approve of. (I have even known accountants too physically afraid of their clients to ask for their money.) If he or she did not, justice could never be done and complicated frauds could never be unravelled.

Some fraudsters combine the air of authority of a judge with the glib tongue of a disc jockey. They can make it seem an exhilarating challenge to circumvent the rules. I had one client like this who was so dynamic that in an hour's meeting he would never actually sit down. He parried awkward questions by insisting on making an urgent transatlantic phone call that minute.

Remember, it is not only you and the punters whom these con men are deceiving. I once read through a client's bank statements for the past ten years. On day one, he persuaded the bank to lend him £10,000. Then another £20,000. Then another £50,000. And so on, until the debt totalled £1 million without him having paid back a penny! Yet the manager was no dumbo either.

With professional con men, even when you know the awful things they have done, even when it is your life savings they have stolen, you still like them!

A colleague who handled only bankrupt companies told me

how he watched one fraudster in action. This smoothie held at bay a hall full of 200 angry **creditors**, every one of whom he had cheated. By the end of his 'explanation' some were brushing tears of sympathy from their cheeks. Yet they knew he had scuttled off to the Caribbean when things grew too hot and had been forcibly returned. My colleague admitted that he felt nothing but admiration. If the same man had held up those creditors at knifepoint on a street corner, they would have been screaming to bring back flogging.

Your only hope is to have nothing to do with known fraudsters at all – ever – or only as little as your job allows. Never part with a penny. As the saying goes: *if you lie down with the dog, you get up with fleas.*

'I had a stranger come in and demand help in laundering,' I told Patrick, who was still unconvinced.* 'He had salted away several hundred thousand pounds of bribes in a Swiss account. How could I show him the door when he claimed to be a close relative of my boss?'

There are ways of coping with this. You can point out to the client the powers of the **Inland Revenue**. Show them that the successful fiddle on which they pride themselves is commonplace, easily detected and certain to be unearthed in the fullness of time. Indeed, the longer it goes on, the more it will cost them to straighten out.

It is possible to frighten someone into being honest, or even coming clean. It is a lovely sight to watch a bully of 6 feet 6 inches and a known record of violence reduced to a quivering jelly by an innocent letter from the Revenue computer.

On the other hand, it is possible to be led on and on, sinking in deeper and deeper until the courts would consider you as guilty as your client.

---

*'Laundering' means hiding money that the owner would rather not explain inside a genuine business, so that they can pretend they earned it in the business.

How many husbands come home worried, snap at their wives and drink too much because of what they have been forced into at work? Now they are afraid of exposure. They are too ashamed to share their worries with a wife who thinks being honest the simple matter of not touching a penny from someone else's purse.

Having dishonest clients is one thing; having a dishonest boss or partner is another. Again, you may work together for years before you realize what is going on, especially as women are kept clear of anything dubious. You can gauge a lot about your boss by the way he reacts to what you think dishonest, just as he can tell a lot about you and what you will tolerate for the future.

If nothing else, you must protect yourself. Keep written records of everything to show that what you did was either legitimate or at least under orders. You don't want to be the fall guy, the scapegoat, when all is revealed. If this happens too often, leave.

Remember, it is possible to jump from the frying pan into the fire. Your new employer may be worse. The best you have to go on is the reputation of the firm locally and what professional associations the owners may belong to. All such associations produce a code of ethics which should govern the behaviour of members.

People often muddle tax *avoidance* and tax *evasion*. (We touched on this in Chapter 6.) Both aim to reduce the tax a person may pay. Avoidance is legal; an expert uses a detailed knowledge of the law to find the loopholes and to arrange a client's affairs to take advantage of them. It may be as simple as telling a client not to sell something, or not to come back into the country until after 5 April.

Evasion is illegal and can send you to prison. It involves either hiding **income** or falsifying expenses to claim – as with the beautifully typed invoice I saw for work done by a **limited company** that no longer existed. That invoice charged £80,000. There was a whole sheaf of them.

My client had bought the blank headed invoices from a friend on a building site and had any figures he fancied typed in. He then produced the invoices as evidence of expenditure by his business. Would the typist who typed the invoices be prosecuted? Probably not, unless she was the wife of the owner of the company and a company **director** in her own right.

A CAUTIONARY TALE . . .

Finally, as promised back in Chapter 7, here is the tale of the one female fraudster I have come across.

Stella was pretty and beautifully turned out. She had an adoring husband and a couple of healthy children. She was also greedy. She ran her own boutique but also sold nearly new furs on commission. The owner took two-thirds of the sale price and she kept one-third.

When Stella died, her solicitor visited the shop to list all the stock. He counted everything and returned all the unsold furs to their owners. An entire rack remained unaccounted for. The furs must have belonged to Stella, but she had never mentioned them in her **accounts**. Realizing that she had been on the fiddle in a big way, the solicitor consulted her accountant (my firm), gathered his evidence and headed for the Inland Revenue.

Slowly, painstakingly, we worked together to reconstruct what had happened. Stella had run her boutique for fourteen years. The solicitor discovered traces of so many bank and building society accounts that he wrote to every branch of every organization in the West of England. Even more accounts came to light, some in her married name, others in her maiden name. Yet others, discovered by pure fluke, appeared in completely different names. No doubt there are more accounts that we never discovered beyond the thirty-odd that emerged.

Stella had not just amassed money, she had spent it. She had bought houses, sometimes several in the same street, and shops.

She had collected the rents, lived in the properties or sold them again as the fancy took her.

Her husband could shed some light on this. He recalled one holiday in Switzerland. After an extravagant meal, Stella had called the owner of the hotel to her table. She had asked him flat how much he wanted for his hotel. The owner had sat down beside Stella, and her husband had listened, mouth open, as the two of them discussed details of sale.

But as time went on, her husband knew less and less of what Stella did. She had built him a fabulous house overlooking a lake, but kept her affairs from him. The husband, weak and in poor health, had never suspected anything was amiss and never set foot in the shop anyway.

So what happened to Stella? Her affairs grew to an almighty tangle, some legal, some not. Her illegal gains prevented Stella from sorting anything out, or even discussing them. Her husband now says he noticed signs of mental instability, whatever that means.

Anyway, the fact remains that with a thriving legal business, never mind all the rest, a family and a not-unhappy marriage, with money coming out of her ears, still young and attractive, Stella committed suicide. Which is how the whole thing came to light.

Moral? Women make bad crooks? Money isn't everything? Oh what tangled webs we weave ...? Draw your own conclusions.

Anyway, by selling off everything in Stella's name (her husband kept what he had) the solicitor raised £90,000. This would probably have bought three semi-detached houses at the time. Every last penny went to the Inland Revenue.

20 WHAT YOU LEARNED AT SCHOOL: SOME BASIC ARITHMETIC REVISION

How do you choose an accountant? runs the old joke. *Ask each one what two times two makes. Then give the job to the one who answers, 'What number did you have in mind?'*

They all know two times two makes four, but you want one who will rearrange the figures to suit you.

I am going right back to the beginning too. Why? To make this book useful to as wide a number of women as possible. Of course, we use calculators. But the batteries run down; machines go on the blink; our fingers slip, and we key in an extra figure. Unless you know the basics, you will not be able to check the answers your calculator offers.

If you are quite happy with arithmetic, you will be encouraged to see that this chapter contains all the maths a chartered accountant needs. So you are cleverer than you thought!

If you have never used a calculator, there is nothing to be afraid of. It is easier than setting a microwave oven or the timer on your cooker. Switch on. Press 2. Press ×. Press 2. Press = . The answer comes up on the screen. It is that simple.

ADDITION

Add 123 and 4,564.

Put the figures in columns, one exactly below the other. When you were tiny, you used squared paper to help you, remember? (In France, even adults still do.) Start from the right-hand side. Draw a line beneath the second figure. Then, always starting from the right, add down each column, using your fingers if necessary. Put the answer below:

```
  123
4,564
4,687
```

Easy. The art is to be neat and orderly, and luckily women excel at this.

Now add 123, 4,564 and 89. Arrange your numbers as before:

```
  123
4,564
   89
```

As soon as you add together the first right-hand column, you see that the total is over 10 (in fact, 16). You put the 6 in the answers line (below the line you have drawn) and a little 1 (to represent the remaining 10) in the next answers position, like so:

$$
\begin{array}{r}
123 \\
4,564 \\
\underline{89} \\
{}^{1}6
\end{array}
$$

Add up the next column, then add on the 1, to give 17. Again, put the 7 in the answers line, covering the 1, and put another tiny 1 in the next position:

$$
\begin{array}{r}
123 \\
4,564 \\
\underline{89} \\
{}^{1}76
\end{array}
$$

Add up the next column, add on the 1 and put the answer 7 in the answers line. Finally, add up the last column:

$$
\begin{array}{r}
123 \\
4,564 \\
\underline{89} \\
4,776
\end{array}
$$

Again, easy. If the total of a column had exceeded 20, you would have put a little 2 where you put the 1; or a little 3 if it exceeded 30; and so on.

SUBTRACTION

Is it all coming back now? Let's try subtraction.

Subtract 23 from 645. Again, put the two figures in columns, starting from the right-hand side, with a minus sign to show what you are doing:

```
  645
-  23
```

Starting in the right-hand column, take 3 from 5 and put the answer in the answers line. Then deal with the next column, then the next:

```
  645
-  23
  622
```

Easy. Now prove you are correct. Add the answer, 622, to the number you took away, 23. You should get the number you started with. If not, something is amiss.

Now take 187 from 724. Line up the figures as usual:

```
  724
- 187
```

You cannot take 7 from 4, so you 'borrow' 10 from the next column. Put a little 1 by the 4 to mark the borrowing and a little 1 by the 8 to remind you to pay it back, like so:

```
  72¹4
- 18¹7
```

The little 1 turns the 4 into 14, and 14 minus 7 is 7, so you put that in the answers line. To pay back the 10 you borrowed, add the little 1 to the 8 to make 9. Now you will try to take 9 away from 2. Of course, this is impossible, so you borrow 10 again from the next column, marking the borrowing and repayment in the same way:

```
  7¹2¹4
- 1¹8¹7
       7
```

Now, 12 (the original 2 plus the 10 you borrowed) minus 9 (the original 8 plus the 1 you repaid) equals 3, so put this in the answers line. Then to repay the next borrowing, add the 1 to the 1: 7 minus 2 is 5, so put that in the next answers position:

$$
\begin{array}{r}
7^12^14 \\
- 1^18^17 \\
\hline
5\ 3\ 7
\end{array}
$$

Just to prove you are correct, add the answer to the amount you took away, and you should get back to 724.

Not difficult, so long as you remember to pay back your borrowings and keep your little 1's (it will always be a 1 you borrow) tiny.

MULTIPLICATION

Ready to try multiplication?

For multiplication and division you need to know your tables. There is no substitute for saying them over and over until they come pat. Einstein said learning his tables was the only difficult part of maths. After that it was all downhill.

To save writing out

$1 \times 2 = 2$
$2 \times 2 = 4$, etc.

I have put them into a table. You can read them off by going down each column or by going across if you prefer:

	1	2	3	4	5	6	7	8	9	10	11	12
1 ×	1	2	3	4	5	6	7	8	9	10	11	12
2 ×	2	4	6	8	10	12	14	16	18	20	22	24
3 ×	3	6	9	12	15	18	21	24	27	30	33	36
4 ×	4	8	12	16	20	24	28	32	36	40	44	48
5 ×	5	10	15	20	25	30	35	40	45	50	55	60
6 ×	6	12	18	24	30	36	42	48	54	60	66	72
7 ×	7	14	21	28	35	42	49	56	63	70	77	84
8 ×	8	16	24	32	40	48	56	64	72	80	88	96
9 ×	9	18	27	36	45	54	63	72	81	90	99	108
10 ×	10	20	30	40	50	60	70	80	90	100	110	120
11 ×	11	22	33	44	55	66	77	88	99	110	121	132
12 ×	12	24	36	48	60	72	84	96	108	120	132	144

Don't panic. Take a deep breath. Just sit back and look at the figures and you can trace lots of patterns. For a start, 1 × any number is the number itself. So the 1 times table is obvious.

I have not bothered to put it in, but 0 × anything is automatically 0. Why? Well, twice as much nothing is still nothing, isn't it?

When two even numbers (2, 4, 6, 8, etc.) multiply, the answer is always even. So if you think 8 × 8 = 63, you must be wrong. It is 64.

When two odd numbers (1, 3, 5, 7, etc.) multiply, the answer is always odd. So if you think 9 × 7 = 64, you must be wrong. It is 63.

When an odd and an even number multiply, the answer is always even. Like 4 × 3 = 12.

Some tables are very easy. To multiply by 10, just put a 0 on the end. So 6 × 10 = 60.

Five times anything produces a figure which must end in either 0 or 5. So if you think 5 × 7 = 36, you must be wrong. It is 35.

Eleven times anything falls into a regular pattern until 100 is reached.

Once you are refreshed on your tables, and can repeat them fast without stopping to think, multiply 136 by 9.

Line up your figures, starting on the right-hand side, with an × to show you are multiplying;

```
    136
×     9
```

Start multiplying on the right-hand side: $9 \times 6 = 54$. Put the 4 in the answers line and a little 5 in the next answers position:

```
    136
×     9
    ⁵4
```

Now multiply 9 by 3, to get 27. Add on the little 5 you set aside, which gives you 32. Put the 2 in the answers line over the 5 and a little 3 next to it to use later, like so:

```
    136
×     9
   ³24
```

Now, $1 \times 9 = 9$. Add on your 3 to get 12. Put the 2 in the answers space over the little 3 and, because you have reached the end, the 1 in the column next to it:

```
    136
×     9
  1,224
```

Not bad, so long as you are strict about your columns. If you find you get muddled, draw vertical lines or use squared paper.

In fact, there is an easier way to do this calculation. Nine is nearly 10, so multiply your number by 10. That is, put 0 on the end to make 1,360. Then take away the original number of 136: $1,360 - 136 = 1,224$. If you get the choice, adding or subtracting is always easier than multiplying or dividing.

Now let's multiply 248 by 39. Remember to lay out your numbers in columns, starting from the right:

$$
\begin{array}{r}
248 \\
\times\ \underline{39} \\
\end{array}
$$

Start on the right-hand side and multiply by 9. $9 \times 8 = 72$, so put the 2 in the answers line and a little 7 next to it. $9 \times 4 = 36$. Add on your 7 to get 43. Put the 3 over the 7 and a little 4 next to it. At this stage, your answer should look like this:

$$
\begin{array}{r}
248 \\
\times\ \underline{39} \\
^432 \\
\end{array}
$$

Keep going by multiplying $9 \times 2 = 18$. Add 4 to get 22. Put 2 in the answers column over the little 4 and, because you have finished this part, the other 2 to the left of it. The line should read 2,232.

So far you have multiplied by 9. Now you must multiply by 30. Of course, you don't know your 30 times table. But 30 is only 3×10, and you know that to multiply by 10 you add 0. So, first of all, put 0 in the right-hand column of the next line. Then multiply by 3: $3 \times 8 = 24$, so put 4 next to the 0 and a little 2 next to the 4, like so:

$$
\begin{array}{r}
248 \\
\times\ \underline{39} \\
2,232 \\
^240 \\
\end{array}
$$

Carry on multiplying by 3. $3 \times 4 = 12$. Add on the little 2 to get 14. Put 4 in the answers space to cover the little 2 and a little 1 next to it. $3 \times 2 = 6$; add the spare 1 to get 7 and put this in the next space, like so:

$$
\begin{array}{r}
248 \\
\times \quad 39 \\
\hline
2,232 \\
7,440 \\
\end{array}
$$

I have put a line under the last row because the final stage is to add the two figures: 2,232 is 248×9; 7,440 is 248×30. To get 248×39, you add them both together. The answer then is 9,672:

$$
\begin{array}{r}
248 \\
\times \quad 39 \\
\hline
2,232 \\
7,440 \\
\hline
9,672 \\
\end{array}
$$

This is not really difficult, just very long-winded. No one will bother to work through the arithmetic when they have a calculator. What they should do is look roughly at the figures, say to themselves 248 is nearly 250 and 39 is nearly 40. What is 250×40? That is easy. Add 0 to the 250 to multiply by 10 and then multiply by 4. $2,500 \times 4 = 10,000$. So the answer will be roughly 10,000. As we worked out, it is really 9,672. If your calculator produces 967 or 96,720 or even 967,200, you will know you have made a mistake.

DIVISION

Finally, division: let's divide 8 into 376. Write it down as follows. Leave yourself plenty of space underneath. You will have realized by now that when you know the proper layout you have won half the battle:

$$8\overline{)376}$$

Now, for the first time, you start from the left. Look at the 3 and ask yourself, does 8 go into 3? Of course not. So look at the first two numbers together. Does 8 go into 37? Yes, $8 \times 4 = 32$. So, put 4 above the 7 and write 32 under the 37, like so:

$$\begin{array}{r} 4 \\ 8\overline{)376} \\ \underline{32} \end{array}$$

I have put a line under 32 because you are going to subtract it from 37. The answer is 5, and you write this under the 2. If the answer is 8 or more, you have made a mistake:

$$\begin{array}{r} 4 \\ 8\overline{)376} \\ \underline{32} \\ 5 \end{array}$$

So you are left with 5. Take the 6 from above and rewrite it next to the 5 to give you 56. Does 8 go into 56? Yes, $8 \times 7 = 56$. So write 7 next to the 4 in the answers space. Write 56 under the 56 just to finish the thing off and underline it. You take 56 from 56 and end up with 0, which shows that you have your complete answer, 47:

$$\begin{array}{r} 47 \\ 8\overline{)376} \\ \underline{32} \\ 56 \\ \underline{56} \\ 0 \end{array}$$

Again, in practice, you would say to yourself, 8 is nearly 10. If I divide 376 by 10, what do I get? It is easy to divide anything roughly by 10, you just ignore the last number. This gives you 37. So, when you are working out the real answer with your calculator, you know that if the answer comes up 479 or 4, you have made a mistake.

One last exercise: suppose you have to divide 3,956 by 43. Nobody knows their 43 times table, so you just have to keep guessing:

$$43\overline{)3,956}$$

Because 43 will not go into 3, you look at the first two numbers; 43 will not go into 39 either, so you look at the first three numbers. It must go into 395, but how many times? You scribble on another piece of paper, $43 \times 10 = 430$. Too big. You work out $43 \times 8 = 344$. Is that big enough? Add another 43 to 344, and the answer is 387. So $43 \times 9 = 387$. Great. Write 9 over the 5, and write 387 under the 395 and take one from the other:

$$
\begin{array}{r}
9 \\
43\overline{)3,956} \\
387 \\
\hline
8
\end{array}
$$

Take the remaining 6 and put it next to the 8 to make 86. Does 43 go into 86? Yes. $43 \times 2 = 86$. Write 2 next to the 9 to give you your answer of 92. Write 86 under the 86 and take one from the other. This leaves 0, which shows nothing is left and the answer is complete:

$$
\begin{array}{r}
92 \\
43\overline{)3{,}956} \\
\underline{387} \\
86 \\
\underline{86} \\
0
\end{array}
$$

By now you are probably thanking heaven for your calculator. Don't worry; this is the most complicated sum we shall do. In practice, you would say to yourself, 3,956 is nearly 4,000, and 43 is close to 40. How many times would 40 go into 4,000? Easy, about 100. So the answer will be around 100. In fact, it was 92. If your machine produces 922 or 9 or 9,222, you will know you have slipped up.

If you have kept pace with me so far, I suggest you take a break before we tackle fractions and decimals – not because they are difficult, but to approach them feeling fresh . . .

Ready for the next stage? So far we have looked at complete numbers. Fractions and decimals are bits of numbers.

FRACTIONS AND DECIMALS

A fraction of something is a part of it. Suppose your house has three floors and you occupy two of them, or two floors *out of* three. You occupy two-thirds of the house. That is written $\frac{2}{3}$ or even 2/3.

The bottom number shows how many parts (or floors) there are altogether. There are three. The top number shows how many you occupy; that is, two.

If you live in a block of flats with a flat on each floor, and there are twelve floors, you occupy 1/12 or one-twelfth of the building.

We use fractions in our everyday speech. We all know that one-half means $\frac{1}{2}$, one-third means $\frac{1}{3}$, one-quarter means $\frac{1}{4}$, and so on.

Any number put over 1, say $\frac{6}{1}$, is simply an ordinary complete number; it is just another way of writing 6. $6\frac{2}{5}$ is 6 complete numbers plus 2 fifths of another. You could also write it 32/5. Each whole number has 5 fifths; $5 \times 6 = 30/5$. Then there are the 2 left over, so 32 fifths in all.

Virtually nobody in business ever needs those sums you practised at school with lowest common denominators and highest common factors. So I will not bother you with them here. If we want to add, subtract, multiply or divide bits, or complete numbers with bits in like $7\frac{3}{4}$, we change the fractions into decimals. Then we add, subtract, etc., their decimal equivalents. This is far easier and it suits our calculators better. If we really need the answer to be in fractions, we just change the decimal answer back to a fraction at the end. How?

To convert a fraction to a decimal, simply divide the bottom number into the top. Of course, it will not go straight away (otherwise it would not be a fraction).

Suppose you want to convert a half, that is $\frac{1}{2}$, into a decimal. Remember your division?

$$2\overline{)1}$$

Two into one will not go, so you put a 0 in the answer space, followed by a decimal point (a dot). Put another decimal point underneath it, behind the 1. These decimal points show that you have reached the end of the complete numbers and that what comes after is bits. Any number followed by .0 is simply the same complete number; 1.0 is just another way of writing 1. So put 0 after the 1.

Now look at the two numbers 1 and 0 together as though the decimal point had disappeared and they read 10; 2 into 10 goes 5, so write 5 in the answer space. Your answer becomes 0.5:

$$\begin{array}{r} 0.5 \\ 2\overline{)1.0} \end{array}$$

Decimal bits are measured in tenths. (The Latin word for ten was *decem*.)* You should not be surprised that a half turns out to be five-tenths. What is new is to see it written 0.5.

If there are two numbers after the decimal point, they are hundredths. You meet this every day. £3.25 is 3 complete pounds and 25 pence. There are 100 pence in a pound, so 25 pence represents 25 hundredths of a pound.

If you want to add or subtract numbers with decimals in them it is easy. You follow the same rules as for complete numbers. So 5.5 plus 7.1 is calculated as follows:

$$\begin{array}{r} 5.5 \\ \underline{7.1} \\ 12.6 \end{array}$$

Parts of numbers can borrow and repay just like complete numbers. So 8.3 − 6.8 is worked out as below:

$$\begin{array}{r} 8.^{.1}3 \\ -\ 6^1.\ 8 \\ \hline 1\ .\ 5 \end{array}$$

First, 3 borrowed 10 from 6, so that 13 minus 8 gave 5. Then it repaid, so that 8 minus 7 (6 + 1) gave 1.

When you come to multiplication, be careful. Whenever you multiply complete numbers, the answer is always much bigger than the numbers you multiply. When you multiply by a bit (a fraction or decimal), the answer is always smaller! Why?

*There used to be only ten months in the year, so the last one was called *Decem*ber.

There are 7 days in a week, right? So 5 weeks covers 35 days. Agreed? Put another way, $7 \times 5 = 35$.

In half a week there are only $3\frac{1}{2}$ days. Half is 5/10 in fractions or 0.5 in decimals. Put another way, $7 \times 0.5 = 3.5$.

Written out in full, the sum is:

$$
\begin{array}{r}
7.0 \\
\times \underline{0.5} \\
3.5 \text{ days}
\end{array}
$$

When you multiply by a decimal, you put the first number of your answer to the *right-hand side* of the decimal point, to show it is a decimal you are dealing with.

If the decimal you are multiplying by is even smaller (say, 0.05, which is 5 hundredths, instead of 0.5, which is 5 tenths), you put the first number *two* places to the right-hand side, not one. Five-hundredths is the same thing as one-twentieth. One-twentieth of a week is far smaller than one-half:

$$
\begin{array}{r}
7.0 \\
\times \underline{0.05} \\
0.35 \text{ days, or roughly an afternoon}
\end{array}
$$

If you want to convert a decimal back to a fraction, it is easy. The first figure is tenths, so 0.6 is 6/10. The first two figures are hundredths, so 0.54 becomes 54/100. The first three are thousandths, and so on.

There is no need to know more about decimals than this. Use arithmetic basically to check your calculator. If you have to multiply 245.789 by 97.753, just ignore the decimals. Say to yourself, 245 is nearly 250, and 97 is nearly 100. What is 250×100? Easy; it is 25,000. This is roughly what you expect the answer to be.

PERCENTAGES

Percentages are really easy. *Per cent* means 'out of a hundred'. So 1 per cent (often written 1%) means one out of a hundred, the same as 1/100 or 0.01 or one-hundredth.

So if you want to write 65 per cent as a fraction, simply put 100 under it: 65/100.

If you want to write it in decimals, it is 0.65.

Suppose your employers have agreed to consider a crèche. They tell you that 75 per cent of your colleagues have one pre-school child, and they wonder how many children to cater for. You know that 3,600 women work in your factory. Multiply 3,600 by 75 per cent. You could do it by 3,600 × 0.75, but most calculators have a % (percentage) button that you can press instead. Either way, the answer will be 2,700 children, and your employers may think again!

Perhaps you are considering borrowing £375 at 8 per cent interest APR and want to know how much extra the interest will cost you a year. Multiply 375 by 8 per cent; or, if you don't use the % button, multiply 375 by 0.08. Either way, the answer is £30.

Maybe you are worried after learning that 100 planes were hijacked last year. Perhaps you even talk of cancelling your holiday. Then you discover that there were 15 million flights last year worldwide. So what percentage were hijacked? 100 divided by 15,000,000 gives you 0.0000066 per cent. This percentage is so tiny that you should be reassured. If the newspaper had quoted it this way in the first place, you would never have panicked.

Perhaps a friend offers to lend you £1,000 provided you pay them back £1,100 in three months' time. You think £100 interest sounds very reasonable. What is it as a percentage?

100/1,000 = 1/10 or 10 per cent, which seems fair. Then you remember that you are to repay after three months, or one-quarter of a year; 10 per cent × 4 = 40 per cent annual interest (in fact, a bit more even than that) – far too high to accept.

AVERAGES

Averages are easy to calculate too. Jane tells you she went off with her caravan for the weekend three times last year. Mary tells you she went four times. You went four times, and three other friends tell you they went twice, not at all and five times. You want to know what the average is for all of you. Add together the number of times:

$$3 + 4 + 4 + 2 + 0 + 5 = 18$$

Now divide by the number of people: $18 \div 6 = 3$, so the answer is three times. Now you know the average and also that you are above average.

Unfortunately, averages don't necessarily mean very much. You would have got the same result if two of you had gone nine times and the rest not at all, or if one of you had gone all eighteen times and the rest of you never. So take all those averages bandied about with a pinch of salt. They sell newspapers, delight television producers and worry people.

There you are. That is all the maths you need to be an accountant or to handle your own money matters. Not too terrible, was it?

21 GLOSSARY

As promised, words printed in the text in **bold** type are explained below. A few new words are included, because you will meet them widely. They are straightforward and will enrich your vocabulary even more.

accommodation address – you may be tempted to invest in an organization because of its up-market London address. Any firm based there must be sound, you might think. In fact, whole streets in London operate as accommodation addresses. Each building acts as a post-box for dozens of different organizations, sending on their mail. The actual firm will be based somewhere much less impressive or reputable, so they hide the fact by using an accommodation address. They may have other things to hide as well.

account card – many shops offer one. You use it to buy goods from any branch of the shop. Nowhere else accepts it. Usually you can spend up to a set limit and then repay by instalments which include high **interest**. The shop benefits from giving you this loan because you keep spending with them. On the other hand, your choice is limited to that shop's goods. People who snapped up account cards from every shop in the high street when they first appeared soon found themselves deeply in debt.

accounts – a page or two of figures drawn up by an accountant from your business records, to show you what **profit** your business has made. There will be a profit and loss account (sometimes called an **income** statement) and often a balance sheet.

alimony – regular payments that a court may order one spouse to make to the other to maintain her (very occasionally him) after a divorce. If the husband does not pay, the wife has to return to the court and ask for help in getting the money. If she wants or needs more, she has to go back to court and prove hardship.

amortization – the same as **depreciation**.

annual percentage rate – see **interest rate**.

annuity – a fixed sum you receive every year as long as you live. Perhaps someone arranged to pay you an annuity in their will, or you can buy one for yourself with a lump sum. You get a **quotation** from an insurance **broker**. The quotation varies from day to day.

appreciation – **assets** appreciate when they become worth more. Every time a Van Gogh painting sells for millions, every other Van Gogh painting appreciates in value. Assets appreciate either as they become scarcer or because more people want them. A vintage Bentley, something that once belonged to Queen Victoria or Elvis Presley, a rare book: all are worth more than they have ever been before, even when new.

APR – stands for annual percentage rate. See **interest rate**.

arrangement fee – a charge made by some organizations to arrange a loan or to change it. In theory, the fee covers their costs of paperwork, etc. In practice, it is often a way to squeeze a little more money out of you.

assets – if a woman has pretty hair or shapely legs, one would say those were her assets. In the same way, anything you possess is an asset if it will earn you income – either directly, like cash earning **interest** in the bank; or indirectly, like the table you use to display the antiques you sell in the market on Saturdays. Even more indirectly, assets include the gold necklace you bought because you could always sell it one day if you really needed to. Like the word **capital**, 'assets' cover all sorts of things. Most are tangible (you can touch them), like a car. Others do not look as though they could be worth much – for instance, a **share** certificate, which is just a piece of paper; a few doodles which represent a brilliant new design; or a few squiggles that supply the magic formula for a cream that will give every woman perfect skin. Some assets are intangible, like the fact that you can prove people owe you money for work you have done, or if you have someone's written promise to help you with money if need arises. The opposite of an asset is a **liability**.

audit – auditing is a part of accounting. Auditors visit clients' businesses and check over their records to ensure they are correct and complete. The checking is called an audit. It may take days or weeks.

balance – the amount you have in an account at the moment. If there is money in your account, you are 'in the black'. The bank will say you have a 'credit balance' because you are one of their **creditors**; they owe you money. If you are overdrawn or owe the bank money, you are 'in the red'. They call that a debit balance because you are one of their **debtors**; you owe them money.

balance sheet – this is a snapshot of a business on a given date. It shows just what **assets** and **liabilities** it possessed on that date.

banker's card – a plastic card that most banks issue. It guarantees to shopkeepers that the cheque you give them will not bounce. It is not a **credit card**, **cash card**, **charge card** or **account card**. That said, it may be combined with one; Barclaycard also acts as a banker's card for a Barclays cheque.

bank payment card or **Switch card** – another plastic card supplied by your bank (or incorporated in another), used like a **credit card**. All transactions are charged directly to your bank account.

bankruptcy – if you cannot pay your debts, your **creditors** can take you to court and ask for you to be made bankrupt.

The court orders officials called bailiffs to take over everything you possess. This even includes your children's toys. They sell the lot to pay off your debts. They must leave you with a table, a chair, a bed and the tools of your trade. Being made bankrupt is a nightmare experience. Bankrupt people lose rights. They cannot vote or get credit. If and when they pay off all their original debts, or at the end of a certain length of time, they can ask the court to discharge them. Discharged bankrupts regain all their rights.

base lending rate (sometimes just called the **base rate**) – this is the rate of **interest** which fixes most bank lendings. You find it in the newspapers or displayed prominently in most banks. Depending on how safe a borrower you are, the bank will lend to you at 1, 2, 3 or even more per cent above its base lending rate.

beneficiary – someone who receives money or goods as ordered by a will or a **trust**.

bequest – the same as a **legacy**. You bequeath a bequest.

black economy – wages, sales, etc., which are hidden from the **Inland Revenue** to avoid paying tax on them. In some countries the black economy is bigger than the ordinary, legal one.

broker – a middleman or go-between. There are brokers who buy and sell **stocks and shares** for clients; brokers who arrange insurance policies for clients (sometimes specialist policies like insurance for a film star's bust or a pianist's fingers); brokers who buy and sell raw materials like copper in large quantities.

capital – money or **assets** which you invest or use to make **income**. Capital is like a tree, and income is the apples on it. Capital can be any sort of asset, from banknotes to a yacht that you charter out, anything that directly or indirectly earns you income. So the definition of 'capital' can stretch very broadly.

capital gains tax – if you buy British Telecom **shares**, a field in the countryside or any other **asset** with a long life, and sell it at a **profit**, you pay capital gains tax on the difference. Your home is exempt, and you cannot pay capital gains tax and **income tax** on the same profit. It is either/or.

CAR – compound annual rate. Sometimes called 'compounded annual rate' or 'compound annualized return'. The **interest rate** to use to compare investments.

cash card – a plastic card issued by a bank or building society. It enables you to withdraw money from a machine outside their branches during or after banking hours. Not a **banker's card**, **credit card** or **charge card**.

charge card – a plastic card you can use to buy goods and services – for example, Diners Club or American Express. It differs from a **credit card** because you have to repay everything within a month of receiving your account. So it really represents a very short-term loan. You usually pay a fixed sum each year to get your card.

civil service – thousands of people employed by the government to carry out its work at home and abroad. From the clerk who calculates your old-age pension to the chauffeur-driven ambassador on his way to dine with world leaders under the chandeliers – all civil servants enjoy job security and equal pay for men and women within the same grade. There are also thousands of other jobs in local government (working for your town council, for instance), the armed forces, the police, etc., where employees may enjoy broadly similar pay and conditions of work to civil servants.

clause – a sentence or two in a **contract**. Contracts are made up of clauses. Each lays down a different rule to govern the agreement.

commission – money charged by professional people for performing a service, as when an estate agent sells your house, or a valuer assesses one you long to buy. Sometimes the amount of commission charged is based on the price of the item concerned. Stockbrokers may charge you 1 per cent of the proceeds from the **shares** they sell for you. If so, they are charging 'on a percentage basis'. Sometimes the commission stays the same whatever the value of the item concerned. Your bank may charge you £10 whether they change £100 worth of pounds into pesetas for you to spend on holiday or whether they change £5,000 worth. This is called a 'flat-rate' commission. Sometimes the commission is worked out on a mixture of flat-rate and percentage basis. Estate agents may charge you a flat £100 plus 2 per cent of the value of the house they sell for you. Commissions, sometimes called 'fees', are the bread and butter of the professions.

In your life you have already paid far more commissions than you realize, because many of them are hidden. When you take out an insurance policy, you pay your money to the insurance company. Some of it zooms straight back to the sales agent who sold you the policy. Umpteen people earn commissions: football pools collectors, even some charity collectors. Commissions are also paid on recommendations. If accountant A advises a client to go to broker (or solicitor) B, he will tell B in advance and usually expect commission. Broker B will often hand on one-tenth of the first year's fees from his client. Many firms offer their employees commission for any clients they can introduce from their friends or family. So, if you do this, don't forget to ask for it.

commodity market – a place where people agree to buy or sell commodities like tea, rubber, cotton, sugar and gold in large quantities. These goods are not on display. They may not even exist yet. People agree to buy or sell, either here and now, or on a set date in the future, at a price agreed now. See **futures market**.

compound – if you put money in the bank to earn **interest**, you are free to take out that interest when it arises. (It is called 'simple interest'.) If, instead, you order the bank to add that interest to your **capital**, so that together they earn you even more interest, you compound your investment. Some investments don't allow you to touch your interest as you go along. They add it to your **capital** and it too earns interest. When the investment matures and you receive your interest, it is called compound interest. Compound interest is always higher than simple interest, because you have to wait longer before you can touch it.

compound annual rate – see **CAR**. This is the true annual rate of **interest** paid by investments.

consols or **consolidated stock** – another name for **gilt-edged securities** or **gilts**. Remember safe Sue and how puzzled she was by the different rates of gilts (Chapter 13)? Here is the reason.

Sue may notice a gilt called '1999 3%' and wonder how anyone could invest for such a low return, even if it is safe. But this government stock may have been issued forty years ago when a guaranteed 3 per cent was a good buy. Since then, the **stock** will have changed hands many times, at different prices. If Sue buys stock with a face value (what it is apparently worth) of £1,000, she will receive £30 **interest** a year (3 per cent of £1,000 = £30). If Sue only has to pay £400 for her £1,000-worth, then she is really getting $7\frac{1}{2}$ per cent ($7\frac{1}{2}$ per cent of £400 is £30). A cast-iron $7\frac{1}{2}$ per cent is much more tempting. Besides, when the stock is repaid in 1999, Sue, if she has not sold it, will receive back from the government the full £1,000. So she can look forward to a cast-iron **capital** gain of £600 (£1,000 – £400) as well as guaranteed **income**.

Alternatively, Sue may be tempted by a gilt called '1999 15%' at a time when most investments only pay 12 per cent. If she buys £100 face value, she will earn £15 a year. But she may have to pay £125 to get that £100 gilt. Then the £15 she receives will give her a return of 12 per cent (£125 at 12 per cent = £15). So she is no better off than if she invested elsewhere for 12 per cent. Besides, when the gilt is repaid in 1999, she will only receive face value of £100 although she paid £125 for it. So she faces a capital loss of £25.

Overall, Sue will find one gilt gives her (yields) just the same return as another. The difference between them is whether she wants her money as income or as capital gain and when she wants what. But all are safe.

contract – an agreement which is legally binding. If one of the parties (the people who made the contract) breaks it, the other(s) can take them to court. The court decides whether to make the contract breaker keep his/her part of the bargain or pay compensation to the other(s).

contract for services – an agreement, which need not be in writing, between a self-employed person and the person who wants his/her services. You go to the beautician and pay her for a facial. You don't tell her how to do it. She provides the salon, the couch, the equipment and cosmetics, even the overall and cotton wool. If she damages your skin or stains your clothes, she must compensate you out of her own money. You never employ her, although she is doing something for which you pay her.

contract of service – an agreement which must be in writing between an employer and an employee. It states the work to be done, hours, conditions and pay. All employees have a legal right to such a contract and can take their employers to court if the employers do not stick to its terms.

conveyancing – the legal work of arranging the purchase or sale of a house or flat, business premises or land. The legal document that transfers ownership of land or buildings is called a conveyance. Conveyancing is a solicitor's bread and butter. Most cases are totally straightforward and, with word processors, don't justify the fees that solicitors charge.

corporation tax – a tax that limited companies pay on their **income** and **capital** gains.

cost of living index – the government keeps records of the cost of goods and services. From those details, it calculates how the cost of living has increased or decreased over the year. The change is usually given as a percentage. If the index shows year 1 as 100 and year 2 as 107, then the cost of living has increased by 7 per cent. These indices (indices is the plural of index) can be misleading. See Chapter 17.

credit card – a plastic card which you can use in place of money to buy goods and services. Examples are Barclaycard and Access. It is very convenient, and you can even buy things over the phone, quoting your number. You can do this worldwide because each card-issuing organization belongs to an international 'umbrella' organization. You can use Barclaycard anywhere that accepts Visa, for example. The **interest** charged is high, and no one insists you repay in full by a set date. The only limit is your own credit limit; this is the maximum that the company issuing the card allows you to owe at any one time. If you are very firm with yourself, you can use your credit card like a **charge card** and avoid interest. But it is easy to succumb just this once . . .

creditors – people to whom you owe money. The opposite are **debtors**. In your **accounts**, creditors represent **liabilities**, and debtors are **assets**.

cumulative preference shares – if a company cannot afford to pay a **dividend** one year, it must pay cumulative preference **shareholders** two dividends the next year. So cumulative preference shares are a bit safer than **preference shares**.

Customs and Excise – an enormous government department with branches nationwide. It collects various taxes including **value added tax**. You meet its employees at ports and airports searching through your suitcases. The Customs and Excise Department is both stricter and more powerful than the **Inland Revenue**. Never mess them around!

day-release training – you work for an employer and receive a wage, but the employer allows you a day or more a week at college studying towards a qualification. Sometimes the agreement allows you to work full-time for a term then study for a term. This is called block-release.

debenture – a loan to a **public limited company**. You can buy or sell debentures on the **stock market**. A debenture entitles you to a fixed amount of **interest** which must be paid. Unlike **shareholders**, debenture holders have no say in the running of the company, cannot vote at meetings and don't share in the **profits**. Debentures are safer than **shares**.

debtor – someone who owes you money is your debtor. You are his/her **creditor**.

deed of covenant – a document promising to pay a sum regularly to another person or organization for either seven years or a shorter date. If you regularly drop money into the church collection plate on Sundays or make an annual donation to your favourite charity, you should do it under a deed of covenant. You sign a deed – which is easy – and continue to pay as before. The church or charity can claim a 'repayment' from the **Inland Revenue**. They claim an extra £2.50 for every £7.50 you give them. You get the form from the church or charity, a legal stationer or your solicitor. The latter will draw one up and charge you.

deed of family arrangement – a document drawn up by a solicitor within two years of a death. It must be signed by all those people, called the **beneficiaries**, who would have benefited under the will. The deed changes the terms of the will and takes its place.

deeds – the legal document which proves who owns a house or other building or land.

deflation – the opposite to **inflation**. Prices fall repeatedly. It last happened in Britain in the 1930s but left many people so poor that they did not notice.

Department of Social Security (or **DSS**; formerly part of the Department of Health and Social Security) – a large government department dealing with all sorts of welfare charges, like your **National Insurance** contributions, and welfare payments like pensions.

deposit – a vague word, generally used to mean a small part of the price of something. You pay it to stop the vendor selling the item to someone else. Also called a 'down-payment'. A real deposit is not returnable, so be very sure in advance whether you can get back what you have paid if you change your mind. When buying a house, it is rare – but not unknown – to borrow the full cost of the property. Such a **mortgage** is called a 100 per cent mortgage. If you are offered a 90 per cent mortgage, you must find the remaining 10 per cent from your own savings. That remainder is commonly called a deposit.

depreciating – reducing in value. See **depreciation**.

depreciation – goods don't last for ever; they wear out, so they are worth less. In other words, they depreciate in value. You expect a longer life from some things than from others. A heating boiler should last longer than a stereo, a three-piece suite longer than a comb. Some **assets** never wear out, like a house or land. Some assets even increase in value over the years, like antiques. They are called appreciating assets. When **accounts** are prepared for a business, depreciation is calculated because every asset has suffered wear and tear during the year. I have not shown this in Sally's Salon's accounts (Chapter 5), but it is worked out as explained in Chapter 9. Broadly, Sally would be able to reduce the tax she pays because of the depreciation her business assets have suffered.

direct debit – if you sign a direct debit, you authorize someone, perhaps the electricity company or a **hire purchase** company, to take money from your bank account to pay their bill. You should check that they only take the number of payments they are entitled to. It is easy for direct debits to continue although the debt has been paid in full. See also **standing order**.

director – a person appointed by the **shareholders** to run the **limited company** they own. The chief director is called the managing director. A director is an employee of the company and usually receives a salary. A person can be shareholder and director of the same company or of many companies at once.

discount – a reduction in price. The seller might offer you a discount for cash or because you are buying a large quantity at once or because you are a regular customer.

dividend – **income** which a **limited company** pays out to its **shareholders** from its **profits**. There is no guarantee that a company will pay out a dividend every year, although many do, or how much it will be.

DSS – see **Department of Social Security**.

economics – the study of how resources are used to create and distribute wealth. Economics is too vague to give you any practical help with your day-to-day problems. I say this with a degree in the subject.

There is an old joke about the economist, the mathematician and the physicist. They were marooned on a desert island, starving, with one can of baked beans between them and no tin-opener. The physicist said, 'I can use the rays of the sun to burst open the can.' The mathematician said, 'I can calculate where to stand so that one-third of the beans falls into each of our mouths.' The economist scoffed, 'You are doing this all wrong. You must start off by assuming that we have a tin-opener.'

endowment-linked mortgage – a **mortgage** where you repay only the **interest** on the home loan over the years. You rely on a **life assurance** policy or even a pension policy to produce the money at the end of the agreed time to repay the **capital**. Like **interest-only mortgages**, and for the same reason, endowment-linked mortgages are more expensive than **repayment** ones.

equities – another name for **stocks and shares**. Equity investment simply means investment in stocks and shares. Careful with this word, though: 'equity' has several other meanings not connected with money.

estate – everything you own when you die. It will be allocated according to your will, or according to fixed rules if you did not make one. If the value of the estate is large enough, **inheritance tax** must be paid first. Currently, only estates worth more than £150,000 pay tax, but remember that this includes the value of your home. Husbands and wives have separate estates. If one inherits everything from the other, no tax is paid.

exchange controls – the rules a country makes to stop its citizens and outsiders moving its own currency in or out of the country. The government is often afraid that the wealth of the country will be siphoned outside. Usually governments don't object to **foreign currency** being brought in, although they may restrict the ways it can be spent. Some countries don't allow foreigners to buy property or start businesses. They are afraid of being dominated by foreigners using their money. When one Japanese businessman flew to Australia and bought ninety business premises all in one day, without stepping out of his limousine, the Australian government immediately passed a law forbidding foreigners to buy premises. Britain no longer has exchange controls. Other countries, like Spain, do, and you will have to comply with them if you want to buy that sun-soaked villa.

exchange rate – this tells you the number of pesetas, dollars, etc., your pound will buy you. The rate changes from day to day for each currency. Britain joined the European Exchange Rate Mechanism to put a high ceiling and a low floor on the amount by which our pound changed against European currencies. Not low enough – we left.

FIMBRA – the Financial Intermediaries, Managers and Brokers Regulatory Association. This organization polices independent financial advisers in Britain to protect the investor.

finance – see **financial**.

finance house – an organization that lends money to people by arranging for them to buy goods on **hire purchase**; a hire purchase company, in fact.

financial – simply means to do with money. You finance something when you find the means to pay for it. I knew a girl once who used to call her fiancé her 'finance'.

foreign currency – the notes and coins issued by other countries for use inside their own borders. Some countries limit the amount a visitor can bring in or take out again. Some, like China, even produce a special currency that only tourists can use.

foreign currency mortgage – a **mortgage** where, instead of borrowing in pounds and repaying in pounds, you borrow and repay in another currency, hoping to pay less **interest**. You may borrow in Deutschmarks at 5 per cent when the ordinary pound rate is 15 per cent. But neither rate is fixed. In a year or two, British **interest rates** may fall below German ones. Countries normally enjoy low rates when their currencies are strong and likely to get stronger. Examples are the Swiss franc, the German Deutschmark, the Japanese yen and, historically, the US dollar. Currencies growing weaker include, unfortunately, the pound **sterling** and French franc. But the process does not happen evenly. All currencies pass through strong and weak periods, and fortunes are made and lost as a result. With a foreign currency mortgage, you gamble on the interest rate, on the **exchange rate** at which you pay that interest and on the exchange rate at which you repay the **capital** you borrowed.

Take Elsie. She borrowed £50,000 in Deutschmarks when the interest rate was 5 per cent compared to 10 per cent at home. The exchange rate was 3 Dm to £1, so she borrowed 150,000 Dm and had to find 7,500 Dm interest a year. At

3 Dm to £1, this cost her £2,500. (In Britain, she would be paying interest of £5,000 – that is, 10 per cent of £50,000 – so she is ahead.)

It only needs the exchange rate to change to 2.5 Dm to £1 for the interest to cost her £3,000. If the German interest rate rises to 8 per cent as well, she will find herself paying £4,800 (150,000 Dm × 8 per cent divided by 2.5 to convert it to pounds). So far she is still ahead.

Now suppose, when Elsie comes to repay the capital, that the rate is still 2.5 Dm to £1. Instead of repaying the £50,000 she borrowed, she will have to find £60,000 (150,000 divided by 2.5)!

forward contract – an agreement to buy or sell something at a future date at a price to be fixed now.

futures market – many crops (cocoa, coffee) and metals (tin, copper) are bought and sold in huge quantities in markets in London called the **commodity markets**. People can buy or sell before the crop has even been harvested or the metal mined. There is not a coffee bean in sight; these are simply paper transactions. People can buy or sell for some future date without actually spending a penny. If things go wrong, not only can you lose all your **capital** but you may have to spend more on top to cover your debts. This makes betting on the horses look safe.

futures trading – buying and selling **forward contracts** (sometimes called 'futures contracts'). Many futures contracts are made on the **commodity markets**. They are also made in other areas like **foreign currencies** and even **shares**.

gilt-edged securities (sometimes just called **gilts**) – when a government wants to raise money to finance its activities but it does not want to increase taxes, it will sell gilts. A gilt may be dated or undated. If it is dated, the government will return your money in the year stated. Otherwise, the government does not promise when it will repay. In the meantime, you receive a fixed amount of **interest**. If you want your

capital, you can sell your gilts to someone else on the **stock market**. You will not get the same as you paid for it. How much you get depends on the length of time before repayment and how high your **interest rate** is compared with other interest rates at the time you want to sell. Gilts are safe investments.

goodwill – an invisible **asset**. It represents the difference between a brand-new business and one in full swing. The existing one has regular customers, perhaps in a 'round'. People in the area know it, use it, trust it. It is established. If you buy an existing business, you usually have to pay for the goodwill.

gross – the full amount before anything has been deducted from it. If you take a job at £200 a week, this is your gross pay. The opposite of **net**. See **income**.

guarantor – someone who promises, in writing, that if another person cannot pay their debt, the guarantor will pay it for them.

hire purchase (or **HP**) – an agreement you sign with a hire-purchase company. If you want to buy a car from a garage, the hire-purchase company will buy the car and become its owner. You will pay the company the purchase price plus **interest** over a period of years, by instalments. At the end of the time, the vehicle becomes yours, although, of course, you have been using it in the meantime.

income – first, what you earn through work and, second, what your **assets** earn for you. The income from the money you put in the building society account is the **interest** you receive. The **gross** income from a house or flat you let out is the rent you receive for it. The **net** income is the sum left after you have deducted your expenses from that rent.

income tax – a tax the government charges on all sorts of **income**. It is collected from employees by the **Pay As You Earn** (**PAYE**) system before they receive their wages. The self-employed also pay income tax, normally half in January and half in June. How much they pay is based on how much **profit** they show in their **accounts** with various adjustments.

inflation – a time when prices go up and up. It is more a symptom than an illness. You may suffer from inflation, but as yet no one really knows enough to prevent or cure it. There is nothing new about inflation; people complained about it in the 1500s when all the galleons sailed home to Spain laden with gold from the New World. The Spaniards spent so freely, they forced up prices all over Europe.

inheritance tax – a tax charged on death on the value of **estates** over about £150,000 at present. This figure includes your home and virtually all you possess. Husband and wife are treated separately for inheritance tax. What a husband leaves to his wife, or she to him, is exempt. This means the **assets** are not included in the total value, and there is no tax to pay on them. When people talk generally about 'death duties' they mean inheritance tax.

Inland Revenue – a large government department concerned with collecting **income tax** and other taxes. Not **VAT**: this is collected by the **Customs and Excise** Department. Both departments have offices nationwide.

instant access – if a bank or building society account offers this, it means you can withdraw your money at any time without telling them beforehand and you don't lose any **interest**. Interest is paid right up to the day you draw out your money.

interest – what you receive for lending your money to someone, like a bank, for a while; or what you pay when you borrow. For centuries in Europe, charging interest was considered wicked and unChristian. As a result, the only lenders were Jews. Some grew very wealthy. Time after time, Christians throughout Europe found it cheaper to kill off Jews than repay their debts.

interest-only mortgage – unlike with a **repayment mortgage,**

you only pay **interest** through the life of the **mortgage**. At the end, you still owe all the **capital** you borrowed. You pay it off in one lump – perhaps by selling the house or flat itself and using the profit left after repaying the capital (if there is enough) to buy somewhere else. This sort of mortgage is not popular in Britain and is usually more expensive. You borrow *all* the capital for the full length of the mortgage, so you have to pay more interest on it. People prefer **endowment-linked mortgages** so they can use the sum they receive to pay off the capital on the mortgage and keep their home.

interest rate – this is always shown as a percentage. It is the amount of **interest** you receive (or pay) if you lend (or borrow) money. The interest figure is meaningless unless you know the period. Usually, the rates quoted are annual – in other words, how much you would receive (pay) if the money was lent (borrowed) for a year. **Credit cards** like Barclaycard often quote a monthly rate. To calculate the annual rate roughly, you multiply that by 12. Then you realize that the annual rate looks jolly high and understand why they quote a monthly rate. To get roughly from a quarterly rate to an annual rate, multiply by 4. Chapter 11 describes how the government tries to protect borrowers from misleading rates by insisting that the **APR** is always shown as well. Chapter 13 describes how the government tries to protect lenders by insisting that the **CAR** is shown. As far as I know, there is no legal upper limit to the interest rate people can charge. Some of the small advertisements in the newspapers which don't demand **security**, and will even lend to people already overwhelmed by debts, demand a horrific 65 per cent. You should be quite desperate for money to consider paying more than 20 per cent. Even at this rate, you borrow £5 but pay back £6. If **base lending rate** rockets that high, you may have little choice.

investment trust – a **limited company** set up to invest in the shares of other companies. Members receive shares.

invoice – a bill.

job-sharing – where two people, usually female, do one job. One may work mornings, the other afternoons, or both alternate days. Some jobs lend themselves to this, like factory production-line work, some social work jobs, copy-typing and nursing. Others do not – for example, jobs where each individual deals personally with their own clients, or where events move so fast that continuity is vital, or where you are overseeing the work of others.

lease – a written agreement to rent a property (house, flat, shop, etc.) for a set length of time. The person who owns the property is called the 'lessor', the person who will be paying the rent and using the premises is called the 'lessee'. If you lease a whole house and only want to use one floor, you may – if the lease allows it – sub-let the rest. The original lease is then called the 'head lease', and the new one between you and your tenants is called a 'sub-lease'. Obviously the sub-lease cannot last longer than the head lease.

lease purchase – a variation on **hire purchase** which can take many forms. It can involve paying a huge first instalment or a huge final instalment; or there may be an agreement that the vehicle be sold at the end of the period, or a difference in the date when you as borrower finally own the article. Unlikely to be cheaper than hire purchase, although the repayment times may suit you better.

legacy – money paid out or goods handed over after someone's death because this is what the will ordered. The person leaving the legacy is called the 'legator'. The person who receives it is called the 'legatee'.

liability – the opposite of an **asset**. It is a disadvantage, a present or future responsibility. All the debts you owe others are your liabilities. These people are your **creditors**.

life assurance – you pay regularly over a number of years. If you die, your dependants receive a sum of money. If you are still alive and kicking at the end of the policy, say at age 60, you receive a sum of money. Either way, someone gets paid.

life insurance – you pay regularly over a number of years. If you die, your dependants receive a sum of money. If you survive, you have been protected throughout the period, but your contributions are lost. Also called 'term insurance', it is far cheaper than **life assurance**. Building societies usually insist on term insurance. Then, if you die during the course of your **mortgage**, your dependants receive the money and use it to pay off the mortgage and keep a roof over their heads. Sometimes this is called **mortgage protection insurance**.

life interest – if you have a life interest in an **asset**, you can use it for as long as you live. It does not belong to you, so you cannot sell, change or destroy it. You can leave someone a life interest in your will, like so: 'I leave the country cottage to Great-Aunt Jane to live in as long as she chooses, and on her death I leave it to my children.'

limited company – people talk loosely about a company when they mean any sort of business run by a person on their own or by a group of people. A limited company means a legal person, set up by **shareholders**, to run a business. The shareholders appoint **directors** – often themselves – to do the actual work. The company continues to live even though the shareholders and directors may change and the trade finish. It only dies when it is 'wound up'. It is called 'limited' because, if the trade fails and the company owes more money than it can find, the shareholders' loss is limited to their original stake. That is the money they put up to buy the **shares**. All their other **assets**, like the family home, stay safe.

liquid asset – an **asset** that is easily turned into cash.

liquidity – how quickly you could turn your **assets** into cash if necessary. The more liquid, the better. Many firms have gone bankrupt because, although they had plenty of assets – far more than their **liabilities** – the assets could not be sold quickly enough to meet a sudden need for cash, and the firm could not borrow enough to tide itself over. This is called a 'liquidity crisis'. Sometimes at this point firms get bought up cheaply by rivals or by asset strippers. I explain asset stripping in Chapter 14.

the market – all the other buyers and sellers.

maturity – when a policy or investment finishes. If you invest in a ten-year scheme in 1985, it will mature in 1995. This is when you will get your money.

MIRAS – stands for **mortgage** interest relief at source. People used to pay the full amount of **interest** due on their house or flat mortgage and then get a subsidy from the government by paying less tax. This roundabout way was scrapped for most people by the introduction of the MIRAS system. You fill in the appropriate forms and pay a reduced amount of interest. The government makes up the difference to the building society or bank without involving you or the tax you pay.

mortgage – a very long-term loan, sometimes for as much as thirty-five years, usually to buy a house or flat, a business or a farm. Building societies give mortgages; so do banks and some insurance companies. They all demand **security** for the loan. They keep the **deeds** of the property or land (the legal document proving you own it). If you cannot keep up your repayments of **interest** and **capital**, they can make you sell the property. They take the money owing out of the proceeds before they release the deeds. See also **foreign currency mortgages**.

mortgage protection insurance – a **life insurance** policy that a borrower takes out. If he or she dies before the **mortgage** is repaid, the insurance company pays off the mortgage and the spouse or other dependants can keep the family home.

mutual – restricted to members only. A credit union only borrows money from members and only lends money to members. When you open a building society account you become a member of the society. This is why you receive lots of rubbish in the post about elections and voting to light the fire with.

National Insurance – money the government takes from employees (through PAYE before you receive your wages), the self-employed and employers. The money pays for the National Health Service, old-age pensions and other benefits like unemployment benefit. The system is operated by the DSS with hundreds of local offices nationwide. In addition, they store everyone's pension details in a vast computer in Newcastle.

net (sometimes spelt **nett**) – the amount of a sum left after the deduction of whatever has to be deducted. Employees receive their wages net of tax. The opposite is **gross**.

offshore – means based anywhere abroad or in the Channel Islands or the Isle of Man. These last two have their own tax rules and are **tax havens**.

onshore – the opposite to **offshore**. It means based in mainland England, Scotland, Wales, Northern Ireland or any of the British islands except the Channel Islands or the Isle of Man. Onshore organizations are covered by British tax rules.

option – if you possess a legal option, you have a **contract** giving you the right to do something in the future. Perhaps you rent a house and the rental agreement gives you the right to buy it for a set price. An option is a choice. You don't have to buy. If you do, you 'exercise your option' or 'take it up'. Options can be very valuable. One of my clients had an option to buy an aerodrome for £1 million. The land must be worth ten times that. For the moment he has no intention of buying, but his option is a valuable **asset**, increasing in value all the time. Sometimes **limited companies** offer their **shareholders** the right to buy extra **shares** at a special low price. Depending on the contract, you may be able to sell your option to others. You may come across options under the name of 'warrants'.

overdraft – you agree this with your bank in advance. The manager allows you to withdraw more money than you actually have in your account, up to a certain limit. An overdraft can turn out cheaper than a loan because you don't start paying **interest** until you actually spend the money. With a loan, you pay interest from day one on the full amount, whether you have spent it or not. Sometimes you can agree, at a later stage, to extend your overdraft – this means increase the limit, to allow you to draw out another £1,000, say.

overheads – the background expenses of a business to provide the setting for the owner to earn money, such as payments for electricity, water, gas and rent. Sometimes people are even vaguer and call any running cost of a business an overhead.

p.a. – see **per annum**.

partner – someone who joins with one or several others to run a business. They pool their **capital** and expertise and share the **profits**. Each partner has joint and several **liability**. This means any one partner is responsible for their own debts and also for the debts of all the other partners.

partnership – see **partner**.

Pay As You Earn (or **PAYE**) – a system that employers must operate on the wages of employees. Employers calculate how much **income tax** and **National Insurance** to deduct for each employee, using tables and a tax code given them by the Inland Revenue. They pay over the net wages to the employee. They pay the tax and NI deducted to the **Inland Revenue**, together with their own NI contributions for each employee. Britain invented and has operated PAYE successfully for nearly fifty years. The French are fighting tooth and nail to prevent its introduction there. They claim it will never work!

PAYE – see **Pay As You Earn**.

PEP – see **personal equity plan**.

per annum – a year. Sometimes written 'p.a.'.

personal equity plan (or **PEP**) – these plans are relatively new. They started in 1987 and have proved very popular. The government allows an individual to invest up to £9,000 a year (£18,000 for a married couple) in such a plan. Your money will be invested in **equities**, either directly or through a **unit trust** or **investment trust**. The generous tax treatment allows gains and **dividends** to build up tax-free. An investor can withdraw the proceeds from the very first year if they wish. The management charges are relatively low. PEPs can only be arranged by people authorized under the Financial Services Act – that is, members of **FIMBRA**.

personal guarantee – a written promise, made by the **director** of a **limited company**, for example, that if the company cannot pay its debts, he or she will pay them out of his or her own pocket.

portfolio – if you stock up at the supermarket, you end up with a shopping-basketful. When you buy various different **shares**, your shopping-basketful is called your portfolio.

preference shares – these are **shares** in a company which must receive their **dividend**, or be repaid their **capital**, before ordinary shares. So they are a bit safer.

premium – a payment or instalment you pay, for instance, to take out an insurance policy. Sometimes, as with a **lease**, the premium means the first payment only. It is the lump sum you pay to get the lease.

principal – the original sum lent, invested or borrowed.

private limited company – one where the **shares** belong to a small number of people, often just one family. The shares are not bought or sold on the **stock market**.

professional indemnity insurance – this is insurance taken out by members of a profession like chartered accountants. If a member or their employee makes a mistake or is dishonest, as a result of which the client loses money, the insurance reimburses the client. Such insurance often forms a condition of membership of the profession. The sum covered may run into millions. Mistakes come expensive.

profit – first, the amount of **income** a business earns, less all the expenses of earning that money; second, if you buy and sell an **asset**, the difference between what you paid for it and what you received, after deducting the costs of purchase and sale, like legal fees. There is a world of difference between these two sorts of profit. Business profits suffer **income tax**, and profits on the sale of assets may suffer **capital gains tax**. In everyday speech, people describe both as profits. The opposite is a loss.

profit and loss account – this records what came into and what went out of a business in the year. The difference between the two is the **profit** (or loss). This account is a history of the business. It includes **income** items not **capital** ones.

property trust – like a **unit trust** but it uses investors' money to buy property, often office blocks and business premises. **Income** comes from rents received and **profits** from the sale of premises.

prospectus – a glossy brochure encouraging you to invest, say, in a new company.

public limited company (or **PLC**) – a company that the public can buy **shares** in through the **stock market**. Such a company has thousands of **shareholders**.

quotation – like an estimate but fixed. The price someone will charge to do a job; or, if you tell them how much you want to spend or invest, the amount they calculate your money will earn you.

rate of interest – see **interest rate**.

repayment mortgage – the normal sort of **mortgage** where you repay **capital** as well as **interest** as you go along. Alternatives are **interest-only mortgages** and **endowment-linked mortgages**.

risk – with an investment, the likelihood of losing the original money you invested (the **capital**) as well as the **income** you should have earned on the investment. The more risky an investment, the higher the income you want from it to justify the risk.

securities – any piece of paper that represents money, such as **stocks and shares**, **debentures** and **gilts**.

security – what a lender demands from a borrower to guarantee that the borrowings can be repaid. A building society will keep the **deeds** of a house so that the borrower cannot sell it and run off with the building society loan.

self-employment – if you start up your own business, you become self-employed. There is nothing to stop you being an employee in the daytime and self-employed in the evening, if you have the energy. You cannot be self-employed at the same time as unemployed; the **DSS** will soon stop your unemployment benefit and may even prosecute you for not telling them. Self-employed people have a **contract for services**, probably many, and receive their **income** in full. They pay **income tax** and **National Insurance** later, separately.

selling forward – you agree to sell something at a future date at a price which is fixed now.

settlor – someone who sets up a **trust**.

share – ownership of a small part of a **limited company**, like Woolworths or British Telecom. As you own it, you have a say in how the company is run and can vote to appoint the **directors** to run it. You are entitled to receive a share of the company's **profits**. What you receive is called a **dividend**. If the company runs up debts it cannot pay, you are not responsible for paying them. If the shares become worthless, you lose what you paid to buy them in the first place. The shares of **public limited companies** are bought and sold on the **stock market**.

share certificate – the piece of paper that proves you own a share.

shareholder – someone who owns a **share** or shares in a **limited company**.

sole trader – someone who runs a business on their own. A sole trader may employ other people but is the only owner.

spot rate – the going rate if you buy or sell here and now. The alternative is called the 'future rate'. Similarly, the spot price of something is the here-and-now, present price – like the one you pay in any shop.

standing order – an instruction you give your bank by filling out a form, to pay a certain bill regularly for you on a certain date, perhaps your **mortgage** payment. Watch your standing orders, because it is easy for the bank to continue paying although the debt, say **hire purchase**, has been paid in full. This is not the same as a **direct debit**. You keep more control over a standing order.

sterling – the name for the British currency, pounds and pence.

stock – the goods that traders buy to sell in their shop. If you buy a shop you often have to buy the existing stock with it. Stock must be counted and valued before **accounts** can be prepared. This is called 'stock-taking'.

stock market – traditionally men called jobbers and brokers met to buy **stocks and shares** in **public limited companies** for their clients. The building used was called the Stock Exchange. As well as the original one in London, provincial stock exchanges exist in large towns like Bristol. The United States one in New York is called Wall Street. Nowadays with modern technology you can buy and sell through your bank too. All the people occupied in buying and selling shares are known collectively as the stock market.

stocks and shares – in practice, the same thing. See **share**.

subsidiary company – just as human beings can have children, so can **limited companies**. A 'parent' company can set up a subsidiary company to form a 'family' or group of companies. A subsidiary may have its own subsidiaries. Some 'families' can have hundreds of member companies, all owned by the 'parent' company.

supply and demand – the basic rule of the subject of **economics**. The more people supply an item, the cheaper it will be. When there is a glut of tomatoes, they are very cheap. The more people demand an item, the more expensive it will be. When everyone is clamouring to see the latest Lloyd-Webber show or the men's singles final at Wimbledon, touts can sell tickets for many times more than their original value. The same rules apply to the supply and demand for services. Brain surgeons receive high wages because there are few of them. If typists earned as much as pop stars, the colleges would not be able to cope with the rush of people eager to learn to type.

tax exile – a very wealthy person who decides he or she does not want to pay British taxes and goes to live in a **tax haven**. Tax exiles need move no further than Jersey.

tax haven – somewhere abroad where you can put your money or even live; and, because the local tax rates are low, you pay a lot less tax than you would if you lived in Britain. The world is dotted with tax havens, such as Andorra, although some are rather unpleasant, unstable places to live. You can imagine the sort of sharks they might attract. Someone once called them 'sunny places for shady people'.

tax return – the form sent out by the **Inland Revenue** in April on which you enter details of all your **income** for the last year. You also enter any **profits** or losses you have made on selling **assets**. In practice, the Revenue often don't need to send returns to employees every year. The self-employed complete and return them annually with a copy of their business **accounts**.

time share – a developer builds a holiday complex or splits up an old house and sells holiday-makers the right to use a flat or villa in it for one week each year, say, for ten years, or for ever. People can sell their right if they want to. There are exchange schemes where you can swap your week in Cyprus, or Scotland, for a similar week in Italy. The developers make a lot of money from sales and management fees. Generally, time shares are a way of enjoying your money rather than an investment. Whether it is worthwhile depends on how much you spend on your holidays. Prices may increase yearly, and so can management fees. If your week is out of season, you may find your management charge higher than you would have had to pay to rent the flat as an outsider.

top-up mortgage – a second **mortgage**, usually at a higher **interest rate**, often offered by banks or solicitors, to top you up to the amount you need to buy the house or flat you want.

traveller's cheques – you buy them before you leave Britain. You can cash in any left when you return. Each cheque is for a fixed amount; you sign it in advance and then again when you change it for local currency. Unlike cash, if your traveller's cheque is lost or stolen, you can claim your money back from the organization (like Thomas Cook or American Express) that issued them. So traveller's cheques are safer than cash.

trust – a legal arrangement where one person looks after another's assets. A toddler may inherit, but adults will need to manage everything until he or she comes of age. Some trusts last for ever – perhaps the person who owns the property is incurably disabled. The people who manage the trust are called 'trustees'. Some trusts allow the trustees wide powers to spend trust money as they see fit; others strictly limit them. Originally designed to protect the weak, trusts are now used widely to avoid tax. Most wealthy families set up one or several trusts. You can set up a trust at any time or leave instructions in your will for one to be set up after your death. The **settlor** can also be a trustee. A trustee cannot be a **beneficiary**.

trustee – see **trust**.

unit trust – an organization which allows a lot of small investors to invest in a wide range of **shares**. It takes in their money, giving them a number of 'units' in return. It employs experts to use this money to buy shares in different companies. These shares will yield **dividends** and also **capital profits** (or losses) when they are sold. This **income** is handed on to the investors after deducting the management expenses of the unit trust.

value added tax (or **VAT**) – a tax collected by the **Customs and Excise** department. It is a straight percentage of the price of many of the goods and services you buy, like dinner in a restaurant. Customs and Excise are much stricter and more powerful than the **Inland Revenue**. They have the power to enter and search premises, and will prosecute for the slightest delay. Never mess them about.

VAT – see **value added tax**.

Incidentally, you will not find a reading list at the end of this book. Why not? Because, by and large, the sort of knowledge you need is not found in books. Finding out what is on offer now, in the real world, means asking and listening, picking up snippets from journals and advertising bumf – and generally growing more aware of the world around you. You cannot do that with your nose in a book.

22 CONCLUSION

My grandmother never knew what Grandfather earned or even exactly what he did. She accepted the housekeeping she was given, with no questions asked. Worse, she had to save towards the weeks when Grandfather was on holiday. She dreaded holidays. He received no money, so he could give her no housekeeping at all.

My mother fared better. Before marriage, she earned her keep and a pittance besides. Afterwards, at least she knew how much Father earned. He alone decided how much housekeeping to give her. Mother had retired before she attained the pinnacle of her own financial life; she wrote her first cheque.

I have managed bank accounts in England, France, Spain and New Zealand. I have bought houses in all four countries, three on forward exchange contracts. I have negotiated on behalf of clients in multi-million affairs, and I retired at 40.

Progress? Of course. But it did not come easily. Who could forget the male bank clerk pleading with my husband not to open a joint account? Then, when he insisted, begging him at least to countersign any cheque I wrote!

There is still a long way to go.

You have already taken a great stride towards financial emancipation if you are still with me in Chapter 22. Armed with your new knowledge, where do you go from here?

Wherever your compass points.

BE REASONABLE

'I think it's really rotten of banks not to lend to single mothers living on social security,' complained Angela, who, although herself a barrister, had no idea about money.

'With no income and no security, how are they going to pay back their debts?' I asked.

'What's that got to do with it?'

You need to understand how the world works first. Then you can think about changing it. Or you may throw out the baby with the bath water.

It is unreasonable to expect to be treated as a financial equal unless you put in the homework that men do.

You cannot expect to be treated as a financial equal if, the minute things go wrong, you flutter your eyelashes, profess congenital ignorance of all things financial and turn to the nearest male to sort you out. The first time, he may feel flattered. The second, he will be annoyed. Besides, you need real charm for it to work beyond 30. Tears, sulks and flirting may win a battle at the expense of losing the war. And don't expect to play the helpless little widow if you are confronted by a single woman of your own age who has had to fight her own battles in life.

Priscilla was like that. She swanned into the office, trading on her father's name. She believed that a quick flourish of her handkerchief would melt all hearts.

Priscilla had set up three limited companies. She got into an almighty tangle through her own pig-headedness. Then she opted out completely, tore up all letters, refused to answer the phone – until she found herself in court for tax bills of tens of thousands on profits she had never made.

'I'm so glad *you're* dealing with my little problem,' she smiled bravely through her tears. 'A woman is much more understanding.'

I understood all right. She thought everyone would yield to her, that every rule would bend. Someone would make her path easy, just like Daddy always had. If I had been male, it would have been, '*Men* are much more understanding.'

In the end, Priscilla had to go sobbing to make a clean breast of her misfortunes to her latest husband. He came to see me, his jaw tightly clenched. I will swear he was muttering, 'Bloody fool of a wife,' under his breath. He confessed that this was not the first time he had listened to a tale of woe and bailed her out, even in their short marriage.

In fact, it did not take me long to straighten out Priscilla. She had caused the tangle by refusing to do anything at all. But she could never face me again, and we had difficulties getting our money.

Priscilla also had a long career in public life. I hope she did not act in the council chamber the same way she ran her businesses.

Be reasonable. When you are confronted with apparent injustice, ask the reason. There may be one. Tax law used to deem (treat for practical purposes) all a wife's income to belong to her husband. So they sent him a tax return to cover both. Processing one return per family saved the country a vast sum. This meant that taxes did not need to be so high; it was a valid reason.

Yet it had some cruel consequences. A wife had to tell her husband all her income, while he did not have to tell her a thing about his. A wife could not even save up in secret to surprise her husband, other than slipping money under the mattress. If she kept quiet, she risked him getting into trouble for hiding 'his' income.

Even worse sufferers were unmarried mothers who had passed themselves off as widows, divorcees, etc. Also, married women had to confess to their husband if they received money from the child's father under a paternity order. You can imagine the body-blow this could strike at a marriage, especially if the husband was already being badgered by the Inland Revenue for lying about this hidden income, of which he knew nothing.

Before now, sympathetic female tax staff have done everything possible to hide such facts from husbands – even to the extent of phoning the wife each year to say the bill has been posted so that she could intercept it on the doormat and pay it secretly herself!

There were good reasons why only one tax return was completed for each married couple, then, but they were not good enough. 'Good reasons must, of force, give place to better,' as Shakespeare says.* Now, in the interests of equality and because more women have their own money, everyone completes their own form.

It was also reasonable for shopkeepers to refuse to give hire purchase to married women when, as the law stood then, they were not responsible for their own debts. Both they and their husband could easily wriggle out of paying altogether. This has changed too.

A lot of energy is wasted by targeting 'reasonable' discrimination rather than the unreasonable. For instance, a wife might run her own business, but if she paid too much tax and a repayment was due, the cheque was always posted to the husband, and made out to him! Nobody ever complained about that.

The only justification was that the wife's income was deemed to belong to the husband, so her repayment was *his* repayment. Infuriating! But few women knew the system well enough to know when they were being hard done by. This example has now been rectified.

When you are turned down – for a loan, say – it hurts. You are naturally upset. But try not to take it personally. Many men get turned down too. Their remedy is often to get drunk; a woman is more likely to go sick. Of course, if there is real

* *Julius Caesar*, Act 4, scene 3.

evidence that you were turned down *because you were a woman*, this is a different matter, although difficult to prove.

Be reasonable with what you expect from your money too. Money can offer you peace of mind, something a little bit different, temporary importance while you are spending it, novelty, comfort, entertainment, even power if you have enough of it. Money can never give you real friends or good relationships – it may even make them more difficult – or youth.

Be reasonable with what you expect from your adviser. Even the best adviser cannot transform your affairs if you ignore their advice, only follow the bits you like, make later changes without a word to anyone or bluntly refuse to change a thing. I have known all happen.

When seeking advice, you must constantly watch out that your own interests remain paramount, even when you are footing the bill. Hilda came to us in great distress. Her husband and sons ran a business which she suspected was in trouble but they refused to seek advice.

Hilda dragged her menfolk to the first meeting with our male partner. She badgered them into admitting their problems and then, relieved that something was being done, never came again. The partner and the men got on fine together. He gave them advice totally in their own interests, although Hilda was paying for it. Poor woman, she thought their interest was her interest.

The accountant, our partner, investigated the business and arranged its sale. Imagine Hilda's shock when her husband suddenly skedaddled to Spain with a girlfriend. The accountant channelled all the sale proceeds directly abroad to her absent husband, and Hilda was left out in the cold.

Why? Surely she could sue the accountant? No. He had done nothing wrong. He had simply arranged everything from the male viewpoint. He deals with men all day long. To do things this way was as natural as breathing.

What should Hilda have done? Been more involved all the way along and insisted on being informed. Admittedly, this is often far easier said than done.

Personally, I find it hard to understand how women marry men they know they cannot trust with money. If you already know you dare not trust someone with something as simple as money, is it wise to rely on them for your future, your children or even – given that your husband is statistically the person far most likely to murder you – your life?

On the other hand, when it comes to money, being female does bring advantages:

- You live longer, so you are more likely to inherit wealth.
- You can admit your ignorance and ask for an explanation or even pay for help. Often a man's pride will not let him.
- If you are married, most men still consider you must be dependent on your husband. The Inland Revenue are less likely to investigate your affairs, and if anything is wrong, you are less likely to be punished. Unscrupulous husbands and a few unscrupulous women play on this for all it is worth.
- If you are a married woman who starts a venture, there is less at stake if things do go wrong. You and your family will not starve.
- You are more sceptical of get-rich-quick schemes, especially those bordering on illegality.
- You take the long view, not the here-today-and-gone-tomorrow approach, and it pays in the long run.

THE WICKED PROSPER, BUT NOT FOR LONG . . .

You will be handling money for the rest of your life. Take courage. With investment, with accounting, as with any review of your past life, whether you conclude you have succeeded or failed depends greatly on when you stop to do your sums. Today's apparent success may shrivel into tomorrow's flop. Today's failure may slowly blossom into a long-term success.

We women have come a long way in our struggle to get and keep our own wealth. We have not arrived there yet. Liberation remains a sham while men still tell us how to use our money. It means they are still telling us how to live our lives. Who was it who claimed that an independent mind starts with an independent purse?

INDEX

account cards 74, 235

accountants 50, 41–4, 54, 83–4, 142

accounts 33, 39, 43–8, 123, 235; interpretation 46, 49–61

addition 219–20

alimony 10, 108, 172, 235–6

amortization 236

annual percentage rate *see* APR

annuities 182–4, 236

antiques 92, 93, 100, 202

appearance, personal 121–2, 169

APR (annual percentage rate) 74, 117–18, 252

arithmetic 2, 218–34

art 93, 143, 164, 202, 236

assets 6–7, 91–3, 202, 236–7, 245; statement of 44, 47–8; stripping 171, 255

audits 237

averages, calculation of 234

balance sheet 44, 47–8, 235, 237

banker's cards 74, 101, 237

banks: accounts (budget) 72, (current) 146, (deposit) 81, 140, (money market) 140; business advice 118; interest 72, 81, 118, 120, 140; safety 153–4; *see also* loans; overdrafts

bargains 95, 196–8

base lending rate 122, 207, 238, 252

bed and breakfast 120–25

benefits, state 11, 30, 72

black economy 21, 238

bonds 155–6; *see also* gilts

bookmakers 86–7, 87–8

brokers 238; insurance 82, 182; investment 139–40, 177; stock 6–7, 157

Budget, beating the 163

budgeting 43, 52, 72

building societies: investment 81, 83, 150, 154; mortgages 114–15, 127–8; traveller's cheques 195

capital 5–6, 32, 62–79, 128, 238; growth 143–8; payments 46–7; *see also* legacies; windfalls

capital gains tax 82–3, 161, 238–9, 259

capital transfer tax 67–8

CAR (compound annual rate) 151, 239, 252

cars: company 23–4, 25, 28, 58; costs 77, 91, 92–3, 97–9;

cars – *contd*
   loans for 118; self-employed
   and 35–6, 38–9, 49
cash cards 239
catering trade 52, 120–25
charge cards 74, 119, 195–6,
   239
charities 207–8
child care 12–13, 26
Citizens' Advice Bureau 72,
   107
Civil Service 14, 18, 21, 101–2,
   105, 169
clothing 24, 25, 89, 100
commodity market 165–6, 240,
   249
companies *see under* limited
compensation 30, 69–70
compound annual rate *see* CAR
computer programming 14, 16,
   19
confidence, market 7, 116
consolidated stock 155–6, 241–2
Consumers' Association 80, 135
contingencies 96, 147
contracts 242; forward 249; for
   services 33, 242, 260; of
   service 20–21, 33, 242
conveyancing 131, 242
corporation tax 57, 58, 242
cost of living index 200, 242–3
covenant, deed of 244
credit cards 74, 101, 113, 119,
   195, 199, 243; abroad 195–6;
   interest rate 101, 117, 243,
   252
credit companies 115
credit unions 114, 256

creditors 47, 243

death 148, 182, 186; *see also*
   estate; inheritance tax;
   legacies; wills
debentures 155, 175, 244
debts 43, 48, 60, 61, 77, 118,
   237
decimals 230–32
deeds: of covenant 244; of
   family arrangement 81, 188,
   189, 244; property 115
deflation 202, 244
Department of Social Security
   22, 30, 40, 104, 244–5
depreciation 91–3, 202, 245
direct debit 245
directors 31, 57, 58, 173, 246
disabled people 27
discounted cash flow 99
discounts 101–2, 158, 246
dividends 57, 152, 157, 246
division 226–9
divorce 10–11, 69, 132, 171–9;
   see also alimony
drawings from business 46

economies 95–6, 97–102
emergencies 96, 147
employment 9–31; black
   economy 21, 238; child care
   12–13, 26; conditions 18, 25–
   30; contract 20–21, 33, 242;
   definition 20–22; of family
   37–8, 42, 54; home-based 27;
   loans through 25, 114;
   National Insurance 21, 24,
   34; part-time 10, 13–14;

'sham' self-employment 34, 40, 141; tax 21, 33, 39, 257; training 14, 27, 28–9, 169; *see also* perks; return to work; unions

equipment 29, 36–7, 99

estate 183, 247

Eurocheques 195

exchange controls 247

exchange rate 84, 130, 192–3, 194, 247; inter-bank 195, 196

exchange schemes 27

expectations 150, 151–2

expenses 35–9, 43, 45

family: businesses 185; employment of 37–8, 42, 54; gifts 66–7; investment to suit 145–6, 147–8; loans within 72, 114, 136–7; *see also* deeds (of family arrangement)

FIMBRA 141, 163, 208, 247–8

finance houses 72, 118, 248

flexitime 26–7

foreign countries 18–19, 84, 108, 192–8; *see also* foreign currency

foreign currency 130, 164, 192–6, 247, 248, 249; mortgages 130, 248–9; *see also* exchange rate

forward trading 249, 260

Foster & Cranfield 162

fractions 229–32

fraud 75–7, 119, 174, 175–6, 195, 206–17

freehold 133–5

furniture 91, 92, 93, 100, 197

futures market 165–6, 249

gambling 84–8, 166

gifts 66–8

gilts (gilt-edged securities) 155–6, 207, 241–2, 249–50

goodwill 61, 250

grants, public 40

gross 250

guarantee, personal 33, 59, 258

guarantor 74, 116, 250

hairdressing 32–3

health 25, 78, 169

health and safety 21, 34

hire purchase 28, 47, 118, 125, 126–7, 250, 268

hiring equipment 99

hobbies 50

home, work from 13, 14, 27, 134

household appliances 96, 100

houses *see* property

ignorance, admitting 3–4, 270

incentive schemes 29

income 5–6, 44, 62, 250; investment for 143–8; *see also* wages

income tax 21–2, 82–3, 250–51, 262; employee's 21, 24, 25, 33, 39, 257; low pay and 21–2, 38; self-employed 34, 35, 36, 39, 43, 83

index-linking 105, 182, 202

inflation 80–81, 83, 90, 147, 199–205, 251; pensions and 105, 182, 202 inheritance *see* inheritance tax; legacies

inheritance tax 65, 112, 132, 184, 185–7, 251; *see also* deeds (of family arrangement)

Inland Revenue 21, 22, 25, 71–2, 251; and fraud 174, 175, 176, 214

insurance 147–8; compensation 30, 69; health 25, 78; and house purchase 129; household 78–9; life 82, 111, 147, 161–2, 186, 254; mortgage protection 132, 147, 254, 255; permanent health 147; professional indemnity 208, 258–9; refunds 77; term 254

interest 251, 252; in accounts 47–8; bank 72, 81, 118, 120, 140, 146; building society 81, 154; compound 240–41; credit card 101, 117, 243, 252; credit, interest-free 83; fixed 156; hire/lease purchase 125, 126; on investments 6, 72, 81, 140, 149–50, 151, 154; on loans 72–5, 115, 116, 118, 120; mortgages, interest-only 251–2; realistic 207, 270; on reducing balance 73–4; *see also* APR; base lending rate

investment 138–69; charitable link-up 207–8; diversification 163; ethical 159; family and 145–6, 147–8; income or capital growth 143–8; in oneself 168–9; profits 167–8; prudent 156–63, 177; reckless 163–7; safe 153–6

investment trusts 160, 253

invoices 43, 253

jewellery 93, 100

job-sharing 14, 26, 253

land 70–71

landlords 135, 160–61

laundering money 214

lease purchase 125, 126–7, 253

leasehold 133–5, 253

legacies 63–5, 69, 78, 143–4, 171, 184–8, 253; *see also* inheritance tax

liability ix–x, 55, 57, 59, 253

life assurance 111–12, 115, 186, 253–4; *see also* mortgages (endowment)

life interest 254

limited companies 254; buying existing 42, 60, 164; buying trade of 60–61; fraudulent prospectuses 206; as legal person 56–7, 60; liability ix–x, 57, 59; off the shelf 42, 58, 61; private and public 58–9, 258; pros and cons of becoming 54, 56–61; tax 57, 58, 59; *see also* debentures; directors; dividends; shares

limited editions 100–101

liquidity 6–7, 254–5

loans 113–37; bank- 25, 59, 116, 118–19, 126, (house

purchase) 25, 129, 130, (interest) 118, 120, (new ventures) 41, 120–25, 178; conditions 115; from employer 25, 114; family and friends 72, 114, 136–7; fees 82; guarantors 74, 116, 250; and inflation 202; for investment 120; and life insurance 82; sharks 75, 118, 252; *see also* interest; property; security

local authorities 40, 155

London allowances 18

losses 168

lump sums 3; on divorce 10–11, 69, 176–9; pension bought by 109; on retirement 181–2, 183

marriage 172, 173, 179, 270; home ownership 131–2, 171; inheritance 171, 186–7; pensions 103–4, 107–8, 173; tax 170–71, 267–8; *see also* divorce; separation

maternity leave 26

MIRAS 128, 255

money market accounts 140

money-lenders 118

mortgages 10, 255; building society 114–15, 127–8; endowment-linked 112, 129–30, 246, 252; extension of 82; foreign currency 130, 248–9; hardship 127; interest-only 129, 251–2; for lender's employees 25; MIRAS 128,

255; protection insurance 132, 147, 255; repaying early 82, 128, 131, 183; repayment type 128, 130, 259; second (top-up) 114–15, 130–31, 156–7, 177, 263; single women 132; size 127, 245; tax relief 128

multiplication 222–6

mutual concerns 114, 256

National Insurance 256; for employee 21, 24, 34; low pay and 21–2, 38; married woman's reduced rate 103–4; self-employed 34, 38; voluntary contributions 104; *see also* pensions (state)

negotiating skills 27–8, 120–25

net (nett) 256

new ventures 40–41; background knowledge 50–51, 121; estimates 41, 123; loans 41, 115, 120–27, 178; pricing 52; timing, for tax 42, 83; *see also* accounts

nursing 14, 19

offshore operations 42, 68, 153–4, 256

old age *see* retirement; widows

options 256–7

overdrafts 47, 101, 116, 119, 257

partnerships 42, 54, 55–6, 257

part-time work 10, 13–14

pawnbrokers 115, 119

pay *see* wages
PAYE (Pay As You Earn) 21, 33, 39, 257
pensions 103–9; dependants' 182; after divorce 173; frozen 181; index-linking 105, 182, 202; lump sums 181–2, 183; married women and 103–4, 107–8, 173; occupational 105–8, 181–2; private 11, 24, 104, 108–9, 181, 183, 202; for self-employed 108–9; single-premium 109; state 11, 103, 180–81; transferability 106–7; with-profit 183; voluntary contributions 104, 107
PEPs 162–3, 258
percentages 233–4
perks 19, 23–30, 101–2, 158, 173
personal equity plans 162–3, 258
Post Office accounts 155
poverty 72
premises, low-rent 40
Premium Bonds 77
premiums 134, 258
pricing policy 52
principal 6, 258
professions 12, 14–15, 20, 208, 258–9
profit and loss account 44–7, 123, 235, 259
profits 6, 46, 123, 167–8, 259
promotion prospects 18
property 127–36; annuities 183–4; appreciation 92, 110–11, 129, 202; buying 131–3, 135, 160–61; cost of moving 95; deeds as security 115; divorce and sale of 178–9; extensions 110–11; freehold and leasehold 133–5; joint ownership 131–3, 171; being landlord 135, 160–61; loans 25, 127–31 (*see also* mortgages); new houses 94; sale 7, 132–3, 135–6, 178–9; in trust 190; widows and 183–4, 190
property trusts 160, 259
prostitution 19–20
public houses 51, 52–3

record-keeping 39, 43
redundancy payments 69
refunds 77, 101
regions 18, 40
retail price index 200
retirement 50–51, 91, 143–4, 180–91; *see also* pensions
return to work 10, 12, 14, 20
risk 144, 148, 149–50, 260

sabbaticals 27
salary packages *see* perks
Save As You Earn 109–10
saving 103–12
secretarial work 19
security for loan 74, 115–16, 252, 260
self-employment 32–61, 260; capital payments 46–7; contracts 33, 242, 260; debts 33, 43, 48; drawings 46; employees of 33, 37–8, 39;

expenses 35–9, 43, 49;
guarantee, personal 33;
income tax 34, 35, 39, 43;
limited company 54, 56–61;
National Insurance 34, 38;
nature of 33–4; partnerships
54, 55–6; pension schemes
108–9; record-keeping 39,
43; 'sham' 34, 40, 141; tax 33,
34, 35, 36, 39, 43, 83; see also
accounts; home
separation, legal 132, 179
settlor of trust 189, 260
shares 6–7, 58–9, 157–8, 207,
260, 261; preference 157–8,
243, 258
shopkeeping 50–51
shopping 94–5, 96–7, 101–2,
196–8; second-hand 89, 93,
99–100
single women 132
skills 15, 16–17, 19
social security 11, 30, 72; see also
Department of Social
Security
sole traders 54, 261
solicitors 77, 131, 133, 142,
156–7, 177
spot rate 261
standing orders 261
start-ups see new ventures
stock market 155, 157–8, 261
student unions 101–2
subtraction 220–22
supply and demand 116, 192–3,
203–5, 262; employment 14,
16–17, 18
Switch cards 237

takings 46
tax: avoidance 6, 53–4, 80, 83,
189, 215–16; budgeting for
43, 52; deductible items 28,
29, 35–9, 43, 45; evasion 36,
53–4, 75, 171, 215–16;
exempt investments 110, 162;
on gambling 85; on gifts 67–
8; marriage and 170–71,
267–8; mortgage relief 128;
offshore 42, 68, 256, 262;
year 35, 42, 83; see also
individual taxes
Tax-Exempt Special Savings
Accounts 110
teaching profession 14–15
telephone 25, 37
tenants, sitting 161
term accounts 83, 150
TESSAs 110
theatre, investment in 164
theft 75–7, 119
time share 262–3
tipping 88–9
Tolley's 30
trade, buying of 60–61
training 14, 27, 28–9, 51, 169,
243–4
travel 25, 29–30, 38–9, 192–8
traveller's cheques 193–5, 196,
263
trusts 160, 188–91, 259, 263–4
Tyndalls 150

unemployed, grants to 40
unions 15, 24, 25–7, 101–2, 107
unit trusts 158–60, 177, 264
United States of America 196

Unlisted Securities Market 58
unmarried couples 132–3, 171
utilities 155, 157

VAT (value added tax) 28, 33,
    39, 43, 243, 264
victims, payments to 69–70

wages 14–20, 172; low 9, 13–14,
    14–18, 21–2
welfare benefits 11, 30, 72
widows 63–5, 132, 179, 184–91
wills 81, 188, 189, 244
windfalls 69–72, 140

Discover more about our forthcoming books through Penguin's FREE newspaper...

Penguin
Quarterly

It's packed with:

- exciting features
- author interviews
- previews & reviews
- books from your favourite films & TV series
- exclusive competitions & much, much more...

Write off for your free copy today to:
Dept JC
Penguin Books Ltd
FREEPOST
West Drayton
Middlesex
UB7 0BR
NO STAMP REQUIRED

READ MORE IN PENGUIN

In every corner of the world, on every subject under the sun, Penguin represents quality and variety – the very best in publishing today.

For complete information about books available from Penguin – including Puffins, Penguin Classics and Arkana – and how to order them, write to us at the appropriate address below. Please note that for copyright reasons the selection of books varies from country to country.

In the United Kingdom: Please write to *Dept. JC, Penguin Books Ltd, FREEPOST, West Drayton, Middlesex UB7 0BR*

If you have any difficulty in obtaining a title, please send your order with the correct money, plus ten per cent for postage and packaging, to *PO Box No. 11, West Drayton, Middlesex UB7 0BR*

In the United States: Please write to *Penguin USA Inc., 375 Hudson Street, New York, NY 10014*

In Canada: Please write to *Penguin Books Canada Ltd, 10 Alcorn Avenue, Suite 300, Toronto, Ontario M4V 3B2*

In Australia: Please write to *Penguin Books Australia Ltd, 487 Maroondah Highway, Ringwood, Victoria 3134*

In New Zealand: Please write to *Penguin Books (NZ) Ltd, 182–190 Wairau Road, Private Bag, Takapuna, Auckland 9*

In India: Please write to *Penguin Books India Pvt Ltd, 706 Eros Apartments, 56 Nehru Place, New Delhi 110 019*

In the Netherlands: Please write to *Penguin Books Netherlands B.V., Keizersgracht 231 NL–1016 DV Amsterdam*

In Germany: Please write to *Penguin Books Deutschland GmbH, Friedrichstrasse 10–12, W–6000 Frankfurt/Main 1*

In Spain: Please write to *Penguin Books S. A., C. San Bernardo 117–6° E–28015 Madrid*

In Italy: Please write to *Penguin Italia s.r.l., Via Felice Casati 20, I–20124 Milano*

In France: Please write to *Penguin France S. A., 17 rue Lejeune, F–31000 Toulouse*

In Japan: Please write to *Penguin Books Japan, Ishikiribashi Building, 2–5–4, Suido, Tokyo 112*

In Greece: Please write to *Penguin Hellas Ltd, Dimocritou 3, GR–106 71 Athens*

In South Africa: Please write to *Longman Penguin Southern Africa (Pty) Ltd, Private Bag X08, Bertsham 2013*

READ MORE IN PENGUIN

A CHOICE OF NON-FICTION

Citizens A Chronicle of the French Revolution Simon Schama

'The most marvellous book I have read about the French Revolution in the last fifty years' – Richard Cobb in *The Times*. 'He has chronicled the vicissitudes of that world with matchless understanding, wisdom, pity and truth, in the pages of this huge and marvellous book' – *Sunday Times*

Out of Africa Karen Blixen (Isak Dinesen)

Karen Blixen went to Kenya in 1914 to run a coffee-farm; its failure in 1931 caused her to return to Denmark where she wrote this classic account of her experiences. 'A work of sincere power ... a fine lyrical study of life in East Africa' – Harold Nicolson in the *Daily Telegraph*

Yours Etc. Graham Greene
Letters to the Press 1945–1989

'An entertaining celebration of Graham Greene's lesser-known career as a prolific author of letters to newspapers; you will find unarguable proof of his total addiction to everything about his time, from the greatest issues of the day to the humblest subjects imaginable' – Salman Rushdie in the *Observer*

The Trial of Lady Chatterley Edited By C. H. Rolph

In October 1960 at the Old Bailey a jury of nine men and three women prepared for the infamous trial of *Lady Chatterley's Lover*. The Obscene Publications Act had been introduced the previous year and D. H. Lawrence's notorious novel was the first to be prosecuted under its provisions. This is the account of the historic trial and acquittal of Penguin Books.

Handbook for the Positive Revolution Edward de Bono

Edward de Bono's challenging new book provides a practical framework for a serious revolution which has no enemies but seeks to make things better. The hand symbolizes the five basic principles of the Positive Revolution, to remind us that even a small contribution is better than endless criticism.

READ MORE IN PENGUIN

A CHOICE OF NON-FICTION

Bernard Shaw Michael Holroyd
Volume 2 1898–1918 The Pursuit of Power

'A man whose art rested so much upon the exercise of intelligence could not have chosen a more intelligent biographer ... The pursuit of Bernard Shaw has grown, and turned into a pursuit of the whole twentieth century' – Peter Ackroyd in *The Times*

Shots from the Hip Charles Shaar Murray

His classic encapsulation of the moment when rock stars turned junkies as the sixties died; his dissection of rock 'n' roll violence as citizens assaulted the Sex Pistols; superstar encounters from the decline of Paul McCartney to Mick Jagger's request that the author should leave – Charles Shaar Murray's *Shots From the Hip* is also rock history in the making.

Managing on the Edge Richard Pascale

The co-author of the bestselling *The Art of Japanese Management* has once again turned conventional thinking upside down. Conflict and contention in organizations are not just unavoidable – they are positively to be welcomed. The successes and failures of large corporations can help us understand the need to maintain a creative tension between fitting companies together and splitting them apart.

Just Looking John Updike

'Mr Updike can be a very good art critic, and some of these essays are marvellous examples of critical explanation ... a deep understanding of the art emerges ... His reviews of some recent and widely attended shows ... quite surpass the modest disclaimer of the title' – *The New York Times Book Review*

Shelley: The Pursuit Richard Holmes

'Surely the best biography of Shelley ever written ... He makes Shelley's character entirely convincing by showing us the poet at every stage of his development acting upon, and reacting to, people and events' – Stephen Spender

READ MORE IN PENGUIN

A CHOICE OF NON-FICTION

1001 Ways to Save the Planet Bernadette Vallely

There are 1001 changes that *everyone* can make in their lives today to bring about a greener environment – whether at home or at work, on holiday or away on business. Action that you can take *now*, and that you won't find too difficult to take. This practical guide shows you how.

Bitter Fame Anne Stevenson

'A sobering and salutary attempt to estimate what Plath was, what she achieved and what it cost her ... This is the only portrait which answers Ted Hughes's image of the poet as Ariel, not the ethereal bright pure roving sprite, but Ariel trapped in Prospero's pine and raging to be free' – *Sunday Telegraph*

The Complete Book of Running James F. Fixx

Jim Fixx's pioneering book has encouraged a sedentary generation to take to the streets. Packed with information for the beginner, the more experienced runner and the marathon winner, it explains the many benefits to be reaped from running and advises on how to overcome the difficulties. 'This book is a boon and a blessing to the multitudes who jog and run throughout the world' – Michael Parkinson

Friends in High Places Jeremy Paxman

'The Establishment is alive and well ... in pursuit of this elusive, seminal circle of souls around which British institutions revolve, Jeremy Paxman ... has written a thoughtful examination, both poignant and amusing' – *Independent*

Slow Boats to China Gavin Young

Gavin Young's bestselling account of his extraordinary journey in small boats through the Mediterranean, the Red Sea, the Indian Ocean and the Malaya and China Seas to China. 'A joy to read, engaging, civilised, sharply observant, richly descriptive and sometimes hilarious ... a genuine modern adventure story' – *Sunday Express*

READ MORE IN PENGUIN

A CHOICE OF NON-FICTION

When Shrimps Learn to Whistle Denis Healey

Taking up the most powerful political themes that emerged from his hugely successful *The Time of My Life*, Denis Healey now gives us this stimulating companion volume. 'Forty-three years of ruminations ... by the greatest foreign secretary (as the author quietly and reasonably implies) we never had' – Ben Pimlott in the *New Statesman & Society*

Eastern Approaches Fitzroy Maclean

'The author's record of personal achievement is remarkable. The canvas which he covers is immense. The graphic writing reveals the ruthless man of action ... He emerges from [his book] as an extrovert Lawrence' – *The Times Literary Supplement*

This Time Next Week Leslie Thomas

'Mr Thomas's book is all humanity, to which is added a Welshman's mastery of words ... Some of his episodes are hilarious, some unbearably touching, but everyone, staff and children, is looked upon with compassion' – *Observer*. 'Admirably written, with clarity, realism, poignancy and humour' – *Daily Telegraph*

Reports from the Holocaust Larry Kramer

'A powerful book ... more than a political autobiography, *Reports* is an indictment of a world that allows AIDS to continue ... he is eloquent and convincing when he swings from the general to the specific. His recommendations on the release of drugs to AIDS patients are practical and humane' – *New York Newsday*

City on the Rocks Kevin Rafferty

'Rafferty has filled a glaring gap on the Asian bookshelf, offering the only comprehensive picture of Hong Kong right up to the impact of the Tiananmen Square massacre' – *Business Week*. 'A story of astonishing achievement, but its purpose is warning rather than celebration' – *Sunday Times*

READ MORE IN PENGUIN

WOMEN'S INTEREST

A History of Their Own Bonnie S. Anderson and Judith P. Zinsser
Volumes One and Two

This is an original and path-breaking European history, the first to approach the past from the perspective of women. 'A richly textured account that leaves me overwhelmed with admiration for our fore-mothers' ability to survive with dignity' – *Los Angeles Times Book Review*

Our Bodies Ourselves Angela Phillips and Jill Rakusen
A Health Book by and for Women

'The bible of the women's health movement' – *Guardian*. 'The most comprehensive guide we've seen for women' – *Woman's World*. 'Every woman in the country should be issued with a copy free of charge' – *Mother & Baby*

Women's Experience of Sex Sheila Kitzinger

Sheila Kitzinger explores the subject in a way that other books rarely aspire to – she places sex in the context of life and writes about women's feelings concerning their bodies, and the many different dimensions of sexual experience, reflecting the way individual attitudes can change between adolescence and later years.

The Past Is Before Us Sheila Rowbotham

'An extraordinary, readable distillation of what [Sheila Rowbotham] calls an "account of ideas in the women's movement in Britain" ... This is a book written from the inside, but with a clarity that recognizes the need to unravel ideas without abandoning the excitements and frustrations that every political movement brings with it' – *Sunday Times*

READ MORE IN PENGUIN

WOMEN'S INTEREST

When a Woman's Body Says No to Sex Linda Valins

Vaginismus – an involuntary spasm of the vaginal muscles that prevents penetration – has been discussed so little that many women who suffer from it don't recognize their condition by its name. Linda Valins's practical and compassionate guide will liberate these women from their fears and sense of isolation and help them find the right form of therapy.

Against Our Will Susan Brownmiller
Men, Women and Rape

Against Our Will sheds a new and blinding light on the tensions that exist between men and women. It was written to give rape its history. Now, as Susan Brownmiller concludes, 'we must deny it a future'. 'Thoughtful, informative and well researched' – *New Statesman*

The Feminine Mystique Betty Friedan

First published in the sixties, *The Feminine Mystique* was a major inspiration for the Women's Movement and continues to be a powerful and illuminating analysis of the position of women in Western society.

Understanding Women Luise Eichenbaum and Susie Orbach

Understanding Women, an expanded version of *Outside In ... Inside Out*, is a radical appraisal of women's psychological development based on clinical evidence. 'An exciting and thought-provoking book' – *British Journal of Psychiatry*

Psychoanalysis and Feminism Juliet Mitchell

The author of the widely acclaimed *Woman's Estate* here reassesses Freudian psychoanalysis in an attempt to develop an understanding of the psychology of femininity and the ideological oppression of women.